BUYING TIME

SECOND EDITION

BUYING TIME

TRADING YOUR RETIREMENT SAVINGS
FOR INCOME AND LIFESTYLE
IN YOUR PRIME RETIREMENT YEARS

SECOND EDITION

DARYL DIAMOND

John Wiley & Sons Canada, Ltd.

Library and Archives Canada Cataloguing in Publication Data

Diamond, Daryl, 1953-

Buying time : trading your savings for income and lifestyle in your prime retirement years / Daryl Diamond.—2nd ed.

Includes index.

ISBN 978-0-470-15422-9

1. Retirement income,—Canada—Planning. 2. Retirement income—Canada. I. Title.

HQ1062.D52 2007   332.024'014   C2007-906090-0

Production Credits

Cover design: Ian Koo

Interior text design: Mike Chan

Printer: Tri-Graphic Printing Ltd.

© Recycled · Recyclé
Supporting responsible use of forest resources
Contribue à l'utilisation responsable des ressources forestières
FSC   www.fsc.org   Cert no. SW-COC-1352
© 1996 Forest Stewardship Council

John Wiley & Sons Canada, Ltd.

6045 Freemont Blvd.

Mississauga, Ontario

L5R 4J3

1 2 3 4 5 TRI 11 10 09 08 07

To Karen, Geoff, and Kelly
For all of their support and encouragement

Contents

Acknowledgements

The author would like to gratefully acknowledge the following for their generous cooperation and assistance in helping to put this project together.

John Wiley & Sons, Inc.
The Knowledgebureau
Michelle Bullard, Editor
Dynamic Mutual Funds
CANNEX Financial Exchanges Limited
Morningstar Canada
Franklin Templeton Investments

Thank you for your support and your enthusiasm for this project.

Preface

The purpose of this book is to provide an opportunity for retirees and those soon to retire (otherwise known as the baby boomers) to experience a more fulfilling and meaningful retirement. We will examine how to make the most efficient use of your time and your assets during your retirement years.

In the four years since this book was first published, there have been many changes. Tax rates and tax credits have been adjusted. There is new and amended taxation legislation, including the most exciting of all—the pension-splitting rules for retirees. And new products have been introduced to provide retirees with investment options they previously did not have. These changes allow us the opportunity to examine new strategies and solutions to help you make the most efficient use of the assets and benefits you have taken a lifetime to accumulate. It is important to remember that even a few small improvements, applied to a block of capital and multiplied over a number of years, can add up to a very large number.

I have been in the financial services business for more than 30 years. The last 18 of these have been dedicated to helping people consolidate their retirement income in the most efficient manner from the assets they have saved and the benefits they have earned. This includes individuals who are within 10 years of a target retirement date, those about to retire, and those who are already retired. Our business practice, which is composed of qualified planners and support staff, is dedicated to serving this group of people.

Most people retire only once, but we have had the experience of being able to retire several hundred times through the clients we serve. This has afforded us the opportunity to live through the experiences of many people and has allowed for some of the conclusions that form the planning concepts and strategies found within this material. There is much to be said for knowledge and information, but there is no substitute for experience and the resulting insight when it comes to providing meaningful advice and direction.

The bottom line is that our experience has shown us that people currently in their retirement years have a very different attitude about spending and using their assets than does the generation that follows them. Within the group of current retirees, we see tremendous waste in terms of asset use and taxation, and too many missed opportunities. Having experienced many retirement scenarios over the last 18 years, we have concluded that there is a way for retirees to make better use of their resources, readily meet other financial objectives, and take advantage of the time afforded them during their best retirement years. Stated another way, retirees could do a much more effective job in spending their assets while covering off health-risk and wealth-transfer objectives.

Time and time again, we see people who did not do the things they wanted to do after retirement because suddenly either they or their spouse started to lose their health, needed care, or passed away. We see large retirement accumulations sitting idle, held by people who do not even spend their government benefits on a monthly basis. This in turn leads to larger personal liabilities to fund their long-term care and larger-than-necessary income and estate taxes.

We hope to bring together various concepts and strategies and, in doing so, show how a comprehensive planning process can help you achieve more enjoyment from your retirement years. We will also show you how to make more efficient use of the assets you have to create the income you need. Given the book's space constraints, it will not be possible to cover off all the planning areas in the type of detail that would be possible if this book was dedicated to simply one particular planning stream. This conceptual resource will, however, assist people, in conjunction with their advisors, to investigate the individual and integrated planning concepts available.

We will accomplish this by bringing together the various multidisciplinary planning channels and by laying the groundwork for meaningful discussions between you and your financial advisor. It is not designed to be a "do it yourself" book. It is intended, by facilitating more comprehensive communication between individual and advisor, to be a "do it properly" and "do it better" manual.

The contents of this book apply to the baby boomers and their currently retired parents. In many instances the principles involve both groups simultaneously since there are familial responsibilities and financial links between the generations. Yet there are also many differences between these two groups, especially when it comes to the value and use of money.

There is no question that each retirement situation is unique. The material presented in this book is based on the general trends we have witnessed through our work. We are able to share with you our experience and insight into this process. In addition to this, we have a strong conviction about where we, as a nation with an increasing number of aging citizens, appear to be heading and the resulting planning issues that need to be addressed, and we will touch on these subjects throughout the book.

Introduction

This book begins where most other retirement planning books end. Many well-written books deal with the subject of accumulating money for your retirement; however, there are very few that give direction from that point forward—that time when you are drawing upon your assets to create the income you will need in retirement.

We may ultimately spend from one-quarter to one-half of our adult life in retirement. It is very common for people to think of retirement as one phase in life, when in fact it is comprised of many different stages over a 20- to 40-year period. Some of these stages may include:

- Starting your retirement
- The early or prime years of retirement
- Children leaving home or moving away
- Arrival of grandchildren
- Changes in your health
- Disability or failing health of a spouse or partner
- Caring for adult children
- Caring for aging parents
- Changing your place of residence/type of accommodation
- Breakdown of marriage
- Second marriage and a resulting second family
- Death of friends
- Loss of a spouse or partner

The stages identified above tend to involve health-related events, changes in family situation, and sometimes both. We refer to these as life-altering events. The reason we call them this is that what follows one will always be different from the way things were before the event occurred. It is also important to note that the vast majority of retirees will go through any number of these events in their lifetime. Granted, some of these events can and do occur before we retire, but most of the events listed above are typically associated with aging. These are retirement realities, and they need to be included in the setting of objectives, the consideration of asset use, health-risk management, and wealth transfer.

The fact that these changes impact our situation is one of the reasons why we emphasize using an advisor, someone with whom you discuss and work upon your financial, lifestyle, investment, and health-risk management issues. The main reason for using an advisor is because the creation of a plan is not what makes things happen. It is the *implementation* of the plan that makes things happen. Your advisor's role should also include assisting you to take the steps necessary to put the plan into action and turn your objectives into reality. Your relationship with your advisor, and the role he or she plays, will constantly change, just as your needs change through the various stages of retirement.

With the boomers and their parents we have one retired generation and one about-to-retire generation. While they have retirement in common, they also have some significant differences between them. Compared to their parents, the boomers expect to retire earlier, live longer, and do more in their retirement. However, most do not know how much money they will need to do this, and they are not as financially prepared as they need to be. This book contains technical and practical concepts designed to help you get the most from what you have been able to accumulate. These are proven strategies that work when implemented in conjunction with comprehensive planning.

In working with the parents of the boomers, we find that there is a great deal of inefficiency in how money is used for personal objectives, is taxed by the government, is used to pay for health-related expenses, and is ultimately passed on to future generations. What this book delivers is a combination of technical information and solutions that addresses the different yet connected problems of two generations moving through retirement at the same time. By employing an integrated approach involving four distinct planning channels, it also serves as a blueprint for planning between the generations. There is in excess of one trillion dollars of wealth to be transferred to the baby boomer generation over the next 25 years. How efficiently this is done will have a direct and profound impact not only on the retirement of the boomers, but on the generations that follow. Use this book to make a positive difference for you, your heirs, and future generations.

A FEW QUICK NOTES

We will use the term "couple" throughout descriptions in this book to refer to married couples, common-law couples, or individuals.

Also, we will use the term "advisor," not "advisors," although you may have more than one person with whom you work. We will not tell you that this is a mistake, but we strongly suggest that there is particular merit in coordinating all of your planning activities with one person or institution. We refer to it as consolidation and believe it delivers more effective planning and better results.

HOW TO USE THIS BOOK

There are three key steps you must take in order for this book to have the potential to make your retirement more fulfilling. They are:

Gain Awareness of the Process—and Yourself

The technical and strategic information in this book will provide you with a general knowledge base and understanding of retirement income planning. The exercise of establishing your objectives and priorities will allow you, and your partner, to better understand and emotionally relate to what it is you wish your retirement experience to be. Through our integrated planning process known as the Prime Approach™, you will find out how you can fulfill your objectives and enhance your best retirement years.

Align Yourself with an Advisor

The use of an advisor is a significant factor in successful planning. You may want to engage the services of someone who can help you in all four of the planning channels involved in this process. To assist you and your advisor in the planning process, we have included two important tools in the back of this book. First are the data forms. These will assist you to gather all of the information you will need to provide to an advisor in order for a comprehensive retirement income plan to be written for you. Second is a checklist that pulls together the key points covered in this book. Whether you are just having a plan constructed or you are reviewing and improving an existing plan, the checklist is an essential and valuable tool in the integrated planning process.

Our recommendation that you work with an advisor is not in any way to suggest that you are inept or unable. It is, however, to contend that you are better served over time by using the services of a professional to help you along this journey.

Put the Plan into Action

All the knowledge, awareness, and planning in the world is not of much benefit unless action is taken. This is also an area where working with an advisor is key. The joint efforts of you and your advisor will help ensure that the action steps you need to take are actually implemented. Just as importantly, the ongoing relationship with your advisor will enable you to make the appropriate adjustments to your financial plan as your priorities change or as life-altering events occur. While it may currently be your desire to handle your retirement planning on your own, there will likely come a time when either this will no longer be of interest to you or you will not be fully capable of handling your own affairs.

PART ONE

In Preparation

Fundamentals of the Prime Approach™

THE TIME HUB AND THE MONEY HUB

Everyone has a Time Hub and a Money Hub through which respective time priorities and money priorities are defined. The Money Hub pertains to those assets, benefits, and entitlements that will be used to create income, and the priorities we attach to their use. It is segmented into income priorities and asset priorities. The Time Hub, on the other hand, is composed of key personal needs. The priorities within this hub are driven by a combination of emotional and physical well-being. Both hubs are dynamic in size and driven by the factors of reality—the income/asset relationship to spending for the Money Hub, and the health, time, and emotional priorities for the Time Hub.

The Money Hub can be objectively and technically planned. The Time Hub, however, is the unknown in the equation because the most dramatic, life-altering events occur here, and they are primarily driven by emotion. Although the two hubs work in tandem, the priorities of the Time Hub are ultimately what determine the priorities of the Money Hub. It is the use of assets and income in relation to the Time Hub objectives that is the central premise of the Prime Approach to retirement income planning.

Establishing Your Time Hub Priorities

Whether you think of retirement as "the long holiday" or a "never-ending weekend," it is the period in our life when we have greatest discretion as to how to use our time. What do you plan to or want to do with your time when you have the choice? It is the Time Hub priorities that will influence these decisions.

- LOVE
  This is the strongest emotion we have. To what extent does this factor drive the prioritizing and setting of your objectives? Is the focus here on love of spouse, children, grandchildren, self, someone else, or something else?

- PURPOSE/FULFILLMENT
  Does your dreamed-of retirement provide you with the opportunity to pursue activities that will allow you to realize your potential or passion in a given pursuit, interest, or cause?

- RECREATION
  Whether it's golf, gardening, travel, volunteer work, or helping the children, what recreational activities will take priority for you in your planning?

- SECURITY
  What needs to be in place to ensure you maintain your sense of well-being as it relates to your safety and surroundings?

- HEALTH
  Are there health issues for you, your spouse, or someone else that set a different priority or order for how you wish to use your income or assets? Health issues are directly connected to time, both in terms of quantity and quality.

- ACCOMMODATION
  Just as the other priorities interrelate, the issue of where you are living will be influenced by health, security, love, and even recreational issues. Where you choose to or need to live involves house, apartment, or facility. It also refers to city or country.

Often the retirement income planning exercise focuses only on what the income needs are. For example, "How much income do you need to have each month?" This is indeed necessary to know and the planning process requires that this be identified and provided to your advisor to help put your financial plan together. But what are the factors that have driven the need for this level of income at this point in time? It is more than just a numerical calculation. It is essential you know the answer to other key questions, most of which are connected to the Time Hub priorities.

Some Time Hub questions include:

- In addition to financial plans, what other plans have you made?
- If you had all the money you could ever use or want, what are the first five things that you would do, and why?
- What are the 10 things you want to do while your health permits you? What is their order of priority for you, and what is the time frame within which you want to accomplish each of them?

Those baby boomers coming into retirement expect that their retirement will look very different from the one that their parents enjoyed. Yet, for the vast majority of boomers, what they have seen their parents go through is the only comprehensive frame of reference that they have on the subject. Since their own retirement is not going to be the same, they had better develop a clear and defined picture of what this is going to look like.

The Time Hub questions are included with several others in the data forms at the end of the book.

Time Hub priorities are not "measured" per se, but rather are defined. Identifying the priorities in this area, as is evident from the questions you need to consider, is really a subjective exercise. You will need to invest some thought and effort to accurately answer the Time Hub questions. That is what makes them worthwhile. If you are married, it is very possible that for any number of reasons, the Time Hub priorities may differ between you and your partner. It is important that you work through this exercise together to address your combined needs.

Once the priorities have been addressed, they are reflected on the financial side where things can be quantified. Stated another way, the Time Hub priorities express the "what," and the Money Hub defines the "how."

If the understanding and alignment of Time Hub priorities between the two generations could be achieved earlier, there would be a considerable number of benefits to be realized by all parties, including:

- More structure for both the parents and boomers in terms of future financial decisions
- More flexibility to use or reposition assets
- Less emotional stress on all parties from decisions that would otherwise have to be made in the future
- Less costs in terms of expenses and taxes
- Potentially greater wealth transfer
- Fewer family disputes

The Boomers and Their Parents— The "Generation Gap" Persists

Do you remember the expression "generation gap"? The term was used to describe the extreme variance in attitudes between what was at that time the boomers in their teens and early 20s and their parents. Guess what? It still exists, although both sides have mellowed considerably over the last 30 years. The passing of time has narrowed the communication gap, which was a significant part of this disconnect between parents and their children. Yet different attitudes on certain issues still prevail to some extent. The boomers are now entering their pre-retirement years, while their parents have been retired for some time. If we look back through the years, these were some of the key differences between the belief sets of the baby boomers in their younger years and those of their parents.

VARIANCE OF ATTITUDES

Boomers	Parents
Change the world	Respect authority/conform
Never die/never grow old	Go when they are called
Many employers, many jobs	Loyal to one company
Focus on possessions, credit, and debt	Modest/avoid debt
Enjoy now and pay later	This one's good enough
Reluctant to save	Reluctant to spend
Afraid of not keeping up	Afraid of loss

For the parents of boomers, the value proposition is the value of money. For the boomers, it is the value of time.

The boomer generation has focused on material possessions, credit, debt, and the continuous belief in the practice of buy now (enjoy now) and pay later. Nearly everything the boomers possess has a systematic repayment schedule attached to it.

Boomers, on average, have had fewer children than did their parents. Their parents, however, managed to do with less, stretching existing resources to the maximum, and were still able to save money. Granted, there may have been lower tax rates than we have today, higher nominal interest rates through the 1980s, and the benefit of soaring housing values, all of which contributed to the wealth accumulated by our parents. But our parents for the most part were and are practical in what they expect from retirement and what they spend money doing in retirement.

Compared to their parents, boomers want to retire earlier, expect to live longer, and want to do more in their golden years. However, all of these goals require assets to replace the income they will leave behind when they stop working. The boomers are notoriously poor savers. Fewer than 35 percent of all tax filers make a Registered Retirement Savings Plan (RRSP) contribution. The median RRSP account holds less than $50,000, and there is next to no savings in non-registered assets. The main reason for boomers making an RRSP contribution is to get a tax deduction, not to accumulate retirement savings. As they progress into the greying years, the generation that was going to change the world, and to some degree did, is realizing that just like their parents they are moving through to old age and many have not prepared properly for this time in their life.

Boomers are accustomed to borrowing to obtain everything they have and so far this pattern has worked, even though they find themselves swimming in debt. The problem in continuing this pattern is that you cannot borrow to finance your retirement. It is the one thing that you must pay for in advance. One needs to pay now in order to enjoy later. This is a process with which the vast majority of boomers have little experience.

Many boomers are counting on inheritances from parents who did not spend their assets. In fact, there are some boomers who have already "spent" their future inheritance in that they will need the money just to clear debt they are carrying. If this is even partially true, then you, your siblings, and your parent(s) need to do some intelligent intergenerational planning. This is probably a difficult subject for you to handle directly with your parents, which is why you should have an advisor serve as your guide and intermediary.

You may have noticed that the boomers like to put forward to their parents what they truly believe to be valuable suggestions regarding the parents' income, investments, health care, and living arrangements. Why is that? Because they feel that they are far more in tune with what is new, current, and best for their parents. The parents, however, don't necessarily share the view that they should make immediate and radical changes to the way things have always been and to what they have become used to. The boomers walk away from such conversations somewhat frustrated and with a view that their parents are stubborn. In reality, you still have two groups with different value and attitude sets that have grown up in different times. The *key* difference is that each group does not share the other's Time Hub priorities.

The communication gap is back, except it is reversed. It is the parents who, for the most part, are tuning out the direction their children are attempting to provide. They will listen politely and nod, but are reluctant to implement the suggestions put to them. Eventually, however, as aging takes its toll, the parents will likely depend on the direction and actions of their children. It is at this point when both groups reach a common understanding, and their Time Hub priorities are aligned. A common understanding is reached.

Establishing Your Money Hub Priorities

Here are some of the issues of the Money Hub.

- INCOME SECURITY

  Are you concerned that you will outlive your income?

- HIGHEST POSSIBLE INCOME TODAY

  How important is it to you to trigger income from every source and asset that you have? The answer may depend on what resources you have and how much income is to be created. Does your state of health or that of your spouse suggest that there will be limited time to do the things you want to do?

- COPING WITH INFLATION
  This refers to having your income and assets grow in order to maintain your purchasing power.

- TAX REDUCTION
  Is it important to you to explore strategies to pay less tax on your income? It may sound like a redundant question, but how important is this issue to you relative to the others listed here?

- HEALTH-RISK MANAGEMENT
  How important is proper management of health care and long-term care to you? In addition, how significant are the issues surrounding how this care will be funded? Is it important that the use of your personal assets be minimized for this purpose?

- USING CAPITAL ASSETS
  How important is it to you that the initial value of your income-producing assets stays intact? Is it a large concern if, in order to create the income needed, your asset balances decline over time?

- WEALTH TRANSFER
  How much of a priority is it to maximize the transfer of your estate assets to your heirs? How significant is it that planning be done so that more of your money goes to family rather than to the tax department?

  In the data forms at the end of the book, you are asked to rank the above items in terms of their priority to you. Each of these items is key, but you need to know exactly how important they are to you relative to each other. There are trade-offs in this process, and you need to indicate your level of interest in or concern for each option.

  The manner in which you rate these priorities will assist you and your advisor to determine how and when different assets and benefits are used to create income. In addition, the answers you provide will give direction in the areas of risk management and investment strategies.

Getting the Time Hub and Money Hub in Sync

Objectives and priorities first need to be established in the Time Hub in order to most appropriately deploy the resources within the Money Hub. The Time Hub priorities of love, purpose, fulfillment, recreation, security, health, and accommodation are driven almost exclusively by emotional factors. Once established, the Time Hub priorities are quantified through Money Hub planning.

How exactly will priorities change over two or three decades of retirement? Other than to say that there will be many changes and different stages through this time, this is really the unknown. When creating income from assets, the structure should be flexible to allow for changes in priorities throughout these stages.

Take the example of two couples about to commence their retirement, both the same ages, with the same retirement assets and income potential. How would the Time Hub factors, priorities, and objectives differ between these two couples if the husband in one family had just been diagnosed with a life-threatening illness?

Or, consider two people who are retired. One is age 63 and has just spent her first month of retirement in a sunny, tropical location. The other is age 83, and has just lost her partner after 55 years of marriage. How does their view of retirement differ? What is their view of the future? How would their Time Hub and subsequently their Money Hub priorities differ?

As you may be beginning to realize, when we talk about defining objectives at retirement we really need to look in detail at the Time Hub. What is it exactly that people want to do? For example, a married couple will need to discuss how closely their respective Time Hubs align. Their objectives and attitudes in any of the Time Hub areas may vary greatly, especially if there is a large difference in age. Once those issues are identified and prioritized, it is then appropriate to look at how to most effectively use assets and income to fulfill their objectives.

By structuring the income plan with consideration to both the Time Hub and the Money Hub, what we can potentially accomplish is enhanced quality of time, if not the quantity of time. We know it is impossible to plan for all of the changes and stages retirees will experience over the decades. Some changes will be sudden, while some will be gradual and prolonged. However, each of these events will be cause to redefine the Time Hub priorities, and, as a result, reflect those changes in the Money Hub.

The span of years during retirement is much like taking a vacation. Of course, with a vacation we normally have a defined time frame. With retirement, we really do not know what amount of time we will actually have. We plan for and save for a vacation. The same must be done for retirement.

Let's take an example of a two-week vacation. If there is only so much money to spend, you may wait for the last week of a two-week vacation to do things that you really want to do for fear of running out of cash too early. So, during the first week, you limit your activities and spend very little of your money, in anticipation of the second week. For the first three days of the second week, the weather turns quite bad. So, at least you still have the last four days. Then you or your spouse become sick for the last four days, so none of the things you had planned for the last half of your vacation come about. You go home with money in your pocket because it was not used during the best days of the vacation, a time when everyone was in good health and the weather was fine. Could this money have been better employed and the vacation time better used? Well, we can simply plan more effectively for the next vacation. However, we only have one retirement. We cannot go back and do it all over again.

Let's add one more issue for the vacation–retirement comparison. Any money not used in the vacation can be held over until the next trip. In retirement, some of the money that passes through to the estate goes through the hands of the taxman first and then on to beneficiaries.

What are the steps that need to be taken to look at the most effective way to transfer these assets? More importantly, how do we make the best use of our money during our retirement years? You need to align your Time Hub and Money Hub priorities to determine both. This is done through the planning and implementation stages.

BUYING TIME

To be able to trade money for time would be both an intriguing and popular concept. The fact of the matter is that we are only given so much time to live. "Buying time" does not refer to being able, through the expenditure of income and assets, to obtain more time, but rather to apply our financial resources in the best possible manner to make our allotted time better. This is the process we refer to as the Prime Approach to retirement income planning.

Introduction of the Prime Approach Concept

There is a double meaning for this term as it applies to different stages of the retirement planning process. As you *Approach* the 10 years before your target retirement date, these are your *Prime* earning years. There are specific planning strategies that can be employed in this time that will make a substantially positive difference on how your retirement income will be delivered.

The second meaning of this term applies if you are retired or are just about to retire. We want to show you an *Approach* to using your assets and benefits in order to maximize the enjoyment of your *Prime* retirement years. We define the prime retirement years as that period of time from the commencement of your retirement, in whatever manner you engage it, to that point in time where you or your spouse needs care or passes away. Whether you retire at age 52, 62, or 72, the first 10 years of your retirement will likely be the most fulfilling. This is because these are usually the years in which you and your spouse will enjoy the best health of your retirement. This is the time during retirement that is referred to as the "golden years." When health fails or a partner passes away, we may find ourselves in the "olden years."

By helping you define more precisely what it is that you wish to do in your best retirement years, both time and financial resources can be used in the most meaningful and efficient manner. In our practice, we have seen too many situations where people wait to do the things they want to do and then lose their health or pass away. It is a shame that some people are not using the wealth they have built, and not enjoying their retirement years to the fullest. The beneficiaries of this overly frugal behaviour are the heirs and the tax department—and not the individuals themselves. Meanwhile, the heirs want to minimize any estate taxes and realize the maximum value of the estate when it is settled. Luckily, several planning steps can be implemented to help retirees fulfill their objectives during their years of best health, while preserving or even enhancing the transfer of wealth to future generations.

As referred to earlier, there are a number of distinctions between the baby boomer generation and their parents. It is the parents of the boomers that are being referred to here as the inefficient spenders. It appears that baby boomers themselves have very little trouble spending money.

So why is it that current retirees are reluctant to use their assets? Aside from the general attitudes listed previously and the fact that many of these people grew up through the depression of the 1930s, there are three common reasons:

1. **Fear of running out of income**

   This is without question the greatest fear of anyone who is retired. As people move into their late 70s and 80s, though, they tend to spend less money than they did in their earlier years of retirement. They may in fact be accumulating money in savings and chequing accounts as income flows exceed the amounts they are spending.

2. **Wanting to ensure there is money available to cover health-care costs**

   This becomes a larger concern with increasing age and with the onset of health problems. There usually is a twofold concern here. First, there is the issue of having the ability to afford a level of care in an environment that will meet their needs and provide dignity. Second, there is the need to have the resources to do this so that they are not dependent on family or feel that they are a financial burden to their children.

3. **Desire to leave money to future generations**

   This objective becomes more important as people age, and is further strengthened when one partner passes away. The reason for the increasing interest in transferring wealth is to leave a legacy or remembrance of some kind. In other words, if you cannot take it with you, why not "live on" through what an inheritance can do or provide for your heirs? Each generation has traditionally been better off financially than the previous. It is common for retirees to initially regard the transfer of their wealth as an issue to which they do not give great priority. As they often say after looking at the material possessions their children have, "the children are in far better financial shape than we are." What the parents usually don't know is the corresponding level of debt that their children are carrying in order to finance those possessions. There is a tendency for these attitudes to change as the parents' health concerns increase and grandchildren enter the picture. This is another example of how changes in the Time Hub priorities directly alter the priorities of the Money Hub. If the desire to leave an inheritance becomes important, a different set of Money Hub priorities may be established.

Through comprehensive planning and with the use of specific financial tools, it is possible to provide a mechanism for covering health-care costs and guarantee a transfer of wealth consistent with objectives. If these contingencies can be addressed and a plan and process to deliver income be put in place, retirees will gain more discretion over how they may choose to use their assets earlier in their retirement years. Simply stated, more structure provides more freedom.

This is the basis of the Prime Approach to retirement income planning. As stated earlier, we cannot use assets and income to buy more time, but we can use them to buy better time. And people should make the most of their best retirement years. After all, it's true that you are only young once, and that you are never old twice.

The Four Planning Channels

By understanding the relationship between your Time Hub objectives, your retirement income, and risk-management issues, you can enhance your best retirement years while still planning for well-being and lifestyle issues you will face as you become older.

In addition to this, the four distinct planning channels must work in tandem if you are to have your retirement plan work most efficiently in accordance with your objectives. The channels are key components of a comprehensive financial plan.

The four planning channels are:
1. The Structural Plan
2. The Investment Portfolio
3. Health-Risk Management
4. Wealth Transfer

Each of these channels is a process unto itself, and initially people may have a specific need to address only one or two areas. However, the true benefits of integrated planning will only be realized when all four planning areas are working in conjunction. This is because each time a decision is reached and action is taken in one of the planning areas, it affects the other three. For example, an increase in the amount of income withdrawn (structure) will reduce potential inheritances (wealth transfer), and may affect the ability to fund long-term health-care costs (health-risk management), unless the investments (investment portfolio) are adjusted to attract a potentially higher rate of return. The four separate channels are illustrated in Figure 1.1 as gears because when one turns, they all turn. It is therefore essential to understand the impact of an action not only on its own planning channel, but on the other three as well.

FIGURE 1.1

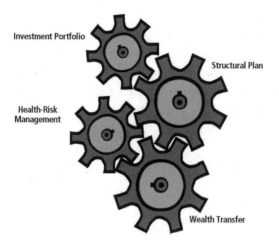

The Structural Plan

This is the formal retirement income plan. It is represented by the largest of the cogs because it is the most important component. It is based on the Time Hub and Money Hub priorities of the couple, as well as the financial resources available to create the income that is needed. A complementary document called the Investment Policy Statement (IPS) will define the purpose and strategy of how money will be invested, income created, management performance assessed, and changes made. The structural plan, in conjunction with the IPS, should serve as the basis for review, decision-making, and any future actions. A comprehensive structural plan should include the following:

GENERAL ITEMS
- Outline of process
- Details of your and your partner's personal situation

- Confirmation of goals, objectives, and concerns
- Net worth statement
- Details of income-producing assets and benefits, incorporating a net worth statement
- Details of business holdings
- Plan assumptions, including rates of return

INCOME-ORIENTED ITEMS
- Cash flow analysis
- Analysis of debt servicing, if any
- An emergency or comfort account
- Optimized cash flow—addressing surplus or negative flows
- Income projections for you and your partner
- Income-splitting opportunities
- Tax illustration of income streams and net receipts
- Cash flow and account balance for each income stream for you and your partner, including pension, RRSP, and non-registered accounts

The Investment Portfolio

There is a distinct income-to-asset relationship. The investment portfolio channel recognizes that your investments cannot stop working at the same time you do. If the rate of withdrawal from your income is greater than the rate of its growth, the portfolio will diminish. As such, an investment strategy must be put in place that applies to all income-producing assets. The structure of the portfolio will be determined by your personal investor profile, the requirements of the structural plan, or a combination of these factors. The investment portfolio channel considers:

- Your risk profile
- Current asset allocation and recommended mix
- Details of investment recommendations
- Your Investment Policy Statement (IPS)

Health-Risk Management

At some point as we grow older we will all require medical help, and there are significant costs associated with incurring a critical illness or requiring long-term care. The personal costs can be financed by your assets or covered by insurance. An in-depth exploration of these alternative funding methods is essential in comprehensive planning. Paying adequate attention to this planning channel will ensure you contemplate:

- Analysis of health and life insurance coverage relative to objectives
- Details of proposed solutions to identified problems including critical illness, long-term health care, and life insurance
- Legal documents such as the will, power of attorney, trust agreements, and health-care directives

Wealth Transfer

What plans and tools are in place to most efficiently put wealth into the hands of future generations? Simple planning strategies and actions can preserve or even increase the amount of wealth to be transferred, and reduce expenses and taxation. The end result for the beneficiaries could be lower taxation for years to come, thereby enhancing the value of the initial inheritance. The wealth-transfer channel incorporates:

- Net worth projections based on income streams
- The effect of estate planning on estate taxation
- Considerations for gifting
- Considerations for charitable bequests

As mentioned earlier, planning or action in any one of these channels has an impact on the others, which may be either positive or negative. For example, lack of attention to the health-risk channel can result in a smaller amount of wealth to transfer. Often people and even advisors do not realize this, and miss out on the many advantageous things that can be done to address contingencies and risks while providing a better lifestyle during the best retirement years.

Completing the Financial Plan

Your financial plan should conclude with some summary comments that not only help direct a course of action to accomplish the plan, but also state the service expectations and other details of the ongoing relationship between you and your advisor. It may include:

- A critical path to implement recommendations
- A proposed schedule of review frequency
- Complete disclosure of compensation to your advisor and related parties
- A waiver of understanding and limitations, to be signed by all parties

This assumes that you and your advisor have completed an initial letter of engagement. Such a document may include some of the components listed above. Given the comprehensive and time-consuming nature of putting comprehensive financial plans together, you should expect to pay a fee for these services. It is important for all parties to be aware of and comfortable with how compensation is made to the advisor and/or the advising institution.

Summary of the Principles of Buying Time

In the Prime Approach, all of the four planning channels are integrated in order to produce a complete financial plan. The end result of this type of planning is that we can move some additional financial resources forward to use in the earlier years when our health is good. What we are doing is buying time. We are using our savings to enhance lifestyle and pursue those things that are most important to us, those things we have defined in the Time Hub. We cannot buy more time, but we can put our assets toward buying better time.

THE SABOTEURS—INFLATION AND TAXES

Understanding Inflation

Inflation, simply defined, is the upward trend in the cost of goods and services over time as measured against a base index. Most people know it exists, but are unaware of how it affects their retirement income and assets.

During your working years, increases in your employment income usually allow you to keep pace or even exceed the price increases caused by inflation. However, when you retire, your major sources of income are not normally inflation adjusted. This is how inflation directly affects retirees—by eroding the purchasing power of fixed incomes. On the positive side, experience with current retirees has shown us that consumer spending during the retirement years tends to be at a lower level than it is during the pre-retirement years, so inflation has a lesser effect.

How Inflation Erodes Your Income

Simply stated, purchasing power is reduced as inflation eats into the value of a fixed income over time. Even if inflation rates are low, a loss is still realized. Over time, inflation is like an insidious form of hidden tax on your income, making you pay more for the same goods and services or make do with less.

Certain sources of income, such as government entitlements, veterans' benefits, and most public service pensions, have an indexing formula that applies and as such maintain their purchasing power.

Consider an example of a retiree drawing $1,500 per month from an account with an initial investment of $200,000. This $1,500 monthly is equal to $18,000 per year, or a rate of withdrawal of 9 percent against the initial principal. If the rate of return on this account is 7 percent, then the investment will exhaust in 20.5 years. In any situation, if the rate of return is lower than the withdrawal rate, eventually the account will exhaust. This is not necessarily a bad thing if that level of income withdrawal is what the financial plan calls for. This scenario makes no adjustment to the withdrawal for inflation.

Now consider that the amount of income withdrawn was increased to adjust for an inflation rate of 2.5 percent per year. This maintains the purchasing power, but shortens the life of the asset by 20 percent to 30 percent, depending on the rate of return. At the same 7 percent rate of return, the asset now exhausts in 15.3 years. Just to keep pace with an inflation rate of 2.5 percent, the original withdrawal of $1,500 must be increased to $1,873 by the beginning of the 10th year. Obviously, since increasingly larger withdrawals are required for each year that we are adjusting for inflation, the accounts will exhaust sooner than in the non-indexed scenario. This is the negative impact that inflation has on your income-producing assets.

It is necessary to provide inflation protection in an income-planning scenario, but discussions between you and your advisor should determine how this will be done. For example, it may be concluded that for a 60-year-old retiree, withdrawals will be fully indexed until the age of 75, at which point the total income withdrawn will be reduced by a percentage (usually

20 to 30 percent). Why? Because people do not maintain the same spending patterns as they get further into retirement. People age 85 do not spend money the same way as do people age 65. There are different objectives, needs, and priorities to which money is allocated as people grow older.

Some financial plans that we have examined do not take this into account, and instead project an income that has been indexed for the entire time that someone is retired. This usually results in an illustration that shows the depletion of income-generating assets. This is not, in reality, how things occur.

Real Rates of Return

Because inflation reduces purchasing power, we must examine the rates of return we receive on our investments after the effects of inflation have been considered. When we take the rate of return we receive and subtract the rate of inflation, we are left with what is known as "the real rate of return."

If we are using a conservative approach in structuring a retirement income investment portfolio, the use of bonds or guaranteed investment certificates (GICs) may be appealing. However, recent returns on fixed-income holdings such as bonds and GICs are in the 5 percent area. Inflation in the last few years has averaged around 2.5 percent per year. Therefore, the real return on these investments is about 3 percent (5 percent minus 2 percent).

If you go back to 1981, the average GIC rate offered through the 12 months of that year was 15.4 percent. This is basically three times what current rates offer. Before we start to wish for the return of those days, however, remember that inflation that year was 12.5 percent, for a real return of roughly 3 percent—the same as we experience today.

The big difference between then and now is that when you factor in taxes it is much preferable to be in a low-interest-rate, low-inflation environment. If our 1981 example of a 15.4 percent return is fully taxable, then at a 40 percent marginal tax bracket the net return after tax is actually 9.25 percent (15.4 percent times 60 percent). Therefore, when we subtract the rate of inflation for that year of 12.5 percent we are actually falling behind with an after-tax, inflation-adjusted return of -3.25 percent (9.25 percent minus 12.5 percent). This is discussed in more depth in the section on taxation.

Inflation and Its Impact on Prices

MENU ITEM	1967	TODAY
Hamburger	$0.20	$1.15
Cheeseburger	$0.25	$1.25
French Fries	$0.20	$0.95
Milkshake	$0.20	$1.45
Soft Drink	$0.10	$0.99
Coffee	$0.10	$0.75

Plus Taxes!

This price list from 1967 and today at a famous fast-food restaurant clearly shows what inflation does—it drives up the cost of goods and services and requires us to pay more to obtain the same things. Then there is the one thing that appears on our bill today that did not show up in 1967—taxes.

The last year when a person could send a first-class letter with a 10-cent stamp in Canada was 1976. Today that same letter costs 51 cents to send, plus an additional 6 percent for the goods and services tax (GST). In fact, by the time you read this, a letter will likely cost more than 51 cents to send (54 cents including GST).

There is a way to avoid paying some GST. If you buy your hamburger at a fast-food restaurant, you pay tax on it. If you buy your hamburger supplies at the grocery store and make the burger at home, you don't pay GST. This is a choice you are able to make. However, when it comes to mailing a letter, you have no choice as to whether or not to expose yourself to paying GST. And so it goes with all government services. You pay what you are told. There is no choice to make, and there is no opportunity to control the cost or to negotiate it.

This is significant because it is very likely that the main cause of future price increases (inflation) for those who are retired will be due to those things that are controlled by government.

Inflation Factors You Cannot Control

- Utilities
- Property taxes
- Income taxes

- Estate taxes
- Dental and medical costs
- Post-secondary education costs
- Funding for social programs
- Prescription drugs
- Health-care premiums
    * Imposed
    * Voluntary
- Long-term health-care costs

Source: *Prime Approach™ to Retirement Planning*

When you look at this list you will probably recognize that these items continue to increase in cost at a faster rate than other goods and services. And we really don't have a choice as to whether or not we will use them.

Inflation Factors Going Forward

The most significant inflation factor revolves around the health-care system and related expenses. On average, one-half of all the health-care costs that an individual will experience during their lifetime are realized in the last year of life and 50 percent of that amount within the last 30 days. When you combine this with the extreme growth in the aging population, it represents unbearable strain on government resources. The current system is buckling under the load, and it will not be able to function in the same manner when the boomers are retired. The economics are impossible.

Advances in medical science and prescription drug research have allowed people to extend the number of years they live and to enhance the quality of those years. Advances in drug therapy have allowed increasing numbers of people to stay at home or return to the workplace rather than convalesce in the hospital. This reduces medical costs and helps keep much-needed hospital beds open.

The result of this, however, is that prescription drug costs in Canada are soaring at a rate of 20 percent and higher each year. In 1999, in Canada, the costs of drugs exceeded the cost of physicians for the first time, and there is every reason to expect that this trend will continue. If there is going to be limited government funding available, those people already in and those heading for retirement had best be prepared to personally fund at least part of the costs that they will incur in this area. This is a serious inflation consideration that applies primarily to those in retirement and those moving into it.

With all levels of government searching for revenue and ways to cut expenditures, there is a general filtering down of expense to the end user. This is not only an inflation issue, but in a real sense is a taxation issue. As discussed above, the increased personal expenses we now absorb, which were previously covered entirely or partially by governments, are, in reality, a form of tax. Indirect taxation is a trend that has been increasing over the years.

Taxation on Income

We experience direct taxation through the visible taxes with which we are only too familiar, such as income taxes levied by federal and provincial governments, and to a lesser degree through consumption taxes, such as sales tax, property taxes, excise tax, GST, etc. Taxation on income is one of the biggest concerns to those who are retired.

There are three certainties in life...

1. Taxes
2. Death
   and, if you live in Canada,
3. Being taxed to death

This section is not designed to be an overview of all aspects of income tax. The intent is to identify basic yet key tax issues as they relate to retirement income. The resulting planning concepts and strategies should be discussed with your advisor. The other major tax component, estate taxes, will be discussed in Chapter 5.

We have found that the number one financial annoyance for retirees is the tax they pay on their income. Aside from the fact that we live in Canada, there may be a number of other reasons for the relatively high level of taxation. Even though there are certain tax credits that are provided to those over the age of 65, there really are no meaningful deductions like when we were working. There are no pension plan contributions, employment insurance (EI) contributions, Canada Pension Plan (CPP) contributions, RRSP deductions, etc. So, without deductions, what comes in as income is pretty much what equates to taxable income. What is also different is that during our working years we have tax deducted by our employer and remitted on our behalf. We are left with our net, take-home pay. In retirement, however, people are likely making quarterly instalments, so the presence of tax and the amount of tax to be paid are constantly in front of them. If you could imagine taking the amount of tax you paid last year, dividing it in four and writing a cheque for that amount once a quarter, you would be able to emotionally connect with those who are retired.

Tax Brackets

After the basic personal exemption to which all taxpayers are entitled, there are four federal tax brackets. Canada has what is called a progressive tax system, which simply means that your rate of tax becomes higher as your taxable income increases. Based on the measure of taxable income for the year, the rate is applied and the amount of federal tax is calculated as shown below. These figures are for the 2007 tax year.

Taxable Income	Federal Tax	Combined Federal–Provincial Tax*	Name
$0 – $9,600	0%	0%	Exemption
$9,601 – $37,178	$0 + 15%	26%	Low
$37,179 – $ 74,357	$5,673 + 22%	37%	Middle
$74,358 – $120,887	$13,942 + 26%	43%	High
$120,888 and higher	$26,040 + 29%	47%	Highest

*Using average provincial rate.

The federal tax column shows the dollar amount payable at the bracket level plus the percentage of tax on each dollar until the next bracket is reached. The combined federal–provincial figures show the resulting amount of tax payable on each taxable dollar when the average provincial tax is added to the federal levy. We have taken the liberty of naming the various brackets for easier reference.

You are entitled to receive a specific amount of income without it being taxed. This amount is known as the basic personal exemption. As shown above, the exemption amount for the 2007 tax year is $8,929.

The low bracket has an increasing marginal rate that moves up from 0 to 26 percent (combined federal and provincial rate) as you reach the upper end. The other brackets are more straightforward. For example, each dollar of income in the middle bracket attracts a rate of tax of 37 percent. The high bracket takes 43 percent of each dollar as tax, and so on.

Very often you will hear the important terms "average tax rate" and "marginal tax rate." Your average tax rate is the total tax you pay as a percentage of your total income. Your marginal tax rate is that which is applied to each new dollar of taxable income. The marginal rate on the first dollar of income is 0 percent (due to the basic personal exemption), while the marginal tax rate on your last dollar of income may be close to 47 percent when federal and provincial taxes are combined. The marginal tax rate is a significant consideration in tax planning since it represents the largest percentage of tax you pay on your income. Many of the strategies within this book are designed to reduce taxes by moving your income out of the higher tax brackets.

Beginning in the year 2000 the federal government began indexing the brackets to match increases to the consumer price index (CPI). This was supposed to have started in 1988.

Tax brackets, exemptions, clawback thresholds, and taxable income limits for determining credits are all indexed to the CPI. This is an important factor as it relates to deferring taxation into the future. It may mean lower inclusion rates and greater tax credits, which would result in a lower amount of tax payable.

Understanding the difference between a tax deduction and a tax credit will enable you and your advisor to apply strategies and employ financial tools to help you reduce the tax you pay on your retirement income.

Tax deductions are subtracted from total income to arrive at the net and taxable income figures. Any deduction serves to lower the net income figure. This has a positive effect on your income tax calculation since it will reduce tax at the highest marginal rate. As such, the value of a tax deduction increases as your income increases.

Tax credits operate differently. Once calculated, the basic federal tax is reduced by federal tax credits, which include the personal credit, age and pension credits, dividend tax credit, spousal credit, and medical expense credit. The resulting number is the federal tax payable at the lowest marginal rate.

A credit is actually more beneficial than a deduction because at the lowest marginal rate, it is a dollar-for-dollar reduction in tax payable.

For the vast majority of those people already retired, their net income for taxation purposes is equal to their total income. This is because there are few deductions that apply to an individual once they have retired. Hence, the main tax relief is found in tax credits to which we are entitled. These credits are maximized by keeping the net income calculation as low as possible. Later on in this book, we will present planning strategies that will lower your net income, thereby enabling you to be taxed at the lowest possible rate.

Quarterly Instalments and Withholding Tax

You will be required to remit tax in quarterly instalments if the difference between your tax payable and the amounts remitted from source is more than $2,000 ($1,200 in Quebec) in both the current year and either of the two preceding years.

The ability to deduct and remit directly from payments is one way to avoid the quarterly instalment process and is one that should be used whenever possible. Direct remittance of tax is available on any form of income, including government retirement benefits.

Especially in the first year of retirement, it is meaningful to approximate the total tax payable and deduct appropriate amounts from the various payments being made. Failure to do this will result in a tax bill in the spring. If you have an open or non-registered investment account, money could be taken from it to pay the taxes due. Some people face a situation where they have to pull money from RRSP accounts, and although this solves the problem it creates larger tax issues for the following year. Direct remittance is particularly important in situations where retirement income is being started mid-year after several months of employment income has been received. It is likely that larger amounts will need to be remitted for the balance of that year.

Institutions issuing Registered Retirement Income Fund (RRIF), life income fund (LIF), and locked-in retirement income fund (LRIF) payments (these plans will be discussed in Chapter 2) are required to withhold and remit taxes based on the level of payments to be made over the course of the year.

The withholding schedule is as follows:

Amount Withdrawn	Amount Withheld	
		Quebec Only
$0 – $5,000	10%	25%
$5,001 – $15,000	20%	33%
$15,001 and higher	30%	38%

For periodic income payments, no tax is withheld until the minimum withdrawal amount is exceeded. So, if only the minimum withdrawal is made, then there would be no automatic withholding. Since the minimum withdrawal amount increases each year, the older the recipient, the greater the amount of income from these sources that is not subject to withholding tax. This can be addressed by requesting, via Government of Canada tax form TD3, that a flat percentage be remitted on the entire payment. The form can be completed and submitted at the time the income stream begins or if payments have already been made. The amount of deduction can be adjusted by simply filing a new form.

It is not the responsibility of the institution or the government agency making the payments to deduct the correct amount of tax for you. Obviously these sources of payments do not know all of the other income you are receiving and what is being remitted from those different sources. The amounts to be deducted and remitted should be determined with input from you, your advisor, and, if applicable, your accountant.

The same withholding formula applies to lump-sum withdrawals from RRSPs; however, the minimum withdrawal exemption does not apply.

Taxation on Different Forms of Income

Your total income may come from many sources, some of which may be fully taxable, some may be tax favoured, and some may be tax exempt.

Fully Taxable Income

Salary, business or rental income, CPP benefits, Old Age Security (OAS) benefits, and EI benefits are all examples of fully taxable income. Interest earned on investments is also fully taxable when earned outside of an RRSP. Furthermore, when earned outside of a registered plan, interest must be declared annually, whether or not it was paid in cash (such as with compounding interest or strip bonds).

Any money coming out of registered vehicles including RRSPs, RRIFs, and pension income is fully taxable. The exception to this is if money is removed from an RRSP for either the Lifelong Learning Plan or the Homebuyers' Plan. Within registered plans such as those listed above, it does not matter whether growth occurs in the form of interest, dividend, or capital gain; whatever is removed as income is fully taxable. Outside a registered plan, dividends and capital gains are tax favoured as described below.

Tax-Favoured Income

There are forms of income that receive preferable tax treatment. For tax purposes, they are not included in income in the same manner as fully taxable sources.

DIVIDENDS

Because dividends are paid out of after-tax corporate earnings, they are taxed to you in a different manner. The amount of dividends you receive are "grossed up" by 45 percent, and that amount is included in the net income calculation. Federal tax payable is then reduced by an amount equal to 19 percent of the grossed-up amount. This allows for an integration of personal and corporate taxes in flowing the income out of the corporation to the shareholders. What this means is that $1,000 of eligible dividends creates taxable income, after the "gross-up," of $1,450. "Eligible dividends" are defined as those dividends paid from Canadian companies taxed at the general corporate rate.

One objective in tax planning is to keep the calculation of net income and taxable income low. For those over the age of 65, higher net income and taxable income numbers will negatively affect the following:

- The age amount
- OAS repayment calculation
- The spousal (and equivalent-to-spouse) amount
- Amounts for infirm dependants age 18 and older
- The caregiver amount
- Medical expenses
- Charitable donations
- Refundable medical expense supplements
- Provincial tax credits
- The GST/Harmonized Sales Tax (HST) credit

If there is no other taxable income, an individual could receive approximately $49,000 of dividend income and pay no tax. But, dividend income may reduce other government entitlements because of the gross-up calculation, especially when added to other taxable income.

The following table entitled "How the Type of Income Affects Net Income" shows how this works. Dividend income actually results in a higher income calculation for net income. If there are no other sources of income or if taxable income is low, then dividend income is advantageous. If you are adding dividend income on top of other income that is exceeding the first tax bracket, there may be a negative impact on those tax credits listed above, as well as potential reduction in OAS.

CAPITAL GAINS AND LOSSES

When you sell something for more than you paid for it, you incur a capital gain. If the reverse happens, you incur a capital loss.

As of October 18, 2000, 50 percent of capital gains are to be included in determining income. These amounts are referred to as a taxable capital gain. Capital gains are reported in the year they are *realized*. Unrealized capital gain is a form of tax deferral. If one of your goals is to defer taxation, but not in the form of registered plans, then investing for growth in the form of capital gains is an ideal strategy. This also provides the advantage of preferable taxation when the gain is realized, and to some extent you have control over when this will occur.

Capital losses can be used to offset capital gains, but not any other form of income (with the exception of losses carried forward from before May 23, 1985). They can be used in the current tax year or carried back three years and can be carried forward indefinitely.

There is a $500,000 lifetime capital gains exemption for qualified farm property or shares in a small business corporation. There is no capital gain on the sale of your principal residence. However, other real estate or property will be subject to capital gain or loss upon disposition.

HOW THE TYPE OF INCOME AFFECTS NET INCOME

Example: $1,000	Interest	**Dividends**	Capital Gains
Amount Received	$1,000	$1,000	$1,000
Tax Treatment	fully taxable	grossed-up	50% taxable
"Net Income" Value	$1,000	$1,450	$500

Source: *Prime Approach™ to Retirement Planning.*

Tax-Exempt Income

Some forms of income are not subject to taxation. Gifts or inheritances, life insurance proceeds, personal injury awards, and lottery winnings are common examples. Veterans' disability pensions and child tax benefits are government-source payments that are non-taxable.

Some social benefits, such as workers' compensation, the Guaranteed Income Supplement (GIS), and Spouse's Allowance, are not taxable but must be considered in net income for the purpose of calculating refundable and non-refundable tax credits.

As mentioned earlier, for each person filing a tax return there is a basic personal exemption. It is adjusted annually for increases in the CPI. For the 2007 tax year, the amount of this exemption is $8,929.

After-Tax Comparison

So what is the relationship between the tax treatment on different forms of income and the various tax brackets? The following table examines this by calculating how much pre-tax money would be needed from each type of income in order to have $1.00 after tax.

WITHDRAWALS REQUIRED

Tax Bracket	Rate*	Fully Taxable	Dividends	Capital Gains
Low	26%	$1.35	$1.00	$1.15
Middle	37%	$1.59	$1.09	$1.23
High	43%	$1.75	$1.26	$1.27
Highest	47%	$1.89	$1.33	$1.31

*For this calculation we are using the marginal tax rate that applies at the top of this bracket.

The above table shows why fully taxable dollars should be used to establish your base income, up to the start of the middle tax bracket ($37,179 in 2007). That is where the lowest tax will be paid. In that lowest bracket, we would need to withdraw $1.35 from a fully taxable source in order to have $1.00 after tax. Once we are in the next tax bracket (over $37,178), a withdrawal of $1.59 would be needed to get that same $1.00 after tax. The increase in the required withdrawal from $1.35 to $1.59 represents a 60% increase in taxation to get to the next dollar to spend. This is why, once we are over the first federal bracket, it is then preferable to use tax-favoured or non-taxable forms of income. You can see how much less of a withdrawal is required for dividends and realized capital gains to end up with $1.00 to spend. This will put less strain on your income-producing assets. From an efficiency perspective, it is usually preferable to have non-registered investment returns in the form of capital gains rather than dividends.

The objective is to "layer" your income streams to create the amount of after-tax income you require while keeping the "net income" figure relatively low. This may also result in preserving available tax credits and other government entitlements. These are actions consistent with the objectives of preserving and making most efficient use of your income-producing assets.

Additional Tax Credits for Seniors

At retirement, when income is being drawn from assets and benefits, few tax deductions are available. Since RRSP contribution room is calculated based on last year's income and applied to the next tax year, there may be a further RRSP deduction after retirement. Similarly, there may also be some RRSP carryforward room that can be used. However, new RRSP contributions and deductions are often unattractive to lower retirement incomes. This is because the tax savings at a lower income and resulting lower tax rate may not be significant. Taking tax-paid capital and turning it into fully taxable registered money may not always be the best strategic move, so opportunities should be examined on an individual basis.

There are, however, various tax credits that are applicable to most seniors.

Pension Credit

The pension credit applies to the first $2,000 of eligible income, which includes private pension income received through a life annuity. The credit will be available at *any age* if this is the source of payment.

Money that was once in a pension plan, but then was transferred into a locked-in retirement account (LIRA) or locked-in RRSP, lost its pension identity at that time. Therefore, if the locked-in account is subsequently converted to a LIF, LRIF, or life annuity, the income is not eligible for the pension credit until the year in which the recipient turns 65 years old.

Income from these sources would also allow a surviving spouse under the age of 65 to claim this credit.

For those individuals age 65 or over, or those under age 65 receiving pension *payments* as the result of the death of a spouse, eligible income also includes:

- Periodic annuity payments from an RRSP
- Periodic annuity payments from a deferred profit sharing plan (DPSP)
- Periodic payments from a RRIF originating from either an RRSP or DPSP
- The taxable portion of a non-registered annuity, deferred or immediate
- Periodic payments from a LIF, LRIF or PRIFF

Payments must be on a scheduled, periodic basis. For example, a monthly, quarterly, or annual payment from a RRIF would be eligible for the pension credit, but lump-sum withdrawals from an RRSP would not.

Government retirement incomes such as the GIS, CPP retirement or death benefits, and OAS payments do not qualify. Non-registered investment income (with the exception of the taxable portion of non-registered annuities) or rental income are also ineligible.

The pension credit is applicable to federal tax. When provincial tax is also factored in, the credit is worth approximately $420 to $580 depending on your province of residence.

Age Credit

Individuals age 65 or older by the end of the tax year will qualify for the age credit. It is applied to the Age Amount and effectively increases your personal exemption. For the 2007 tax year, the Age Amount is $5,177. Once your net income exceeds $30,936, the credit is reduced by 15 percent of your net income over that amount. The benefit is totally eliminated at the point where net income reaches $65,449. Both the amount of credit and the brackets for reduction of benefits are indexed to the CPI.

Like the pension credit, the benefit of the age credit is enhanced when provincial tax is considered.

If you do not need all of the pension credit and age credit to reduce your federal income tax to zero, you can transfer the unused portion of these credits to your spouse.

Medical Expense Credit

All *qualifying* medical expenses over 3 percent of your net income will create a federal tax credit of 15.5 percent. The higher your net income, the larger the 3 percent deductible. For example, consider a retiree with a $30,000 net income who has spent $1,900 on qualifying medical expenses in the calendar year. Since 3 percent of $30,000 is $900, the remaining $1,000 qualifies for the medical expense credit. The federal credit is calculated to be $155 (15.5 percent of $1,000). Provincial credits are applied in the same manner.

A married or common-law couple can combine qualifying expenses and claim them on the return of one spouse. By claiming in one name, the 3 percent exclusion is applied only once. If applied to the spouse with the lower taxable income, there is a larger balance of allowable medical expenses that qualifies for the credit. In the above example assuming $1,900 of expenses, if the lower income spouse's net income was $20,000, the 3 percent limitation is calculated at $600, leaving $1,300 to be applied to the credit—$300 more than if the higher-income earner had made the claim. The resulting credit is a dollar-for-dollar reduction of tax payable, regardless of income or tax brackets.

There is a maximum for the 3 percent exclusion. In 2007, it cannot exceed $1,925. This would represent the 3 percent calculation on a net income of $64,200.

The claim can be made for the best 12-month period ending in the tax year (24-month period prior to the time of death). Hence, if the 3 percent net income limitation wipes out any tax benefits from the credit, it is wise to save the medical expenses for use in the next year.

Some qualifying medical expenses include:

- Payments to medical practitioners and nurses
- Payments to dentists
- Prescription drugs
- Institutional care (nursing homes)
- Hospital fees not covered by public health insurance

- Costs of diagnostic procedures
- Care and supervision of persons with severe and prolonged disabilities living in a group home
- Costs of moving to accessible housing
- Home and driveway alterations to accommodate someone with mobility impairment
- Specific medical equipment and devices

A more detailed listing of the above, plus other eligible expenses, can be found at the Canada Revenue Agency (CRA) website—www.cra-arc. gc.ca.

Caregiver Credit

A tax credit is available for caregivers who provide in-home care for infirm or elderly relatives. The infirm relative must be living in the same home. The credit is factored on the Caregiver Amount, which is $4,019 in 2007. If the infirm relative's income is in excess of $13,726, the credit is reduced. It will disappear entirely if income exceeds $17,745. These are 2007 numbers and will change since both the benefit and income brackets stated above will be indexed with increases to the CPI.

If you are already claiming the amount for an eligible dependant (formerly known as equivalent-to-spouse), you can also claim either the infirm dependant tax credit or the caregiver credit. In other cases, claim either the infirm dependant tax credit or the caregiver credit, but not both. The net income level of the dependant will affect the amount of your claim.

Income-Splitting Strategies

One strategy that can be employed to reduce the tax bite on income is to split the stream of income between you and your spouse. The purpose behind creating two income streams is really quite simple—there are tax savings to be realized if we have two taxpayers instead of one. Each person has their own set of exemptions, deductions, and credits. In addition, when we can move a taxpayer from a higher tax bracket to a lower tax bracket, tax savings follow.

Assume you have a married couple and both people are age 62. One individual has income for the year of $48,000, while the other has no income. If the income is taxable in the hands of only one person, the tax payable is $11,575. If the income is split evenly between the couple, each would have a taxable income of $24,000 and each would pay $4,064 in tax, or $8,128 in total. This represents a difference in tax payable of $3,447 per year ($11,575 minus $8,128), or $287 of tax savings per month. The amount of tax savings will become even larger as personal exemption brackets continue to rise through the years. These calculations use the average combined tax rates shown previously.

This is $287 each month that our retired couple gets to spend and enjoy rather than send to the government. They did not have to save more or have better investment returns. They just split their assets during the accumulation years so they could have two income streams in retirement. For a couple over age 65, the inclusion of the age credit means the same calculations produce an even greater monthly tax saving.

The 2007 federal budget introduced measures that make it easier for pensioners to split income and achieve some of the benefits mentioned above.

Pension Splitting—2007 and Beyond

WHAT IS IT?
The 2007 federal budget introduced a measure known as "pension splitting" for tax year 2007 and beyond. This move represents a large shift from previous federal tax policy and provides the potential for meaningful tax savings for spouses and common-law partners who are in receipt of "eligible pension income" whether they are actually retired or not. There is no age limit for this to apply, nor does employment status have any effect.

These rules apply to calculation of federal tax and it is up to each province to determine if and how they will come onside with this initiative. Quebec is introducing a similar program for pension splitting that will include some features specific to Quebec. The following pertains to the federal initiative that applies to all common-law provinces.

For the definition of pension splitting, "eligible pension income" includes those income sources that qualify for the Pension Amount and Pension Credit (page 35).

WHO QUALIFIES?

A "pensioner" is anyone who is in receipt of "eligible pension income" and resident in Canada on December 31 of that tax year. The "pension transferee" is the person to whom the pension income is allocated. There are pro-rata entitlements to this program in the event of death, marital breakdown, or marriage throughout the calendar year.

HOW DOES IT WORK?

The "pensioner," knowing the amount of eligible income, can determine the amount that is to be allocated to the pension transferee (partner or spouse). The election of whether to split and how much to split is made each year, so a couple can determine what is most beneficial. A maximum of 50 percent of the eligible income can be split and will be prorated for marriage and death within a calendar year. The amount allocated will be added to the income of the pension transferee and deducted from the income of the pensioner.

A joint election must be filed each year that income is split. This is done at the time the tax return is filed. The income payments are not affected. The payor of the retirement income does not issue separate cheques. This is different from the process for splitting Canada Pension Plan (CPP) retirement benefits.

WHAT IS THE SIGNIFICANCE FOR YOU?

One of the objectives within the Prime Approach is to make the most efficient use of your income-producing assets. This means creating the after-tax cash flow you need while keeping the taxable income or net income figure low.

The ability to split income may go a long way toward this goal if there is a discrepancy in the amounts of income between two spouses or partners. There will be an obvious reduction in tax payable if we can move some income into a lower bracket. There is also the potential to further increase the tax savings through preserving some or all of the Age Credit, reducing any OAS clawback, and providing access to the Pension Credit for the pension transferee if this was not previously available to them.

The bottom line is that any time you can keep more of your own income, after tax, it is all very good news. The pension splitting initiative is, in fact, excellent news for most retirees.

The following table, derived from Finance Canada, illustrates the positive impact of this program.

Federal Tax Savings for Couple in 2007 (Both Age 65) —As Calculated by Finance (see note 1)						
Higher-Income Spouse's Eligible Pension Income	$50,000		$75,000		$100,000	
Lower-Income Spouse's Eligible Pension Income	Total Impact	% Reduction in Federal Tax (see Note 2)	Total Impact	% Reduction in Federal Tax (see Note 2)	Total Impact	% Reduction in Federal Tax (see Note 2)
$00,000	$2,586	29%	$5,122	36%	$7,439	37%
$10,000	1,301	12%	4,011	25%	5,130	23%
$20,000	492	4%	3,312	18%	2,872	12%
$30,000	460	4%	2,241	11%	1,304	5%
$40,000	460	2%	1,303	5%	158	1%
$50,000	N/A	0%	341	1%	N/A	N/A
$60,000	N/A	N/A	N/A	0%	N/A	N/A

Note 1: Table assumes each taxpayer is receiving maximum OAS benefits (assumed to be $5,594). The couple is assumed to be sharing CPP benefits. CPP benefits are assumed to be the lesser of assumed maximum benefits for 2007 ($10,298) and 5/12ths of eligible pension income. There are no other sources of income.
Note 2: Federal tax reduction includes savings from reduced clawback of Age Credit and OAS benefits, as well as pension splitting.

Shifting Income on Non-Registered Assets

What if you did not have the opportunity to split income-producing assets and benefits during your accumulation years? There are some strategies that you can employ now to make a difference going forward. The concepts shown here involve non-registered assets only. There is no way to transfer RRSP assets to another taxpayer while you are alive, only the income as described in the above section on pension splitting.

Whether it makes financial sense to initiate income-splitting strategies and, if so, to what extent will be determined by the specifics in each situation.

For our examples, we will assume that we have a married, retired couple, Joan and Dave, where Joan is the higher income recipient. She also has $200,000 of non-registered assets and is looking for some method of having less taxable income in her name.

SECOND-GENERATION INCOME

Joan has $200,000 of invested capital. She can transfer title of these investments to Dave so the assets are now in his name. The attribution rules within the tax department require that any investment earnings are taxed in her hands each year. Let's say, for example, that the taxable earnings are $10,000. Joan will be required to bring this amount into income and pay tax on it.

She can now give Dave up to $10,000 (from earnings) that he will invest in his name. Any subsequent investment returns or taxable events from this money will be in his name. This may not appear to be a significant opportunity, but when done over a number of years, the impact can be quite positive. It also keeps the amount of capital on which Joan is exposed to taxation at $200,000, since investment income is being withdrawn and given to Dave.

SPOUSAL OR FAMILY LOANS

Another option for moving non-registered assets is that of loaning money. This can be done with a spouse or any family member. For the purpose of this example, we'll assume that Joan is going to make a spousal loan to Dave in the amount of $200,000.

Proper documentation must be in place. A signed acknowledgement of the loan should be maintained in your files and should include the following information:

- Date of loan
- Amount of proceeds to be loaned
- Interest rate to be applied to outstanding balance
- Repayment terms to allow interest-only payments
- Date by which interest payments are due
- Structure (a demand loan with no defined term)
- Provision that the loan can be terminated and full repayment made with notice from either the borrower or the lender
- Signatures of all parties involved

The CRA permits this type of loan as long as certain interest rate and payment conditions are met.

Interest Rate The lender must charge interest to the borrower. The interest rate can be set by the lender, but cannot be less than the prescribed rate established quarterly by the CRA. At the time of writing, the minimum or prescribed rate is 4 percent. Of great importance is that once the loan is in place, the rate of interest applies as long as the loan is in place regardless of future changes to the prescribed rate.

Payment of Interest Payment of loan interest must be made and documented. The best way to accomplish documentation is by having loan interest paid by cheque. Interest is calculated to the end of the calendar year and must be paid by January 31 of the next year.

Once the loan is established it can stay in place indefinitely, or it can be easily wound up with repayment to the lender.

So, back to our example...

- Joan loans Dave $200,000.
- Dave immediately invests this money. Any investment returns from this point forward are taxed in Dave's hands, not Joan's.
- Dave will pay Joan $8,000 at the end of the year (assuming a full year's interest).
- The $8,000 is taxable to Joan as income, which she must declare.
- Since Dave used the loan to purchase taxable investments, the interest he pays is tax deductible. This deduction serves as a tax benefit against taxable investment gains.
- Since Dave is the lower income earner, other investment gains will be taxed at his lower rate.

SAVING THE INCOME OF THE LOWER-INCOME SPOUSE

Much like the "second-generation income" strategy, this approach is effective over longer periods of time. It involves saving an amount, each year, in the name of the lower income spouse. The amount "saved" can be up to the pre-tax income of the lower income spouse. This is a way to systematically migrate non-registered assets from one spouse to the other.

THE DOUBLE BITE ON YOUR INVESTMENT RETURNS

Earlier in this chapter, when dealing with inflation, we discussed the calculation of real rates of return. This is the net return realized after subtracting the rate of inflation from the gross or nominal return. As you may now have realized, the other factor that must be considered in determining what your money is actually earning is the tax treatment.

When inflation and taxation are combined, they work together to erode your purchasing power over time and substantially reduce your net, real rate of return.

THE IMPACT OF INFLATION AND TAXES

$10,000 Invested at 5%	Marginal Tax Rate 26%	Marginal Tax Rate 37%	Marginal Tax Rate 43%
Interest Income	$500	$500	$500
Taxes Payable	-$130	-$185	-$215
Net Income	$370	$315	$285
Less Inflation (assuming 2.0%)	-$200	-$200	-$200
Net Purchasing Power	$170	$115	$85
Real Rate of Return (Net of Taxes)	1.70%	1.15%	0.85%

This illustrates why *interest* earnings on non-RRSP holdings are a very ineffective way of taking income at higher tax rates and an even less attractive way of accumulating growth. The preferred tax treatment of dividends and capital gains and the deferral potential of capital gains, as well as their historically higher returns, make a case for equity investing outside of registered holdings.

THE FOUR Ds OF EFFECTIVE TAX PLANNING

The original three Ds of effective tax planning—deduct, divide, and defer—appear in nearly every manual or guide to tax planning. These same principles apply to both the accumulation of assets in pre-retirement years and the income strategies in the retirement years.

Deduct Anything that you have the opportunity to deduct lowers the amount of total income and assists you in arriving at a lower taxable income. A $100 deduction means a tax saving of between $27 and $51 depending on your taxable income and province of residence.

There are a number of allowable deductions, including such major items as registered pension plan contributions, RRSP contributions, and carrying charges and interest expenses on qualifying loans.

Divide Financial strategies that contribute to this type of effective tax planning include the use of spousal RRSPs and jointly held property. If both partners in a marriage have employment income, there is the opportunity to place non-registered accumulations in the name of the person with fewer assets. Although the actual division of assets must be implemented during the asset accumulation phase, there are a number of opportunities to enhance the splitting of income, assets, and entitlements at retirement.

Defer Deferring the realization and ultimately the payment of tax is of benefit to you because it keeps your money working for you longer, rather than reducing it as you go along. By doing so, your investments may have doubled or tripled by the time a disposition occurs and tax must be paid. There may also be a benefit when the tax payable is realized. If the deferral period takes you into your retirement years, or years when you experience a lower taxable income, you may also be in a lower income tax bracket when the tax is payable.

Among those tools that allow you to defer taxation are registered pension plan contributions, RRSP contributions, and DPSP contributions. For non-registered assets, tax-deferral vehicles include the use of capital gains, mutual funds that are legally set up as corporations, and cash value life insurance.

Although the concept of deferral is an important one, it is also worthy to note that we need to be careful which assets we are deferring. As later chapters will detail, there are rules and restrictions on how we can defer registered money. Remember that in addition to restrictions on how we can defer registered money, any income coming from registered sources is fully taxable. There is ample opportunity to effectively tax defer the growth on non-registered investments, and this area is one that more people need to investigate and develop. Strategies for this appear later in the book.

In the context of the Prime Approach to retirement planning and of the concept of buying time, we submit that there is a fourth D that must be included to achieve effective tax planning.

Discount Discounting refers to using insurance dollars to pay for future contingencies and liabilities rather than using our own assets for such costs. For example, you can provide tax-free dollars to cover potential costs of future health-related care and taxes. These benefits can be delivered for pennies on the dollar through insurance vehicles. Whether you are using life insurance, critical illness insurance, or long-term health-care coverage, the dramatically lower cost and the tax-efficiency of these tools create the fourth D in tax planning.

These four Ds are critical elements in attaining an effective tax plan, and thereby limiting the negative effects that taxation has on your income. Deduct, divide, defer, and discount will come up again throughout this book.

SUMMARY OF THE PRIME APPROACH

The emotional objectives of the Time Hub will always determine the Money Hub priorities. It is, therefore, essential to precisely define your objectives as they relate to the Time Hub. Often, this first important step is missed. Dialogue and action tend to wrongly centre solely around the Money Hub. The first step in integrated planning is to get the two hubs working in sync.

Remember as well that your Time Hub priorities will change as you go through the various stages of retirement. As such, the Time Hub priorities are different for the boomers coming into retirement and for their already retired parents.

The Prime Approach integrates four distinct planning channels that work together in order to achieve the desired end result. The objective of this process is to provide you with more discretion to use your income and assets for lifestyle pursuits when you are enjoying your best health. You will have the confidence and freedom to do this if you cover off potential health-risk management costs and wealth-transfer objectives with insurance vehicles rather than using your own money. We referred to this earlier as discounting.

There are a number of barriers that interfere with what we want to do. The two largest saboteurs are inflation and taxes. The preceding material showed how inflation is a form of tax if governments continue to download expenses to us that were previously covered by them. What you will see in the following pages are integrated strategies that help you deal with inflation, and minimize taxation on your income and your estate. Specifically, many of the concepts apply to keeping your net income for tax purposes low in order to take advantage of the lower tax brackets and not lose valuable tax credits.

A more detailed planning approach allows people to more readily reach their objectives, enhances the value of accumulated assets, and minimizes losses due to taxation and costly mistakes. But this is true only if the plan is enacted and followed. This section identified the three main reasons why current retirees do not use their money. The Prime Approach provides solutions to these issues, and allows retirees more freedom and discretion to enjoy their wealth.

PART TWO

The Four Planning Channels

CHAPTER TWO

The Structural Plan

Our first gear, or planning channel, is that of the structural plan. The largest and most important of the cogs, the structural plan is the formal retirement income plan. It takes into consideration the Time Hub and Money Hub priorities of the individual or couple, as well as the financial resources they have to reach their goals, and sets out the "rules" for investment review, decisions, and actions.

INITIAL CONSIDERATIONS

There are a series of points you must understand, questions you must ask, and decisions you must make before delving into the heart of structural planning.

Income Changes upon Retirement

Imagine that it is your last workday before you are retiring. You are handed your last paycheque. What are some of the differences you will experience when you are transitioning from employment to retirement? If you are already retired, you are very familiar with a few of these issues. Some of the changes that occur are subtle and gradual. Some are obvious and immediate. Either way, there is an impact—financially, psychologically, or both. These are issues with which you should be familiar. A handful of the more noticeable changes are listed below.

- Costs related to work disappear. Transportation costs, clothing specific to work, and the cost of meals or lunches are no longer a factor.
- Group insurance benefits (disability and life insurance) are commonly terminated or at least reduced when someone leaves their employer. A key planning point to examine is which, if any, of these benefits may be appropriate to continue on an individual basis. Health considerations also enter into this decision. Someone in poor health may very well want to take advantage of the non-medical conversion option available in group plans.
- With the departure from employee benefit programs, the costs of dental care, some medical requirements, and prescription drugs now fall to the individual. These costs have the potential to be quite high.
- While we are working, it is typical for people to spend most of their discretionary money on weekends and holidays, which is really leisure time. In retirement, a person has 100 percent "leisure time."
- As we go through our working years, we receive a regular paycheque from our employer. Retirement income, however, is created from benefits and drawing income from our own assets. This is a big change in how the creation of income occurs and is a large psychological shift.
- At the time an individual retires, he or she is basically finished saving money. The process now becomes one of drawing income rather than accumulating assets. This may be the point in time when an individual has the greatest net worth.

It's Net Income that Counts

For someone looking at leaving his or her employment situation for retirement, the difference between gross employment income and gross retirement income may appear quite significant. Some analysis of your earnings statement may help you clarify this disparity. Compare what you are bringing home on a net basis with what you will receive in retirement. You may find the difference in net pay is not as significant as you thought.

THE DIFFERENCE BETWEEN GROSS AND NET INCOME

	Employment	Retirement at Age 65	Difference
Gross Income	$4,000	$2,500	$1,500 (-37.5%)
Income Tax	962	494	
CPP	110	0	
EI	78	0	
Group Benefits	72	0	
Pension at 4.5%	180	0	
Parking	125	0	
Group RRSP	200	0	
Net Income	$2,273	$2,006	$267 (-11.7%)

Source: *Prime Approach™ to Retirement Planning*.

Your employment earnings have deductions for CPP, EI, retirement savings, and benefit contributions, although most of these are deductible. This fact, combined with onerous taxation at higher income levels, brings the two net income numbers more closely in line. This example also includes the age credit in the calculation of tax payable, which has the effect of raising the net retirement income.

How Long You Will Need Your Income For

Obviously, "How long will you need your income for?" is a question for which we do not know the precise answer. Life expectancy numbers continue to rise as we become older. We do not want to outlive our assets and income, but should we be running retirement income scenarios that assume we'll live until we are 110 years old?

Certain planners contend that income projections should extend until the younger of two married partners is age 90. That is one option. Certainly, the average longevity numbers suggest that the majority of those about to retire today will make it into their 80s. Seeking a solution to this question is not an attempt to have your money deplete the month after you pass away. Again, it comes down to a practical application of using your assets in a way that provides both security and the option to do more things earlier in retirement.

Other considerations on this point involve your spouse, if applicable. Will your spouse be retiring (or retired) at the same time as you? Is your spouse younger or older than you are?

Income Needs

The closer we get to an actual retirement date, the more our focus seems to shift from the accumulation of assets to what those assets will actually provide for us in retirement.

Income planning is more than totalling the sum of receipts from all sources. There are considerations of asset preservation, tax-efficiency, and inflation protection that must be addressed. To this end we must also determine the sources from which we are going to stream income.

There are three common methods used to determine your income objective.

1. Percentage of Final Earnings

The more accurate we can be in determining the income target, the better we can be in planning to deliver it. However, if we are five to 10 or more years from actually commencing our retirement, it may serve our purposes to approximate the amounts that we might need. Most commonly, this is done on a percentage of current earnings basis. It is not exact, but it does provide us with an indication as to whether or not things are on track. There are different thoughts on what percentage should be used. We often see 70 percent of inflation-adjusted income used as the target. This number may have merit if the retirement age is going to be 65. However, if earlier retirement is an objective, then a higher percentage should be used. The results here provide us with an estimate rather than a precise target, but that is the purpose of this type of calculation.

Ideally the retirement income target should be 100 percent or greater of final earnings. But why is this uncommon? The main reason is that pursuing such objectives means having to save more now. Giving up current lifestyle for this purpose may not be an acceptable trade-off for many people.

2. Matching Income Needs to Income Available

This approach allows us to see what level of income can be created from various benefits and assets. This usually involves establishing a straight rate of withdrawal from assets in a way that will not erode the initial capital value. The point of the exercise is to enable someone to see if they have the resources to be able to retire. The question put forward is "Will I have enough income to do the things I want to do?"

If the level of income is not sufficient, then you know that:

- It is not the right time to retire.
- Your income and lifestyle needs will have to be reduced.
- You will need to find some level of employment income to supplement what can be delivered from existing sources to meet the income target.

Often, there are special circumstances that trigger this type of calculation. Among these may be:

- Potential termination of existing employment (downsizing/layoff/ plant closing)
- Desire to leave or change from current employment environment
- Desire for more control over personal time
- Sudden and radical change of objectives
- Sudden and radical change in the state of your health (or your spouse's)

As suggested by the reasons listed above, the request for this type of calculation is usually the result of changes in Time Hub priorities. If this is the case, often the person will retire even if the actual numbers do not solidly support the move. These are examples of the Time Hub priorities driving the Money Hub priorities.

3. The Budget Approach

By working through a detailed budget to more accurately determine the amount of after-tax income we will need, the more likely we will preserve and even grow the assets that will produce this income. Simply stated, this method provides for the most relevant delivery of income and the most efficient use of assets. It is the preferred approach for determining your income needs in retirement.

The data forms at the back of the book include a budget worksheet for your use. The purpose of this particular worksheet is twofold. First, it will allow you to estimate what your regular expenses are and then compare those estimates to your actual experience. This should be measured over several months to balance out any unusually large or abnormally small allocations to any of these areas. Second, it should be used as a tool to estimate what the level of expenditures will be after you retire, relative to what you are currently spending.

Whichever of the three methods is used, the plan should provide flexibility in its structure to allow for adjustments in the amount of income being delivered. The commencement of retirement involves charting some unknown waters. For all of the care put into planning, expectations, and calculating income needs, there may end up being too much or too little income. Too much income is not tax effective and may hinder the battle against inflation. Too little income means that basic needs and wants are not being met.

Working After You Retire

Often we find that people are looking to be involved in some kind of employment after they retire. There are a number of reasons that drive this decision. The obvious one would be the financial rewards. Less income needs to be drawn from assets if you are receiving a paycheque. This has the added benefit of allowing assets to grow or to at least be drawn upon in a lesser amount. Income earned from employment may go toward a special purchase or purpose such as a vacation. Post-retirement work may also be a form of social activity or recreation. It may be an opportunity to be involved in an area of personal interest.

Work after retirement may, but usually does not, involve full-time employment. There are many part-time, contract, casual, and consulting opportunities available. Most retirees, if they decide to work, will do so on a schedule and a basis that is convenient for them. This is not the case with people who are required to work because they are not in a financial position to retire.

Some people simply have a desire to make a more gradual transition into a full state of non-employment. To this end, volunteer work is also an option.

Where You Are Going to Live

One of the Time Hub priorities is accommodation. We have strong emotional ties to the place we call our home, so one of the important decisions to be made at the time you retire is determining where you are going to live.

Staying in your current house likely means that there is no rent or mortgage payment that forms part of your lifestyle needs. If you sell your home, it will mean that there is a non-registered sum of money to consider for investment and income purposes. On the other hand, you will have a rent payment that must be taken from cash flow. Remember that this payment must be a net after-tax return from the invested proceeds of the house.

The vast majority of the time, the decision people make concerning their home is not solely financial, but is primarily driven by Time Hub considerations. There are a number of questions about the principal residence that need to be addressed at the time retirement begins and the plan is put together. These are included in the data forms. Additional accommodation considerations over the retirement years may include:

- Do you plan to remain in the same city?
- Do you plan to remain in the current residence?
- What are the accommodation options if you move from your current residence?
- Is the size of your house appropriate?
- Is there a need for a different climate?
- Do you have a desire to be closer to family?
- Are you close enough to children/grandchildren who have moved away?
- Is property maintenance becoming too difficult?
- If you or your spouse pass away, what are the intentions of the survivor in regard to the principal residence?

In most situations the principal residence is among the largest assets that a family has. It is important to know what the immediate plans are for this asset.

The Best Use of Your Income

A retiree at age 62 and a retiree at age 82 do not spend money in the same way. And people do not require the same level of income, fully indexed, all the way through retirement. Retirement illustrations that show a fully indexed income all the way through your life are basically misleading.

These illustrations will show that in order to deliver a level of income, assets are going to exhaust.

When they see this kind of retirement plan, retirees immediately fear that they are going to run out of income. With this mindset, why in the world would they ever think of using some of their assets in their earlier retirement years? If the income requirement projection is not adjusted realistically, people may not feel they have enough flexibility and income in the early years when they can really enjoy things.

Most retirees realize that the first 10 years of retirement, regardless of whether they retire at age 48 or 68, will be the best 10 years that they have. Statistically, using the averages in Canada, a male age 65 can expect to live another 15 years, eight of which will be in good health. Females can expect another 19 years after age 65, nine of which will be free from major health problems.

People may put off retirement or delay doing things when retired because they fear running out of money in the later years. They then run the risk of losing the opportunity to enjoy their money if there is a change in the state of health of one of the partners or if one of the partners passes away. Keeping in mind your objectives for your assets, you should plan for your assets to deliver some additional income in the early years of retirement. There are far too many examples of people in their 80s and 90s with hundreds of thousands of dollars in assets sitting idle. These people don't even spend enough on a monthly basis to use up their government entitlements, let alone investment income or capital. The tax department usually ends up being the largest beneficiary in this type of scenario.

As long as it is consistent with your objectives, it may serve you well to consider planning scenarios that include two different levels of income. The first level would be the higher one in the earlier, more active years when additional income is required. The second level is for that time in later retirement where you are not likely to be as active. Both income streams would be indexed but, for example, if at age 75 the income flow were reduced by 25 percent, this would reflect an expected slowdown in spending.

This does not mean that you are planning to exhaust all assets or have income run out at a given age. It does mean that you are bringing some of your assets and income "forward" to use at a time when health and desire make it most appropriate.

Is this a contradiction to earlier comments? The previous chapter spoke of the number of baby boomers soon retiring, looming problems with the health-care system, and a reduced ability for government to fully fund programs. How, then, can it be suggested that people spend some of their money earlier in their retirement? What about concerns of funding long-term health-care costs or leaving an inheritance? An effective approach to solving these problems is found in the integrated planning that encompasses the four distinct planning channels.

Consolidating Your Assets

Making the best use of your income goes hand in hand with making the best use of your assets. The first step in having your assets work most efficiently for you is to consolidate them with one advisor or institution. Having things scattered about between competing advisors is not a form of efficient diversification. Consolidating your assets affords you the following benefits.

- Better planning, no conflicting advice, less confusion
- More control over amounts and sources of income
- More efficient asset allocation/better portfolios
- More opportunity for tax-efficiency/savings
- Less administration—reporting, number of cheques
- More orderly, expedient, and less costly wealth transfer—easier for surviving spouse, beneficiaries, and estate
- Lower investment costs/higher deposit rates

Of course, any advisor or institution would like to attract all of the investment capital you have. Yes, they will gain by having all of your business, but you will be the much larger beneficiary of such action. You cannot achieve the same degree of efficiency for the benefits listed above unless you consolidate your holdings.

Where You Should Draw Your Income From

Your advisor needs to be proficient in "layering" your income. This is the process of putting together your income streams in the most efficient manner to create the after-tax cash flow you need. It involves the "intelligent disassembly" of your assets and incorporates the following considerations.

- Using the least flexible income sources as they are available
- Using the least tax-efficient income sources in lower tax brackets
- Working efficiently within the tax brackets
- Putting the least amount of "strain" on an asset to deliver the next dollar to spend
- Looking for income-splitting opportunities
- Determining which assets are best to use and which are best to defer

There are four basic sources from which income is drawn.

1. Government retirement benefits, including OAS and CPP
2. Pension plans or locked-in accounts
3. RRSP assets
4. Non-registered (open) assets

Income should be drawn from these sources in accordance with one basic rule: use the least flexible, least tax-efficient sources first.

Obviously we have no control over the amount of income that comes from government benefits or pension income in the form of an annuity. If we establish those sources as the base income, we will have discretion in terms of how we handle our accumulated assets. With the exception of minimum withdrawal amounts on registered assets, we will have control, to some degree, over withdrawals that are made from our personal accounts.

The sections that follow look in detail at the various income sources. For the most part, these income sources will be examined in the order in which we believe they should be triggered. This is all part of the structural planning channel within the Prime Approach to retirement planning.

FIGURE 2.1—SOURCES OF RETIREMENT INCOME

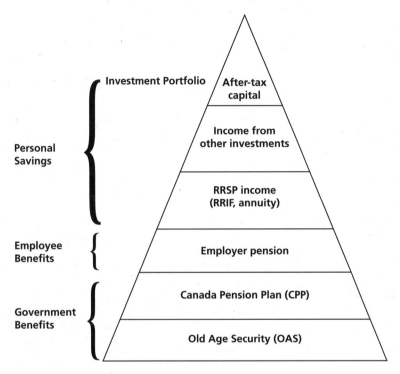

Source: *Prime Approach™* to *Retirement Planning*.

SECTION 1:

Government Retirement Benefits

We feel comfortable in contending that there will always be some form of government retirement income program(s) in place. Currently, there are two primary benefit plans under this umbrella. The first is Old Age Security (OAS), the universal government pension that also includes the Guaranteed Income Supplement (GIS). The second is the Canada Pension Plan (CPP). The main purpose of the CPP is to provide a base replacement of earnings for retirees. Neither program, nor the combination of programs, is designed to serve as the total source of retirement income for an individual or couple.

OLD AGE SECURITY (OAS)
Old Age Security (OAS) is a universal entitlement to Canadians who fall into any of the categories listed below.

- Retirees living in Canada
- Individuals age 65 or over
- Those living in Canada who are Canadian citizens or legal residents at the time their pension is approved
- Those who have lived in Canada for at least 10 years as an adult
- Retirees living outside of Canada
- Those who left the country and were Canadian citizens or legal residents of Canada when they left

The OAS Program
No direct contributions are made to the OAS program. It is funded out of the general revenues of the federal government. The income is fully indexed to increases in the consumer price index (CPI) and adjustments are made on a quarterly basis. There are no reductions if the CPI declines. The amount of income from an OAS full pension is the same for everyone, assuming no Guaranteed Income Supplement (GIS) applies (more on this shortly).

With OAS, there are no survivor benefits, no income-splitting opportunities, and no option to commence this income prior to age 65.

Calculation of Benefit

Technically, there are 40 equal portions in the OAS "pie." Full pension allows you to qualify for all 40 portions each month. Full pension is payable if you have lived in Canada for at least 40 years after turning 18, or if you meet all three of the following conditions:

1. You were born on or before July 1, 1952.
2. Between the time you turned 18 and July 1, 1977, you lived in Canada for some period of time.
3. You lived in Canada for the 10 years immediately before your application was approved.

If you do not meet the criteria in either of the full benefit categories, you may still be eligible for a partial pension. For example, someone who lived in Canada for 10 years would qualify for 10 of the 40 portions of the pie. In other words, he or she would have an entitlement to 25 percent of the full pension.

Amount of OAS Benefit

At May 2007, the monthly income provided from this benefit was $491.93 per month or $5,903.16 per annum.

The OAS "Clawback"

The federal government implemented a ceiling on income at which point OAS would be taken back or "clawed back." It was determined that after a certain level of net income ($63,511, including OAS payments from the previous year) you did not need the full OAS pension. Every dollar of net income over this amount reduces the OAS receipt by 15 percent. It was determined that past a certain higher net income level, you did not need *any* OAS pension. As such, at a net income of $102,865 or above, you will be ineligible for any OAS pension.

The clawback calculation is assessed on an individual income basis, not on household income. There is no repayment of the benefit. It is simply adjusted or eliminated for the following year. Since July 1996, OAS payments are adjusted based on the prior year's net income. There are some planning strategies that can assist you to keep your income level below the point where the clawback of the OAS benefit occurs. After all, it is frustrating, after years of paying taxes, to forgo this payment.

One way for you to avoid this clawback may be to take far more income one year and then far less the next. In this way you could at least obtain the OAS payment every second year. Going through the numbers in detail with your advisor would reveal whether this exercise would be worth the effort.

Payments to Canadian Non-Residents

If you lived in Canada for at least 20 years after the age of 18, OAS payments will continue until your death. This would also apply if you lived or worked in a country that has a social security agreement with Canada—because of that you are considered to meet the 20-year residency requirement. If residency in Canada was less than 20 years, payments are made to you for the month of departure and six months thereafter. Then they cease.

The Guaranteed Income Supplement (GIS)

The income security benefits within OAS extend to include what is known as a Guaranteed Income Supplement (GIS). In order to qualify for any GIS benefits, either you or your spouse must be eligible for OAS. Entitlements also include the Spouse's Allowance and the Widowed Spouse's Allowance. If total income is below a maximum level, pensioners may qualify either as a single person or a couple. To even qualify for partial benefits, your income must be near or below the poverty line. Check with Human Resources and Social Development Canada (HRSDC) to obtain the income schedule by visiting the HRSDC website at www.hrsdc.gc.ca, or by phoning HRSDC, Income Security Programs at 1-800-277-9914 (English) or 1-800-277-9915 (French).

An individual or couple who does receive benefits under the GIS must qualify each year because the entitlement is based on net income from the previous year. All benefits payable under the GIS program are non-taxable.

The Spouse's Allowance

This benefit provides money for low-income seniors who meet all of the following conditions:

- Their legal or common-law spouse is entitled to receive OAS pension and GIS.
- They are 60 to 64 years old.
- They are a Canadian citizen or legal resident.
- They have lived in Canada since age 18 for at least 10 years.

If these conditions apply, but the spouse is widowed, the survivor may apply for the Widowed Spouse's Allowance.

The complete schedule of OAS and GIS payments and qualifying income limits can be found at the HRSDC website.

CANADA PENSION PLAN (CPP)

The Canada Pension Plan (CPP) offers an element of protection to the contributor and his or her family against the loss of income due to retirement, disability, or death. For the purpose of this book, we will concentrate on the benefits that come at retirement.

Calculation of Retirement Benefits

The benefits payable from the CPP are dependent upon the level of contributions made by the employee and employer and the number of years during which contributions are made. This differs from OAS, which is a uniform amount with universal entitlement. The CPP is designed to replace about 25 percent of the earnings that an individual paid into the plan, up to what is known as the Yearly Maximum Pensionable Earnings, or YMPE.

Adjustments are made in the benefit payable calculation through what is known as the dropout clause. This actually increases the benefits payable by eliminating 15 percent of the lowest-earning years from the calculation, and provides a higher income to those who may have had lower or no earnings in certain years or were late in entering the workforce. There is also an adjustment for years when a parent was at home with children under the age of seven. In 2007, an individual age 65, with entitlement to the maximum retirement benefit, will receive a monthly CPP pension of $863.75.

Income Splitting with CPP

Sharing or assignment of pensions allows spouses who are together (not separated or divorced), and are both eligible, to combine their pension incomes and split the total evenly between them. It is a form of income splitting and may offer some tax savings, especially if there is a discrepancy in the amounts they would receive as individuals.

Eligibility

- Both spouses must be at least age 60.
- Both must have applied for CPP retirement benefits if they were contributors.
- The splitting of income is allowed even if only one spouse has contributed (that spouse can apply).

Purpose

- Recognizes the role of both spouses in earning pensions
- Provides each spouse with a retirement pension even if one did not contribute
- An income-splitting opportunity

Assignment Ceases

- When one of the spouses dies
- Upon divorce or after separation of one year
- Benefits will revert to the original entitlement, but a survivor's income may apply.

Applying to Split CPP

To split your CPP, you and your spouse need to apply, together, at an HRDC office. You will be required to complete the request form, have the usual personal identification documents with you, and present a marriage license or certificate.

Early Receipt of CPP Benefits

To qualify for retirement benefits from the program, an individual must have contributed to the plan, be 60 years of age or older, and:

- Have stopped working, or
- Have had no employment income for one month, or
- Have had two consecutive months where for each month employment income is less than the maximum, monthly CPP pension that would be paid at age 65 ($863.75 in 2007)

After commencing the CPP benefit, a person can earn employment income without limits, but he or she will not be permitted to make additional contributions to the CPP. The Quebec Pension Plan (QPP), however, permits additional contributions, adjusting benefits when the secondary employment ceases.

The basic calculation for early receipt is as follows. The amount of entitlement is reduced by one-half of 1 percent for each month (6 percent for each year) that income has been received prior to age 65.

The table that follows shows the factors involved in starting CPP retirement benefits early. The numbers relate to each $100 of CPP income that one would be entitled to at age 65.

Early Receipt of CPP Income

Age	60	61	62	63	64
Months Early	–60 months	–48 months	–36 months	–24 months	–12 months
Percentage of Age 65 Income (Decrease of 1/2% Monthly)	70%	76%	82%	88%	94%
Monthly Payments	$70	$76	$82	$88	$94
Monthly Decrease	$30	$24	$18	$12	$6
Payments Prior to 65	$4,200	$3,648	$2,952	$2,112	$1,128
Make-Up Time (in Months)	140	152	164	176	188
Make-Up Time (in Years)	11.66	12.67	13.67	14.67	15.67
Break-Even Age	77	78	79	80	81

Taking Your CPP Benefits While Working

Changes made in 2005 allow for an individual to commence CPP retirement benefits as long as the conditions stated at the start of this section are met. Why would someone want to have CPP income early if they are still working? The table above shows some of the reasons, but consider some additional points on this strategy.

If you receive your CPP benefits when you are still working, the rate of tax you pay on this receipt may be higher compared to when you are retired. However, the main reason for electing your CPP retirement benefit early, even if you do not need the income, is to allow you to convert an inflexible, tax-inefficient, limited-life income stream into a more flexible asset.

The following table shows the potential benefits of investing the CPP retirement benefit for an individual age 60 until age 65. It assumes Ontario tax rates and a rate of return of 6 percent. The column titled "Sheltered" assumes that the entire CPP payment was put into an RRSP.

Marginal

Rate	Sheltered	Open
21%	$42,571	$33,624
31%	$42,571	$29,367
44%	$42,571	$23,811

The benefits of early receipt become even more meaningful if you have a couple where both people are entitled to CPP retirement benefits. As stated below in "CPP Survivor Benefits," a survivor can receive both a survivor's benefit and a retirement benefit, but the sum of the two cannot exceed the maximum entitlement payable to a retiree age 65. So, if the two individuals were each entitled to the maximum and waited until age 65 to start retirement income from CPP, at the passing of the other there would be no survivor benefit. Starting the retirement income at an earlier age at a lower amount would leave room for a "top up" on this formula.

CPP Survivor Benefits

Survivor benefits will be paid if the deceased made CPP contributions for at least three years. If the contributory period is longer than nine years, the individual must have contributed in one-third of the calendar years in their contributory period, or 10 calendar years, whichever is less.

Death Benefit

A lump-sum benefit is payable to the heir or representative of the estate on the death of a contributor. Currently this amount is a flat payment of $2,500. The QPP pays six times the monthly receipt of the pension, to a maximum of $2,500.

Surviving Spouse's Pension

In determining the survivor's benefit, the following factors are considered:

- The spouse's age at the time the contributor died
- How long and how much the contributor paid into the plan
- Whether the spouse is already receiving a CPP disability or retirement benefit

CPP calculates what the pension entitlement of the deceased contributor would have been if they were 65 at the time of their death. This factor is combined with the age of the surviving spouse at the time of the contributor's death. The following details the benefits:

Spouse younger than 35 (no children/not disabled)
- No entitlement until age 65

Spouse age 35 to 44 (no children/not disabled)
- Full benefit, less $\frac{1}{120}$ per month under the age of 45

Spouse age 45 to 65
- Flat rate, plus 37 ½ percent of the "calculated" retirement benefit

Spouse older than 65
- 60 percent of the "calculated" retirement benefit

Additional Survivor Benefit Points

- If more than one survivor benefit is payable, only the greater benefit will be paid.
- A spouse already in receipt of a CPP retirement income can collect the survivor benefit as well. The sum of the two receipts cannot exceed the maximum income payable to a pensioner age 65.
- Survivor benefits do not end on remarriage.

Children's Benefit

A benefit is paid to a natural or adopted child when a contributor passes away and the child is:
- Under the age of 18, or
- Between 18 and 25, with full-time attendance at a recognized educational institution

Detailed information on these and other government income programs, including entitlements and qualifying criteria, can be obtained through the HRSDC.

APPLYING TO RECEIVE CPP RETIREMENT AND OAS BENEFITS

CPP and OAS benefits must be applied for through HRSDC. Government publications suggest that formal application be made six months prior to the month income is expected/requested to commence.

GOVERNMENT BENEFITS AND THE PRIME APPROACH

Since both the CPP and OAS are a form of annuity with limited, if any, benefits after death, withdrawals should be started as soon as they are available. The earlier table showing the effects of early CPP withdrawal shows that by age 77 or 78, depending on when benefits commenced, one would have received more if they had waited until age 65 to start. The problem is that we have no guarantee that we will live to be in our late 70s.

It makes sense to start government benefits as early as possible for several reasons.

- There are limited survivor benefits.
- They have no capital value to the estate.
- Income from these programs is income that we do not have to draw from our own assets.
- We have no control over how government plans work. There is no flexibility.
- We can convert a limited-life, tax-inefficient, inflexible income stream into an income-generating asset.
- CPP and OAS benefits are fully taxable (with the exception of GIS) and should form part of your income base.

Pension Plans and Locked-In Accounts

The main purpose of a pension plan is to assist employees in creating an income that will help them replace their paycheque when they retire. It is a vehicle that allows the employer to make contributions on the employees' behalf. Usually, but not always, there is some form of employee contribution into the same plan.

It would seem that a pension plan is the most effective accumulation vehicle since it involves employer contributions, but contribution formulas and types of pension plans vary substantially. It is very important for you to be aware of the amount of income that you can realistically expect from this source.

Sometimes formal pension programs have been complemented, and in some cases replaced, by other accumulation vehicles in the pursuit of building capital assets for the employees' retirement. The trend in this area is a move to contribution schemes that still allow for employer contributions and yet provide more flexibility for the employee when the time comes for them to commence income. These vehicles include DPSPs and Group RRSPs. Many companies have implemented Group RRSPs with employer contributions.

In formal pension plans, there has been a gradual move away from defined benefit programs to defined contribution (money purchase) plans. Increasingly, there has also been an opportunity for employees to select specific investment strategies for their own, and their employer's, contributions.

TYPES OF PENSION PLANS

Defined Benefit Plans

As the name of these plans suggests, there is a specific formula that determines what the plan members' financial benefit will be at retirement. As such, the amount of income to be paid out by the plan is known in advance.

A number of different formulas can be used to calculate the income payable, but regardless of the calculations used there are three key factors that will determine the retirement income to be received:

1. Years of pensionable service
2. The defined pension benefit factor, which is usually between 1 percent and 2 percent per year of service
3. A formula to measure your income, such as
   - Career average earnings, or
   - Final average earnings (e.g., the best five years of income in the last seven years of service)
   Currently, the maximum pension that can be paid is the lesser of:
   - $1,722.22 times the years of pensionable service, or
   - 2 percent times the average of your best three consecutive years of remuneration times the number of years of pensionable service

For example, if you work for 35 years and earn the maximum pension allowable, your pension income would be 35 times $1,722.22, or $60,277.70. For those people earning over $86,000 this ceiling would effectively lower the rate of pension paid, relative to their income. Since 2004, the maximum of $1,722.22 has been indexed to reflect increases in the average wage.

Consult your employer benefit or pension booklet for the details of your plan. Providing this information to your advisor will help him or her guide you in your planning.

Features of Defined Benefit Plans

INTEGRATED PENSION
A defined benefit plan may be an integrated pension, which is a plan that includes the CPP/QPP retirement income in the benefit formula. This would take into consideration that, for a working career of 35 years, the benefit provided by CPP/QPP is equivalent to 0.7 percent of the Yearly Maximum Pensionable Earnings (YMPE) for each year of employment. For example, an integrated benefit of 70 percent of final average earnings may see a formula of 1.3 percent of earnings up to the YMPE and 2 percent on earnings thereafter. It is not a common process to use OAS benefits in the same manner; in fact, it is actually illegal to do so in some provinces.

INTEGRATED BENEFITS

This option allows the pensioner, in the case of early retirement, to take into account the amount of government payments they will receive and combine those with their pension to provide a higher income, earlier.

This has the effect of levelling the total pension income, except for any indexing provisions. At the time the CPP/OAS benefits actually do commence, the employment pension is reduced by the same dollar amount. The trade-off for this higher, initial income is that there is no increase in income at the time CPP and OAS commence.

FIGURE 2.2—INTEGRATED BENEFIT

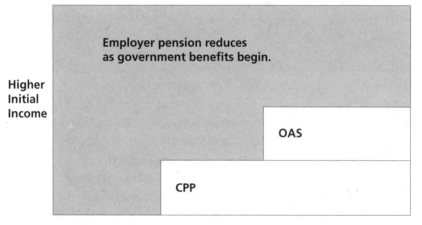

There are certain life insurance companies that will issue a form of personally purchased annuity structured on this same basis. This could be acquired with proceeds of a defined contribution plan (discussed in detail shortly), a locked-in RRSP, or a LIRA.

BRIDGING

Bridge benefits, unlike integrated benefits, are paid after early retirement commences until the plan member turns age 65 and can collect OAS and full CPP/QPP retirement benefits.

What also differentiates this from integrated benefits is that there is not the same reduction factor for electing the value of future benefits early.

The employer pension does not decline, and the full, unreduced benefits of CPP/QPP and OAS are paid in addition to the pension income. The bridge is an additional payment, provided by the employer, that does not impact the future value of the pension income or government entitlements.

The maximum bridge benefit allowed is the total of the CPP/QPP retirement and OAS benefits that the plan member would be eligible to receive if they were 65 at the time the bridge benefit commences.

If the plan member receiving the benefit has not reached the age of 60 or has not completed 10 years of pensionable service, the maximum bridge benefit is reduced by:

- One-quarter of 1 percent for each month that the bridge benefit commences prior to age 60, and
- 10 percent for each year of pensionable service less than 10 years

INDEXATION

These are adjustments made to the amount of pension income to allow it to keep pace with inflation. Indexing formulas vary. Normally they are stated as a goal rather than a commitment, and often the target amount of indexing to apply to the income will be a fraction or percentage of the actual inflation rate. Application of the indexing feature in whole or in part will be contingent on the overall health of the plan, including actuarial soundness, surpluses, etc. This benefit is most common in public sector plans and is very seldom found in the private sector. Bridging and benefit integration are enhancements found only in defined benefit plans.

Defined Contribution (Money Purchase) Plans

The other pension plan option is far less complicated than the defined benefit model. In a defined contribution plan, the employee, employer, or both contribute a fixed percentage of income. Usually, but not always, the amount of contribution is the same from both parties.

The account value of these plans is the combination of employee and employer contributions plus investment growth (or loss). Assuming any vesting requirements have been satisfied, the employee is entitled to the account value to create his or her income. When the time comes to commence retirement income, the choices are identical to those available in a defined benefit program. Life annuities, the LIF, and its cousin, the LRIF, are discussed in detail later in this chapter.

Employers are moving away from the defined benefit form of pension since their *liabilities* are undefined. With a defined contribution model, they know exactly what their costs will be. By moving to a defined contribution arrangement, the responsibility for retirement planning now shifts to the employee. The employee chooses how the pension money will be invested, and will need to do some planning around what may or may not be successfully provided by the pension plan.

READING PENSION STATEMENTS

As a member in a pension plan you will receive an annual statement.

In the case of a defined contribution plan, the account balance of the pension plan will be shown along with activity for the year, such as contributions and investment results. There may also be a commuted benefit value in the event of termination, and an amount that would be payable in the event of the plan member's death.

Defined benefit plan statements often include the same information listed above and will show the pension earned to date that will apply at the normal retirement date, usually age 65. Also included is the commuted value of that benefit, plus information on death benefits. What you should know is that the future monthly income amount that is shown on your pension statement will quite likely not be the amount that you receive. Why is that?

The annual statement of a defined benefit plan commonly projects the future income payable on the basis of a single life annuity with a five-year guarantee. What you need to be aware of is how this income is calculated. As you will see in the pages that follow, if you choose a joint life annuity, a longer guarantee period, or both, your actual pension payable may be 15 percent to 25 percent lower than the amount shown on your statement.

Since pension benefits can represent a large percentage of your retirement income, such a reduction could have a major impact on your plans. Discuss this with your advisor. Understand what it is that you can ultimately expect from your pension.

COMMUTING PENSION VALUES

Whether you have come to the point of retirement or of termination of employment, you will be presented with options regarding your pension plan entitlement. At retirement, one of the choices that may be available is the option to commute the account into a lump sum within a locked-in RRSP or LIRA. Since this is likely a large sum of money, it is highly appropriate to explore your options to make the best decisions.

Larger issues surface in defined benefit pensions. By law the commuted value must reflect any *guaranteed* enhancements in the policy, such as indexing or early retirement subsidies. What is not included in the calculations are any future ad hoc improvements, such as pension contract changes, which positively affect current members and current annuitants of the plan, and increases in income due to plan surplus allocation. Commutation also means that there is no opportunity for integration of benefits with CPP/OAS, and no option of bridging, which is a supplement that provides a level income until the commencement of CPP/OAS.

There may be restrictions within the plan that preclude you from commuting your pension after a certain age (age 55, for example). In this case your only option is to transfer your pension to a life annuity when you wish income to commence. This is common in defined benefit programs.

If you are employed in the public sector, you may participate in a pension plan where income is adjusted to the CPI or some portion thereof. This is known as an indexed pension. As described above, the commuted value would reflect any provision such as indexing, and other guarantees and enhancements. Long-time employees who participate in such a plan would have a rather substantial sum that potentially may be available to them for commutation.

Before a long-time employee makes this move, however, it is important for him or her to consider what the key issues are regarding the use of this asset. If the most important factors are the amount of income to be received and the fact that it is guaranteed, then the annuity option would be the logical choice. There would need to be some unique and compelling objectives other than those mentioned above to even consider commuting the value. This may change if we are ever in a situation where locking-in rules no longer exist, such as in Saskatchewan. This issue is discussed in more detail later in this chapter.

Another point to consider is that the transfer value has an interest rate applied to it for purposes of calculation. The rate can change significantly over short periods of time, and when applied to large sums of capital can result in a large change in value.

In certain employer plans, commuting the pension benefits precludes the retired employee from participating in health benefit plans that are otherwise available to those who have chosen a formal pension income. This point should be investigated, as it may be a key consideration for some.

THE COMMUTATION TEST

If you have participated in a pension plan for only a short period of time prior to leaving your company, you may be able to simply cash in the balance or move it to an RRSP. This is because the requirement to have it moved to a locked-in vehicle is dependent on the size of your pension balance. Currently, in Manitoba, if either of the two tests listed below is met, there is no need for a locked-in account; the money can be rolled to an RRSP for tax deferral or taken as cash.

1. The *sum* commuted is less than 4 percent of the YMPE, or
2. The calculated, *deferred income* payable in the normal form of pension at the normal retirement age, as defined by the master pension document prepared by your company's human resources department, is less than 4 percent of the YMPE

The percentages used differ from province to province and are becoming more liberal, meaning that larger and larger pensions will be allowed to avoid being locked in.

The ability to keep assets flexible is important. The numbers above would represent a very small pension accumulation, but it is still important that you be aware of your options and how they apply to your assets. Investigate before taking action.

PENSION INCOME OPTIONS AT RETIREMENT

You contribute to your pension plan to accumulate funds for retirement. When the time comes to create income from this asset, the role of the pension plan actually ceases.

The income you receive from pension plan accumulations is delivered by one of two financial tools that provincial pension legislation permits you to use, a life annuity or a Life Income Fund (LIF). In certain provinces, there is a third option called the Locked-In Retirement Income Fund or LRIF.

Income from a pension source must, by law, provide payments for the lifetime of the pension plan member, so pension funds cannot be rolled into a vehicle that can be exhausted or cashed out, nor can lump-sum withdrawals be made. Pension accounts must be converted to an income-delivery vehicle by the end of the year in which the plan member turns age 71.

The exception to this pertains to members of pension plans in the province of Saskatchewan. More on this point later.

The restrictions described above apply to *all* monies deemed by provincial pension legislation to be locked in. This includes not only money from a pension plan, but also money that was formerly in a pension plan and was transferred by you into a locked-in RRSP or into a LIRA. These are basically the same vehicles, with the only notable difference being that, in some jurisdictions, LIRAs are preregistered with the government supervisory authorities. There is no difference in the options available at the time income is to commence.

The income-delivery tools we will examine apply to all of the assets mentioned previously, including initial income options for both defined contribution and defined benefit pension plans. For LIF or LRIF options, the values of the plan must be commuted.

Life Annuities

Whether the annuity income is coming from a defined contribution or a defined benefit plan, it will be paid in the form of a life annuity. Until the early 1990s, the life annuity was the most common and, to a large extent, the only option for commencing income from a pension plan or locked-in asset.

A life annuity is a stream of future payments composed of a combination of principal and interest. Think of an annuity as a loan in reverse. When you borrow money, you arrange a repayment schedule of so much per month until principal and interest are completely paid off. With a life annuity, instead of borrowing capital we are lending our pension plan value to the institution or plan trustees. They are repaying us on a monthly basis. These payments to us are known as pension income.

Instead of a set period of time for repayment, as we are used to when we borrow money, the income schedule for a life annuity is based upon average life expectancy. Some individuals pass away before that date and "subsidize" the amount of payments to those people who live longer than the average.

Remember that you can never outlive the income to be paid to you from a life annuity. Regardless of how long you live, the income will be paid. In a very real sense, the pensioner is "purchasing" his or her income with the capital accumulating in the plan.

Life Annuity Options

There are different forms of life annuities and various features that apply to each of them. This recognizes that pension plan members have different financial circumstances and objectives. When the time comes for you to assess your pension options, there are a number of decisions that you must make in choosing your lifetime income.

SINGLE OR JOINT LIFE
You can choose a life annuity based on your life only (single life annuity) or on two lives (joint life annuity) with the second individual not necessarily your spouse. Normally, if a single life annuity is chosen, a guarantee period is attached in order to provide both some form of income continuance to a survivor and some potential estate benefit.

LEVEL OR REDUCING SURVIVOR INCOME
In a joint life annuity, the income to the primary annuitant (pension plan member) is normally level for life. Income for a surviving annuitant can be level or it can reduce by 25 percent, 33 percent, or 50 percent. In many, but not all annuities, the reduction in the survivor's income does not occur until the end of what is called "the guarantee period," which will be discussed next.

Is a reducing survivor benefit an appropriate choice or should it always be level? The answer to this depends on a number of factors, many of which are financial. Consider the following. Are there other assets that can replace the income reduction? What is the age difference of the two people involved? What is the state of health of each?

What we are emphasizing with these questions is that every financial decision is contingent upon a number of factors, all of which fall into either the Time Hub or Money Hub. No decision about income and assets, especially involving your pension, should be made without full consideration of the big picture.

GUARANTEE PERIOD

Think of the guarantee period like a warranty on a new toaster, DVD player, or car. Basically it provides repair or reconciliation should something happen early in the life of your purchase. The same applies to an annuity. The guarantee assures that a certain value will be paid out either in the form of income, balance of payments to the estate, or both.

Let's use an example of the joint life, level income annuity with a 15-year guarantee. Fred is the pension plan member and Bev, his wife, is the other annuitant. Exactly five years after the annuity starts, Fred passes away. The income continues in the same amount to Bev. She passes away exactly five years from the date of Fred's passing. In total, 10 years' worth of payments have been made. A 15-year guarantee means that five years' worth of income payments would still be paid to the estate, since both annuitants passed away within 15 years of starting the annuity. If either of them lived past 15 years and then passed away, payments would continue until both Fred and Bev passed away, but there would be no residual payment to the estate.

The guarantee period is a totally separate issue from the fact that the income is guaranteed for life. Whether a single or joint life annuity is elected, it is prudent to attach a guarantee period. The guarantee period can be five to 15 years for pension-source annuities and, when added to the age of the planholder, cannot exceed the number 90. Alternatively, the calculation may use the age of the spouse. This issue does not have much application for someone age 65, but if the pensioner at an older age is converting a LIF or LRIF to a life annuity it may be a factor.

The guarantee period may serve to:

- Provide a time period during which benefits could continue to a survivor
- Ensure that a reduced benefit does not comes into effect for a specified time frame (check your annuity contract for this provision)
- Ensure that a minimum number of payments will be paid either to the pensioner, their survivor(s), or the estate rather than left with the trustee or insurer
- Provide a lump-sum payment of unused pension values to the estate in the event of an unexpected, early passing of a pensioner and spouse

Your employer pension options may or may not have guarantees attached to them. This is worth looking into and may have a significant impact on your ultimate decision regarding what you do with your pension asset at retirement. You may find that if the annuity is the option you want, it may be better to purchase the annuity outside of the plan in order to obtain the guarantees you feel are important. Normally, but not always, the income from the plan will be slightly higher than the level of income that can be obtained in the marketplace.

The election of the joint life rather than single life option, the level of survivor benefits, and the term of the guarantee period all serve to extend the payment duration of an annuity. Going back to the loan analogy, if, when borrowing money, the loan payback period was extended, it would end up reducing the amount of the monthly payment. The table below shows the same effect of these differences in annuity options.

SAMPLE MONTHLY INCOMES: Assumptions: Male age 65, female age 62, pension value $100,000

	Guarantee Period	Pensioner	Survivor
Single Life	0 years	$851	N/A
	10 years	$802	N/A
	15 years	$761	N/A
Joint Life	0 years	$681	$681
• level	10 years	$679	$679
	15 years	$676	$676
Joint Life	0 years	$729	$487
• reducing to 66.7%	10 years	$717	$478
	15 years	$708	$468

Note: The above numbers will be used in illustrations throughout this chapter.

Choosing Your Annuity Option

Most people's pension entitlement is the largest single asset they own. Once the form of pension income (annuity) is chosen, it cannot be changed, so it is very appropriate to ensure that you take care when making this decision.

As stated before, the more guarantees you attach to your income option, the lower the income amount. You do not want to choose an option that will disinherit your spouse, but there are more considerations that impact this decision.

- What is the state of health of you and your spouse?
- What are the survivor needs of your spouse?
- Is your spouse also in a pension plan?
- What other income-producing assets do you have?
- Is it your desire to generate some estate value from your pension?
- Do you have or could you acquire enough life insurance to replace all or part of your pension income? The following example shows how this might work. If the example below represented your options, which one would you choose?

SAMPLE MONTHLY INCOMES: Assumptions: Male age 65, female age 62, $100,000 of pension proceeds

	Monthly Income Before Tax	Net at 26% Tax	Net at 37% Tax
Single Life Annuity	$851	$630	$536
• zero guarantee			
Joint Life Annuity	$676	$500	$426
• level income			
• 15-year guarantee			
Difference	$175	$130	$110

The single life annuity provides an increase of 25.88 percent over the income delivered by the joint life annuity. If you are married, however, the practical option in most cases is to choose a joint annuity to provide an income for both lives. The joint annuity provides an income to your surviving spouse, but if your spouse predeceases you:

- You have taken a reduced income for the rest of your life, for no reason.
- You cannot name a replacement joint survivor to receive income at your passing, other than as a beneficiary of any guarantee period remaining.
- You will receive no additional benefit, such as a cash value.

Despite all this, you don't want to disinherit your spouse.

The vast majority of married people select the joint life option. However, it may make sense to investigate one other option before making a final decision on a joint annuity. A possible solution may be in a strategy known as pension maximization. It works in the following manner:

1. Select the single life annuity with no guarantee period to create the highest possible income.
2. Apply the difference between the single life and joint life income toward the acquisition of a life insurance contract.
3. Have the insurance proceeds purchase an annuity for the survivor.

Here is how the numbers work out, using the same monthly figures from the previous example for a male age 65 and a female age 62.

		Net Income	
	Before Tax	Marginal Tax Rate 26%	Tax Marginal Rate 37%
Single life annuity zero guarantee	$851	$629	$536
Joint life annuity level income 15-year guarantee	$676	$500	$426
Difference between a single and joint life annuity	$175	$129	$110
Amount of non-registered capital required to create the net income of the joint life annuity described above*		$82,637	$70,018
Insurance premium required to create that capital**		$213	$182
Difference in net income between joint option and insurance strategy		($84)	($72)

*A single life annuity, guaranteed 15 years, was used to create this income.
**Term-to-100 insurance contract.

When the numbers are examined, there seems to be no distinct advantage to using a life insurance policy to complement income from a single life annuity. In fact, you would realize an income that is lower by $84 or $72, depending on your marginal tax bracket.

Remember, though, that these numbers would be those in effect if the pensioner died at his or her current age. For each year that goes by, the surviving spouse grows older and therefore could buy a higher income with the original amount of insurance proceeds—a definite benefit.

With this in mind, the annuitant in this example could take the difference in income between the single and joint annuity and simply acquire the amount of insurance that this would buy. In our example, the actual monthly difference ($129 at a 26 percent marginal tax rate) would purchase an insurance contract that cost just in excess of two-thirds of the amount required ($213) for full coverage from day one. It would be important to examine other assets that may serve to bridge the income in the event of the annuitant passing away in the short term.

The most common mistake in considering this option is assuming that the amount of insurance must be the same as the amount of initial retirement capital. As the table shows, you only need the amounts of non-registered capital required to create the net income of the joint life annuity described above at the different tax rates, not $100,000 to replace the after-tax benefit of the joint annuity income. This is because the pension income would be fully taxable, while the prescribed annuity income would be only partially taxable (this is explored in more detail later on in this chapter). The amount of insurance coverage represents 70 percent to 80 percent of the original capital. To insure the entire amount of non-registered capital would not only be incorrect, but would represent an additional 20 percent to 30 percent premium in after-tax dollars.

The Benefits of Pension Maximization

The comparative, net income calculation should not be the only consideration in this exercise. The planning concept of pension maximization includes a number of significant benefits to both the pensioner and the survivor/estate. Several of these may dovetail with other objectives the pensioner has apart from the delivery of income, including wealth transfer and tax strategies. All of the merits of this strategy should be considered.

If the insurance can be purchased before retirement, the premium will apply to a younger age and as a result be lower. This obviously improves the net income position. Depending on the amount of non-registered capital that is available, there may be an opportunity to pre-fund the insurance. Although a term-to-100 product was used in the above illustration, there is merit at looking at some of the additional features that a universal life contract would bring to your situation. Some of these are mentioned below.

For you, the pension plan member:

- You enjoy the maximum level of income for life from your annuity.
- You know your spouse will have ongoing income equal to the after-tax receipt from the joint annuity option.
- You can accelerate deposits to an insurance contract to have premiums vanish in five to 15 years.
- You can apply one lump sum to have the contract fully paid for.
- Your cash values within the contract accumulate on a tax-deferred basis and may be an additional source of income at some point in time.

If your spouse predeceases you:

- You can choose a new beneficiary for the insurance contract.
- You can dispose of the contract for its cash value, if any.
- You can use the cash value to provide a future income supplement, or a lump sum of cash.
- You have the option to maintain insurance coverage for other estate conservation purposes.

For your survivor and your estate:

- The insurance proceeds are non-taxable to the beneficiary.
- Your survivor receives tax-effective guaranteed income. Other sources of income to which they may also be a beneficiary—RRIFs, CPP survivor benefits, etc.—are fully taxable.
- Your survivor may choose to use the capital for purposes other than income.
- At the subsequent passing of your spouse, any remaining insurance proceeds or non-registered annuity value are not taxable to the estate as pension values would be.
- There may be a better opportunity for the estate to realize receipt of some of the pension proceeds, given the new guarantee period that is established with the purchase of the new annuity. Normally a prescribed annuity contract (PAC) is purchased to provide the income needed. These are non-registered annuities that have some taxation advantages over regular annuities. They are discussed in detail in the section on investing non-registered assets.

THINGS TO CONSIDER IN PENSION MAXIMIZATION

DO NOT select any form of annuity until you have obtained insurance issued on terms that are satisfactory to you and to this strategy.

You may be wondering why you should even worry about this issue when you can acquire a LIF or LRIF. Doing so would eliminate the single or joint life decision, yet a large number of the stated benefits of pension maximization could still be realized.

There are several reasons why the annuity may be the best or even the only consideration for you.

- Your pension contracts may not allow for a commutation of benefit after age 55.
- You may feel more comfortable with the guarantees provided by life annuities and want to use that vehicle.
- Commutation would preclude you from participating in contractual indexing if this is provided in your plan.
- Commutation would not allow you to participate in bridging or benefit integration, or in positive income adjustments through reallocation of pension surplus.

Remember that the purpose of this exercise is not necessarily to realize greater net income, but to allow some additional flexibility for you and your survivor, and ultimately give some distinct tax advantages to the estate.

Shopping for an Annuity

Values accrue to the pension plan member during their working life as they and the employer make contributions. There will be a trustee (let's use an insurance company as an example) to administer the plan and invest the contributions. When the plan member retires and wishes to take their pension income in the form of an annuity, it need not necessarily be acquired from the same company that manages the pension. Why is this an important thing to know?

At different times, different insurance companies are seeking capital. To attract money they offer attractive income purchase rates. As such, *the relative rank of companies is constantly changing*. The table that appears below is not an endorsement of any particular company, but is included to show that it is worth taking the time to have your advisor canvas the market prior to making an annuity purchase.

There are no changes permitted to an annuity once it is purchased. There will be no additional features, options, conversion considerations, etc. Since it is basically an amount of income paid out in exchange for an amount of capital put in, comparisons are very simple and very accurate.

Take, for example, the case of a $100,000 joint life annuity, level income to survivor, with a 15-year guarantee. The husband is age 65, and the wife is age 62.

Rank	Company	Monthly Income
1.	AIG Life of Canada	$527.14
2.	Equitable Life	$518.75
3.	Canada Life	$513.60
4.	Transamerica Life Canada	$513.44
5.	Desjardins Financial Security	$512.89
6.	Great West Life	$509.90
7.	Standard Life	$508.16
8.	Sun Life Assurance Company of Canada	$507.45
9.	Empire Life	$498.76
10.	Manulife Investments	$495.82

Reprinted with permission of CANNEX Financial Exchanges Limited. Data as of October 2007.

The above table shows an increase of 6.31 percent between the highest and lowest ranked offering. This difference of $31.32 would be realized every month for life. Using the above figures, the difference in total income paid out to the retiree over 25 years between the first place company and the last place company in this particular quote would add up to $9,900.

Since the annuity purchase decision cannot be altered once elected, it makes sense to investigate your options thoroughly with the help of an advisor. Keep in mind that this is the ranking of companies for a particular day and that this ranking among companies changes daily.

ASSURIS LIMITS ON ANNUITY INCOME

Assuris, the insurance industry's consumer protection program, covers life insurance policyholders against loss of benefits due to financial failure of their insurance company. Annuity income is protected to a maximum of $2,000 per month, per annuitant, per institution.

LIFE INCOME FUNDS (LIFs) AND LOCKED-IN RETIREMENT INCOME FUNDS (LRIFs)

Another income option for pension-source proceeds is the Life Income Fund, or LIF. Although it is not available in every province, the cousin of the LIF, the Locked-In Retirement Income Fund, or LRIF, has also been made available. The two vehicles are very similar, so this section will deal primarily with the LIF in detail and then identify the differences and enhancements within the LRIF.

If you purchase an annuity from the proceeds of a pension plan, you will be subject to the interest rates in effect at the time of purchase for an extended period of time. If interest rates are low, annuities will be unattractive. But what if you want or need the income?

Both the LIF and LRIF allow you to receive income from a pension or locked-in asset, but also enable you to have more flexibility.

- You have control in how your money is invested.
- You can control income flow within limits—there is an annual withdrawal maximum permitted.
- You can receive income without initially having to purchase an annuity.
- There is no single or joint decision to be made at the time of a LIF/ LRIF purchase as there is with an annuity; LIFs and LRIFs are issued in the name of only one person.

As in all facets of retirement income planning, your health and that of your spouse is a key consideration. Certainly in a situation where the health and longevity of the pensioner are questionable, the use of a LIF or LRIF will provide needed flexibility for survivors and the estate. Realize, however, that some pension plans may not permit commutation as an option after the employee reaches a certain age.

Income Options

There is a legislative requirement that income from pension-sourced assets, including locked-in RRSPs and LIRAs, must provide an income that the planholder cannot outlive. The exception to these rules, currently, is in the province of Saskatchewan, where locked-in holdings, including pension plan amounts, can be rolled directly into RRSP accounts if certain conditions are met.

The income that can be removed from a LIF is based upon several factors, including the age of the individual, the balance in the account at January 1 of each year, and a factor know as the CANSIM rate. The CANSIM rate changes every December based on the average rate of return on a Government of Canada 10-year bond. LRIFs do not rely on the CANSIM rate, but do have other factors that determine what level of income constitutes the maximum payable in a given year.

There is a minimum income that must be paid out from a LIF on an annual basis. There is also a maximum income that is permitted to be paid. You may elect an income anywhere between the minimum and maximum. You also have the option to change the amount of income at any time. LIFs and LRIFs follow the same minimum withdrawal formula as a post-1992 (termed "non-qualified") RRIF, which means there are no required payments in the year that the contract is created. A table showing RRIF minimum withdrawals appears later, in the section on RRSPs and RRIFs. The following example shows the range of monthly income that would be generated by a LIF for an individual age 65, using $100,000 of locked-in capital and an investment return assumption of 7 percent.

LIF MAXIMUM WITHDRAWAL PERCENTAGES

Age at January 1	Maximum %	Age at January 1	Maximum %
50	6.27	65	7.38
51	6.31	66	7.52
52	6.35	67	7.67
53	6.40	68	7.83
54	6.45	69	8.02
55	6.51	70	8.22
56	6.57	71	8.45
57	6.63	72	8.71
58	6.70	73	9.00
59	6.77	74	9.34
60	6.85	75	9.71
61	6.94	76	10.15
62	7.04	77	10.66
63	7.14	78	11.25
64	7.26	79	11.96

Because one of the factors in determining the maximum amount removable from a LIF is the value of your account on January 1 of each year, there will likely be some variance of income from year to year. This is significant if you use investments other than GICs. Although LIF and LRIF illustrations assume an average rate of return over a long time period, the returns on a LIF or LRIF account made up of variable investments will definitely vary from year to year. This will have some effect on your account balances and ultimately on your income.

As restrictive as pension plans and their resulting income streams are, LIF/LRIF incomes do provide you with some flexibility.

You have the option to convert the LIF/LRIF back into a LIRA and suspend income payments from this source. This is permitted as long as you are under the age of 71 and the minimum withdrawal requirements have been paid out for that year. This has great potential application if you are drawing income from this source at an early age. Your initial plans may be to rely upon a locked-in or pension-source asset to provide your floor of income; however, if the situation changes due to an employment opportunity, realization of an unusual taxable receipt, or something of the like, this conversion opportunity may come in handy.

Investment Options

Unlike an annuity where the income is *purchased*, LIFs and LRIFs have an account balance. Initially, this account balance is the amount transferred from the pension plan. The future values in the account will vary depending on withdrawals made and the rate of growth from the investment choices.

A LIF/LRIF account can be invested in GICs, bonds, investment funds, or any combination of these instruments. Provincial rules dictate that all investments that would qualify for use in a RRIF are also acceptable in a LIF/LRIF, with the exception of a self-directed mortgage.

Ongoing investment decisions will ensure growth in the account. In a LIF, such decisions would be necessary until the time the account is converted to an annuity, which must occur before the individual turns age 80. The comparisons below illustrate the relationship of investment returns to the income provided and the capital value of the plan. We have illustrated the LIF only.

This table illustrates that as investment returns increase, so do the amounts of income that can be withdrawn, as well as account balances. If GICs or bonds at a rate of 5 percent are used exclusively, incomes *and* account balances will decline.

LIF INCOMES AND ACCOUNT VALUE: $100,000 Maximum Withdrawal

	5% Return		6.5% Return		8% Return	
	Monthly	Year-End	Monthly	Year-End	Monthly	Year-End
	Income	Value	Income	Value	Income	Value
Age	($)	($)	($)	($)	($)	($)
65	615	97,461	615	98,914	615	100,368
66	611	94,835	620	97,681	629	100,570
67	606	92,134	624	96,312	643	100,616
68	601	89,458	628	94,804	657	100,496
69	597	86,493	634	93,134	672	100,177
70	592	83,543	638	91,301	686	99,652
71	588	80,496	643	89,288	702	98,892
72	584	77,347	648	87,080	718	97,871
73	580	74,091	653	84,667	734	96,566
74	577	70,715	659	82,024	752	94,938
75	572	67,224	664	79,151	768	92,974
76	569	63,604	669	76,020	786	90,626
77	565	59,846	675	72,613	805	87,857
78	561	55,949	681	68,918	824	84,636
79	558	51,900	687	64,906	844	80,910

Occasionally, planners may want to encourage the use of segregated funds for LIF investments. (Very briefly, segregated funds are professionally managed pooled funds, offered by life insurance companies and mutual fund companies, that have investment features similar to mutual funds but that provide investors with unique features and guarantees not generally available in traditional market-based investments.) This is for a couple of key reasons. First, at the owner's death, the value of the plan transfers by operation of law. The result of this is that, with a named beneficiary, the LIF will avoid probate. The second reason is that there is an element of creditor protection for the assets if you have named a beneficiary for the preferred class (wife, children, parent, grandparent, etc.).

These points are not exclusive to segregated funds. Any registered asset with a named beneficiary transfers by operation of law at the passing of the planholder, and avoids probate. Equally important is that any pension-source asset, including pension values, LIRAs, locked-in RRSPs, LIFs, and LRIFs are already secure from seizure by creditors. The additional management fees associated with segregated funds may not warrant their use on these points alone, unless the other guarantee features, such as the death benefit guarantee, are of significance to you. Segregated funds and their unique guarantees are discussed in more detail in Chapter 3.

Additional LRIF Features

- The CANSIM rate does not apply to an LRIF in calculating maximum withdrawal.
- The calculation of LRIF maximum income can cause real problems in years of low and negative investment returns. The maximum income calculation is based on the greater of:

   The January 1 value of this year, minus the January 1 value of last year, minus the value of funds transferred in

   The previous year's investment return

   The minimum withdrawal calculation

   In times of good investment returns, LRIFs have the ability to deliver larger amounts of income when compared to LIFs. In times of flat or negative investment returns, the LRIF may end up only being able to pay out the minimum income.
- In an LRIF, there is no requirement to convert to a life annuity, so the account will require ongoing management.
- LRIF income is usually restricted to a flat withdrawal amount of 6 percent in the first two years.

Survivor Options

If you are unmarried, the proceeds of the LIF/LRIF will flow to either your named beneficiary or to your estate at the time of your passing. With no surviving spouse to whom this money can be transferred, the full balance will be taxable to your estate as income in the year of your death.

If you are married and your named beneficiary is your spouse, then there are several options when you pass away:

- Continue the plan in the same manner with a change of ownership
- Convert to an annuity
- Convert the plan to a personal RRSP*
- Convert the plan to a personal RRIF*

  *For a spousal beneficiary, the locked-in restriction on the balance within the LIF/LRIF is removed and the option to roll to an RRSP/RRIF becomes available.

ANNUITY/LIF/LRIF INCOME COMPARISON

The structure of an annuity, as previously defined, is to create income payments that are a combination of principal and interest, amortized over the period of average life expectancy. It is by design a principal-encroachment vehicle. That is why, in comparison to LIFs/LRIFs, which have specific limitations on the rate of capital encroachment, the incomes from a single life annuity will initially tend to be higher. The most accurate comparison when looking at the delivery of income would be between a LIF and a joint life annuity with level income to survivor and a 15-year guarantee.

Here is just such a comparison. For this example, the LIF/LRIF and joint life annuity are $100,000 plans. The joint life annuity covers a male age 65 and female age 62. Incomes are payable for life and the annuities have a 15-year guarantee. The investment returns for the LIF and LRIF are assumed to be 7 percent.

MAXIMUM MONTHLY INCOME

At Male's Age	Single Annuity ($)	Joint, Level Annuity ($)	LIF ($)	LRIF ($)
65	765	678	615	513
66	765	678	623	582
67	765	678	630	582
68	765	678	637	582
69	765	678	646	582
70	765	678	653	582
71	765	678	661	636
72	765	678	670	641
73	765	678	678	645
74	765	678	687	650
75	765	678	696	655

76	765	678	705	659
77	765	678	714	663
78	765	678	724	668
79	765	678	734	673

ESTATE TRANSFER COMPARISONS

Conversely, the *estate values* in the annuity will be lower than those estate values found in the LIF/LRIF. This example uses the same assumptions as above.

MAXIMUM MONTHLY INCOME

At Male's Age	Single Annuity* ($)	Joint, Level Annuity* ($)	LIF ($)	LRIF** ($)
65	89,283	80,267	100,000	100,000
66	85,328	75,624	98,603	100,809
67	81,268	72,025	97,679	100,838
68	76,964	68,211	96,601	100,838
69	72,402	64,168	95,345	100,838
70	67,566	59,882	93,909	100,838
71	62,440	55,339	92,720	100,195
72	57,006	50,523	90,412	99,453
73	51,246	45,418	88,320	98,602
74	45,141	40,007	85,966	97,637
75	38,669	34,272	83,345	96,540
76	31,810	28,192	80,424	95,315
77	24,538	21,746	77,182	93,948
78	16,831	14,916	73,598	92,425
79	8,660	7,675	69,641	90,736
80	0	0	65,276	88,871

*Commuted present value estimates. **Alberta legislation.

SUMMARY OF PENSION INCOME OPTIONS

Annuity
- Guarantees income for life
- Does not allow for inflation adjustments
- Inflexible contract once purchased
- No ongoing investment decisions required
- Joint annuitant cannot be changed

LIF and LRIF
- Automatically single life; no option for joint
- Ongoing investment decisions required
- Potentially higher or lower income than annuity
- You control income flow within limits (up to age 80)
- Locked-in status waived for spousal beneficiary*
- LRIF permits larger income in earlier years
- No annuity purchase is required with LRIF

*Refers to the locked-in status being waived if the beneficiary is the spouse of the planholder. As of *January 2008, this is not allowed in British Columbia.*

THE BEST OF BOTH WORLDS
You may find that there are appealing features in each of the retirement income tools that we have discussed here. You may appreciate both the guaranteed and structured nature of annuities, and the flexibility and estate benefits of a LIF or LRIF. Assuming there are no pension plan restrictions, you may consider allocating some of your pension values to an annuity and some to a LIF or LRIF. In this way there is a secure base for your income and the benefits of flexibility offered through the LIF or LRIF.

It may not have to be an "all or none" type of decision. It is worth discovering, through your employer, what all of your options are when you are getting close to the time you will start taking income.

Also remember that if you have money in a locked-in RRSP or LIRA, there is no requirement that you use all of the funds at once. You may, for example, choose to take half of your locked-in account and create income through an annuity, LIF, or LRIF. The other half of the account can remain in the locked-in RRSP/LIRA until you decide to create additional income. You can defer this election until the end of the year in which you turn age 71.

CONVERTING LOCKED-IN MONEY

Because flexibility within our assets will better allow us to address the priorities and objectives within our Time Hub, any opportunity to free up locked-in account values is constructive. On the surface, it may not seem like meaningful amounts can be moved. But when it's done year after year, the total adds up. And gaining more control over your money is always beneficial.

This can only be done after locked-in money is transferred into a LIF or LRIF. In most provinces, the earliest age at which this could happen is age 55. Some provinces have no restrictions on age, meaning that this transfer may occur at the planholder's discretion.

Once income from these plans commences, you are allowed to transfer the difference between the minimum and maximum payments into your own RRSP. You can do this each year up to and including the year in which you turn age 71.

You are required to take the minimum withdrawal amount into your taxable income. However, you can defer being taxed on this income if you have RRSP contribution room. You could put the minimum withdrawal amount into an RRSP that was either in your name or the name of your spouse. The minimum withdrawal amount in the year that the LIF/LRIF is established is zero. A LIF/LRIF does not use the age of the spouse for minimum withdrawal calculations. Instead, the formula for minimum withdrawal on these plans is the same as it is for RRIFs and is discussed in upcoming sections.

These are the necessary steps for converting locked-in money.

- Move locked-in amounts to a LIF/LRIF and commence income on a minimum withdrawal basis.
- Take the minimum withdrawal amount into income.
- Transfer the difference between minimum and maximum income directly to your RRSP. This may be done with Canada Revenue Agency (CRA) form 2030 or, with some institutions, by a signed letter of direction.

- The LIF/LRIF carrier and the receiving RRSP institution issue offsetting receipts. This results in a tax-neutral transaction, except for the minimum payment.
- This is a section 60(I)(v) transfer. As such, there is no effect on RRSP contribution room.

Discuss the merits of this concept with your advisor.

NEW RULES FOR LOCKED-IN MONEY

Rules that effectively lock in pension money were implemented, in part, to prevent individuals from cashing out pension accumulations at the time they left an employer (cashing out is still an option with pre-1985 contributions). The rules support the objective of pension plans, which is to provide an income that an individual cannot outlive. No lump-sum withdrawals are permitted, and no cash-outs are allowed.

However, recent legislation passed in Manitoba, Alberta, and Ontario allows for a portion of the locked-in account to be moved to what is called a Prescribed RRIF (PRIFF). In Saskatchewan, the locked-in status of pension money at retirement age and beyond has been removed completely. This type of legislative change allows more flexibility and discretion in how the pension funds are used. Yet, it still prevents early cash-out of accounts by younger workers.

For most individuals who have contributed to pension plans for an extended period of time, the value of the account likely represents one of the largest capital assets they own. Those who contribute to RRSPs have choices in how they remove money and/or income, and our feeling is that pension plan members should be treated in exactly the same manner.

Governments need to continue to evaluate approaches that can accommodate their objectives, while at the same time allowing individuals at retirement to have more discretion in how their pension assets are used.

By providing this additional flexibility for locked-in money, people will be better able to tailor their income streams to their changing priorities and objectives throughout the various retirement stages. The current system is far too inflexible and archaic. Expect to see more, significant changes over the next few years that will allow us greater access to locked-in assets.

DEFERRED PROFIT SHARING PLANS (DPSPs)

You may participate in a deferred profit sharing plan, or DPSP, in addition to or instead of a pension plan. These plans allow employers to make, within limits, tax-deductible, tax-deferred contributions to an employee's account.

There are many reasons why employers who wish to contribute to an employee's retirement account would choose to use this vehicle. One of the key features for the employer is that with the exception of an annual minimum, there is no fixed amount of contribution as there is with a regular pension plan. As a participant in the plan, you should be aware of this. There will likely be varying amounts of contributions to your account depending on the profitability of the company.

A DPSP cannot accept employee contributions, except for transfers from other tax-assisted plans. Full employee vesting (entitlement to the contributions) occurs after 24 months of DPSP membership. Unlike a formal pension plan, locking-in rules do not apply on these accounts, and you have total flexibility and portability upon termination or retirement (if vested).

The total of your contributions to your DPSP (transfers from other tax-assisted plans), contributions to your RRSP, and your and your employer's pension contributions cannot exceed 18 percent of your income from the previous year, unless there is RRSP carryforward room. These amounts are reflected in your notice of assessment and will determine the amount of eligible RRSP contribution room you have. Care needs to be exercised where there is a combination of pension and DPSP so that limits are not exceeded.

Options at Termination or Retirement

At termination, you can roll your DPSP money into a registered pension plan (RPP) or another DPSP, if either of these is available with a new employer, or into a personally held RRSP account.

At retirement, the most practical alternative is to roll the account balance into a personally held RRSP. At this point you have all of the income and cash options that are available to RRSPs. We will cover these in detail shortly.

From the perspective of planning, flexibility is good. So, the fact that DPSP values can be moved to an RRSP and treated accordingly is a real advantage to these programs.

PENSION DECISIONS AND THE PRIME APPROACH

There really are no black and white rules on pension decisions. There are many financial variables and personal priorities that will dictate the most appropriate course of action for an individual or a couple. Some people may have a preference for a guaranteed income for life, while others will accept a variable income level because they want increased flexibility and the opportunity to retain as much capital value of their pension as is possible within their estate.

This is why the features of annuities and LIFs/LRIFs are just that—features. There are no advantages and disadvantages that can be assigned to these financial tools until you know what your preferences and objectives as a pension plan member happen to be.

For example, a single life annuity with a 15-year guarantee may be a very wise choice if the spouse is also in a pension plan that will produce a significant income at retirement. This would provide a higher lifetime income for the couple and yet still ensure a defined number of years of payment should something happen to one of them.

In trying to determine the best course of action for your situation, the following are some of the key points that should be kept in mind:

- Do not make this decision on your own. Discuss this with a qualified financial advisor. Since this is likely one of the largest financial assets you own and you really only get to make this election once, it better be well thought out.
- Do not solicit assistance from your human resource person or benefits administrator. They are very competent in many areas, but financial planning is usually not one of them. You also run the danger of putting them into a position of being liable if they give advice in this area. That is not fair to them. They may, however, have a list of financial planners with whom you could consult if you do not have one of your own.
- You need to consider how the features of each income option fit together with your Time Hub priorities. Since your priorities will change over time, you may want to consider keeping some, if not all, of your pension income in a more flexible form than that offered by an annuity. This has particular merit if you are triggering your pension income at an earlier age.

- Be aware of what benefits, such as bridging, integration, or income enhancements, you may be forgoing by commuting your pension values. Are there any extended group insurance benefits—life, health, or dental—that will be lost if the option is commuted?
- Do not make this decision without taking into account all of the other financial assets and planning issues that are involved in your situation.
- Be aware that should you elect to move pension or locked-in money to a LIF or LRIF, you can always then move to an annuity. In fact, as you become older the amount of income an annuity will provide to you will likely be larger than that provided by a LIF or LRIF. While you can move from a LIF/LRIF to an annuity, you cannot go the other way. Once the annuity is purchased, no changes can occur.

The Prime Approach emphasizes flexibility and access to income streams and assets that will allow you to do more in the earlier years of retirement. Locking-in rules place substantial restrictions on how pension-source assets can be used. Income is also fully taxable. We therefore recommend using this source to create the initial base when establishing income. Remember that we want to use the least flexible, least tax-efficient income first.

As mentioned previously, governments are starting to allow individuals more flexibility and access to locked-in accounts. The trend is clear. Legislators see that people want and are expecting to receive more flexibility and more options in regard to pension accumulations and locked-in accounts. We believe that individuals should have total discretion with how they use their accumulated retirement assets. We are only now seeing legislative changes to permit this. As individual taxpayers, we should demand it. Expect to see many of the archaic locking-in restrictions to be amended or eliminated over the coming years. As the creator of and an advocate of the Prime Approach, we will be cheering loudly as this happens. It's a worthwhile move that will enable those in retirement to have a better opportunity to fulfill their objectives.

SECTION 3:

Registered Retirement Savings Plans (RRSPs) and Registered Retirement Income Funds (RRIFs)

The purpose of this section is to discuss the RRSP options available to you at retirement, with some thoughts on pre-retirement positioning. We'll also look at some withdrawal strategies that can help maximize the benefits you realize from your RRSP accounts.

RRSPs are one of the most effective tools for accumulating retirement assets. We encourage people to contribute to the maximum they are allowed, especially in the early years.

Once the base or floor of income has been established from government benefits, and pension (locked-in) income, the next inclusions should be taxable distributions from non-sheltered assets and then RRSP/RRIF amounts up to at least the amount of the first federal tax bracket.

Remember that any money withdrawn from RRSPs or RRIFs, either as a lump sum or an income stream, is fully taxable as income. It does not matter whether the growth within the plan was in the form of interest, dividends, or capital gains. If it comes out, it's fully taxable. Unfortunately, investment losses that may be incurred over the years cannot be written off for tax purposes. These are the trade-offs for being able to deduct contributions and being allowed years of tax deferral on the growth within the plan.

Reference was previously made to the possibility of having government benefits reduced or clawed back if your taxable income is too high. You may be wondering, then, why we would still suggest maximizing RRSP contributions if the eventual withdrawals are fully taxable.

The main answer is this: The result of deducting RRSP contributions from your taxable income is significant. Think of the tax savings realized as the government helping you to build your retirement nest egg. If you are in the middle tax bracket, you will be taxed at roughly 40 percent on each dollar. What this means in terms of your RRSP is that it takes $0.60 of your "take home" pay to make a $1.00 contribution.

RRSP CONTRIBUTIONS AFTER RETIREMENT

Should you make RRSP contributions after you retire? Aren't you finished saving by the time you get to retirement? Well, the answer to this depends on a number of factors.

For example, do you need the tax deduction? You may. Suppose you have a large taxable receipt from the sale of property, a business, stocks, etc. The ability to use RRSP contribution room, including any carryforward room, to offset an unusual receipt would be a very beneficial tax strategy.

You are allowed, since 1991, to carry forward unused RRSP contribution room. Prior to this provision, "use it or lose it" regulations meant that those who did not contribute forfeited the opportunity. Initially the carryforward was for a moving seven-year period. In 1996 the act was amended so that the carryforward runs indefinitely.

The government actually keeps track of the amount you are allowed to carry forward, and details it on your CRA Notice of Assessment. Contribution room is created from the eligible sources of income from the year previous, minus any pension adjustment, plus any used room from previous years.

This has two distinct benefits for retirees. The first benefit is that since contribution room is based on the tax return of the previous year, there will most likely be some ability to make an RRSP contribution in the first full year of retirement. The second benefit presents itself if a carryforward exists. If there is unused contribution room, it can be used to offset an unusual receipt in the year of retirement or in any year thereafter (subject to the age rules as detailed below). This unusual receipt might be an amount from a retirement package that could not be completely sheltered in the form of a retiring allowance. It may be the disposition and gain realized from liquidating company shares, or some other capital gain that is triggered to turn investments into income.

You can use any contribution room, either earned after retirement begins or from carryforward, for contribution to your own plan until the end of the year in which you turn age 71. You may still make a deductible contribution to a spousal plan after age 71, if you have carryforward room and your spouse is age 71 or under.

The earlier that these catch-up contributions can be made, the better. The luxury in timing for you is that you can make a large deposit to your RRSP, or to a spousal plan, as long as you are within your limits. You can then claim the deduction over any number of years, keeping in mind the age 71 rule for yourself and your spouse. Taking the deductions from a higher marginal rate works more effectively for tax savings than trying to lower taxable income to zero. Tax on the first dollar of net income after $29,590 (the first tax bracket change) goes from an average of $0.26 to an average of $0.37. This is an increase of 42.31 percent on the next dollar. To spread deductions over a time period where we are deducting dollars at a higher tax rate makes more sense and saves far more tax dollars than a one-year "go to zero" strategy.

Because of the complex rules regarding contributions, and the likelihood that errors can be made by even the most well-meaning investors, an overcontribution amount of $2,000 is available to everyone. Amounts over and above this limit are penalty-taxed at the rate of 1 percent per month. Excess contributions under $2,000 are allowed to remain in the RRSP account on a tax-sheltered basis, but the amount is not deductible from income unless new contribution room is created.

The question you face is basically "Do I overcontribute $2,000 for the benefit of sheltering any growth from tax?" You must remember that while you cannot deduct this amount from your income, it is fully taxable when removed. If you are dealing with a long time frame, there may be some merit to the overcontribution of the $2,000. However, to consciously make this over contribution for the benefit of some short-term tax sheltering is questionable. Why would you take tax-paid money and convert it into fully taxable money without a deduction to offset it?

This same questioning needs to be applied to any RRSP contributions made in retirement. If the tax rate at which you will be making the deduction is less than the rate at which the money will be taxed at when withdrawn, it is likely not advantageous.

Final Points on Contributions

RRSP contribution credits are based on eligible earned income. In retirement, the opportunity to create more credits may be small. It is worth keeping in mind that net rental income and royalty income qualifies as earned income for this purpose.

In retirement, any new contributions made to an RRSP can be immediately transferred into an existing RRIF.

We don't want to take additional space in this book to detail contribution limits, but here's the significant point. Contribute as much as you can, as soon as you can. Granted, there is a balance to everything. You can't live in a ditch and save every cent, but neither can you afford not to save. Like everything else in life, there has to be some balance. Let's assume you've paid into your RRSPs over the years. Now let's talk about the best ways for your RRSPs to pay you.

CONVERTING RRSP/RRIF MONEY

You can defer taking money from registered plans, but you will ultimately reach a point where you are required by government to remove certain percentages whether you need the income or not.

Knowing this, you should consider taking out amounts earlier, up to certain tax levels, to gradually make it subject to taxation. Consider bringing in amounts to at least use the personal exemption. Remember, $1 after tax is better than a $1 deduction.

The next step, if we have used up the personal exemption, is to look at taking out even more income, perhaps even to the first federal tax bracket. There are several reasons for this suggestion.

First, if you continue to defer the removal of income from your RRSPs, you will increase the value of the account on a tax-deferred basis. In one sense, this is good. But you may very well run yourself into the trap of being forced to take out more than you want to and end up putting yourself into a higher taxable income scenario.

Second, you are gradually converting fully taxable money into tax-paid money. You are bringing it into income at a marginal tax rate that is lower than the rate at which the contribution was deducted. This is when the RRSP is at its most efficient.

Third, the ability to access tax-paid money as a lump sum or as income will help keep your taxable income low and not put as much strain on your RRSP/RRIF to deliver income at higher tax rates. As was mentioned in the taxation section in Chapter 1, to get one after-tax dollar out of an RRSP or RRIF, after the first federal tax bracket has been reached, requires a withdrawal of $1.60 (assuming a 38 percent rate).

Fourth, once your RRSP/RRIF money has been taken into income, at a low tax rate, there are investment opportunities that will allow for growth of this money at either a tax-preferred or tax-deferred basis. Certainly there is a benefit in deferring tax (remember that "defer" is one of the four Ds of tax planning). But it is also essential to consider which assets to defer and how to go about doing it. This process allows you to defer both registered and non-registered holdings.

The sum of these factors makes RRSP/RRIF conversion a worthwhile goal that may have a place in your planning. Obviously, the amount of income to be withdrawn, as it relates to the above strategy, will be largely dependent upon the total amount of money you have in your registered accounts.

There is no restriction on the earliest age at which income can commence from your RRSP. On the other end of the spectrum, an RRSP is deemed to have matured on December 31 of the year in which you turn age 71. Election must be made with regard to the maturity of the plan by that time. The options will be discussed later in this chapter.

SPOUSAL RRSPS AND RRIFS

Earlier we identified the four Ds of effective tax planning—deduct, divide, defer, and discount. Spousal RRSPs incorporate the first three of these strategies. You and your spouse are permitted, within your respective contribution limits, to structure the ownership of your RRSPs in any manner you choose. As is the case with other assets, RRSP accounts cannot be transferred from one individual to another, with the exception of at divorce or death. The structure must be established at the time the contribution is made.

For example, suppose you and your spouse each have money to contribute. At the time of contribution, you may determine in whose name the amounts will be deposited. Both deposits may be in the name of one person. The deduction, however, can only be taken by the contributor, within his or her limits.

The objective in splitting assets is to create two streams of income in retirement. This is more effective than having the majority of income in the name of only one taxpayer. Each individual has their own set of exemptions, tax credits, and graduated personal rates. The end result is the same flow of total income for the household but greater after-tax income. With the introduction of the pension-splitting rules, one might ask if there is still relevance in balancing the accumulations for RRSPs. Remember that the income-splitting rules for RRSP accounts will only take effect at age 65 and beyond, so there still is merit in having some balance as these assets are being accumulated in case you start your income before age 65.

The Three-Year Rule

If withdrawals are made from a spousal RRSP within three calendar years of the last contribution, income attribution may apply. What this means is that if your spouse withdraws money from the spousal RRSP within this time limit, and you were the contributor, you will have the withdrawal amount added to your taxable income.

These rules were implemented to stop abuses where a higher income contributor could make a deduction and the lower income spouse would liquidate the account and incur little or no tax. Unfortunately, as is often the case, attempts to stop the abuses of the system have meant that those who would employ it properly are penalized.

Let's be clear on how this time period is actually calculated. The measure is the year of contribution, not the year that the deduction is made. The three-year period includes the year of the last contribution and the following two full calendar years.

LAST CONTRIBUTION	TAX YEAR	THREE-YEAR RULE ENDS
Dec. 30, 2007	2007	Dec. 31, 2009
Jan. 3, 2008	2007	Dec. 31, 2010
Jan. 3, 2008	2008	Dec. 31, 2010

The first two contributions shown above are only five days apart and yet the end of the three-year periods is one year apart. Caution should clearly be exercised with spousal contributions as the retirement date draws near.

People are often under the erroneous belief that if a spousal contribution was made 10 years ago, it is permissible to collapse that one account or certificate and not have the attribution apply. This is not correct. The government views it from a point of when the last deposit was made into *any* spousal RRSP with your name on it, not the timing of individual placements.

After the three-year period has elapsed, the spouse can remove whatever amount of income he or she wishes and it will be taxed in his or her hands.

Working Around the Three-Year Rule

As obvious as it sounds, be careful with how contributions are made as retirement nears. Your spouse's regular RRSPs could be used for income or withdrawals in the first two or three years. The attribution rules described above will not apply if your spouse purchases an annuity that cannot be commuted for at least three years.

Attribution does not apply on withdrawals up to the minimum formula. Accordingly, base the minimum withdrawal on the age of the *older of you or your spouse*. This will allow more income to be removed. Equally important to this strategy, create the RRIF in *the year before* the income is to commence, since minimum withdrawal in the first year is zero.

RRSP ROLLOVERS

In addition to the regular contributions we make through the years, some direct rollovers and transfers are permitted. These do not either require or affect RRSP contribution room.

LIF/LRIF Conversion

A previous section on locked-in money discussed the steps you need to take to trigger income from locked-in assets and, within the formula permitted, to transfer sums to your personal RRSP on an annual basis.

Retiring Allowances

You may, at termination of employment or retirement, receive a retiring allowance in recognition of a history of long employment and contribution to an organization. You may be able to roll some or all of this allowance into a personally held RRSP, within certain limits. You cannot move this money into a spousal plan.

You are permitted to transfer $2,000 for each year of service, plus an additional $1,500 per year prior to 1989, if you were not a member of a pension plan, or if benefits under the pension plan were not vested. No credits for the purpose of calculating transfer limits will be given for years after 1995. You and your employer will complete either CRA form TD2 or T1213, or simply compose a letter of direction, to accomplish this direct deposit. The employer then submits this form along with a cheque to the receiving institution.

You may have accumulated unused sick days. In lieu of being paid out for these in the form of taxable income, you can have the value transferred directly to your personal RRSP. Basically the sick days can be transferred directly in the form of a retiring allowance. The calculation for the amount of allowable transfer is the same as described in the previous paragraph.

Accrued vacation cannot be transferred in any form, not even a retiring allowance. Any benefit from this source must be taken as a taxable receipt. You could also, at the discretion of the employer, simply extend the formal retirement date by the number of days of vacation and be paid for that period, also potentially retaining your benefits during that time.

There may be situations in which you have accumulated paid-out vacation, or the allowable retiring allowance cannot shelter all of the money you are eligible to receive. You may be able to be offset these amounts, or at least reduce them, if you have RRSP carryforward room or have not maximized contributions for the current tax year.

Pension Rollovers

When you terminate employment, you can roll your entitlement from the pension plan into a personally held account. The locking-in restriction on pension plan money still applies, subject to the amounts involved. As such, the rollover accounts have a status distinct to regular RRSPs. Depending on the legislative jurisdiction under which the pension plan falls, the account may be a locked-in RRSP or a LIRA.

Depending on the length of time you have been a member of the pension plan, when contributions were actually made, and several other factors, there may be a portion of the pension accumulation that is non-locked. Any non-locked portions can be transferred directly into an RRSP, and take on the character and the rules of RRSP money. Any non-locked amounts are typically identified as such by the pension plan trustee and distinguished from the locked-in values.

RRSP INCOME OPTIONS AT RETIREMENT

By December 31 of the year in which you turn age 71, your RRSP is deemed to have matured. You must decide before that time what you are going to do with these assets. There are four common options for dealing with RRSPs at retirement. You can elect any one of them or any combination.

1. Surrender the RRSP for Cash

An RRSP, or any portion of an RRSP, can be collapsed and taken as a lump-sum withdrawal. The only proviso is that the investments must allow for this. For example GICs issued by some banks, trust companies, and credit unions do not permit you to remove amounts of capital before the maturity of the certificate. As is the case with any RRSP-based withdrawal, any amounts you take this way are fully taxable as income in the year received.

Ideally, in the year that you turn age 65 and each year thereafter, you want to have at least $1,000 of eligible, periodic income to qualify for the pension tax credit. Lump-sum withdrawals from an RRSP do not qualify.

2. Life Annuity (Single or Joint)

These are exactly the same income delivery vehicles that are used to create pension income. All of the features and details of annuities were described earlier in this chapter. As a reminder, an annuity is an investment where the annuitant receives a regular fixed-income payment made up of both principal and interest.

The payments are guaranteed to be paid for life and do not change with fluctuations in markets or interest rates. In exchange for this "maintenance-free" performance, there is no access to capital and very little flexibility.

Life annuities from RRSP proceeds can be indexed on a fixed basis of 1 percent to 4 percent per year. While this does provide for some inflation protection, the initial income is lower than that delivered by a non-indexed life annuity.

3. Annuity Certain to Age 90

This form of annuity would pay the same monthly income up to when you reach age 90. If death should occur before age 90, the balance of remaining payments would be paid to the estate. It is the only form of term-certain annuity permitted for RRSP funds. Mechanically, it would be possible to structure a RRIF to accomplish the same thing without the rigid structure, but the RRIF would not provide the guaranteed income as found in the annuity.

4. Registered Retirement Income Fund (RRIF)

By far, a RRIF is the most common and practical option for delivering income from RRSP accumulations. There are several, well-deserved reasons for this popularity.

- A variety of income options
- An ability to change income amounts
- An ability to make lump-sum withdrawals
- Much greater flexibility than an annuity
- Potential for the account balance to become part of the estate
- Smooth transition from RRSPs
    * Existing RRSP investments can remain the same
    * Amounts remaining in the account grow tax deferred
    * Ongoing investment decisions are required

When the RRIF was introduced in the early 1980s it became an alternative to an annuity, which was the main income delivery vehicle for RRSPs up to that time. When first available, they provided only one form of income—the minimum withdrawal—and were therefore inflexible. The withdrawal formula also dictated that the entire account would be exhausted by age 90. Another negative point for RRIFs was that an individual could own only one.

By the mid-1980s, changes to the withdrawal formula still required that the calculated minimum amount be removed, but basically did away with any limit on the maximum amount that could be removed. The restriction on owning only one RRIF was also done away with. In 1992, the requirement that the account be depleted by age 90 was eliminated. In addition, a new schedule of minimum withdrawal for those contracts issued after 1992 was put in place. The old schedule still applies to pre-1993 contracts, with some amendments that allow those contracts to extend beyond age 90. The changes:

- Allowed the RRIF plan to continue for a lifetime
- Accelerated the payout from age 71 to age 77 on post-1993 RRIFs, to allow governments to make up the tax revenue that would now be able to be deferred past age 90

Today, RRIFs have tremendous flexibility, and income can be received in a number of ways. Since there is no longer a restriction on how many RRIF contracts an individual can own, it is common to employ a number of plans with different withdrawal options to meet specific objectives. For example, you may have a need for a RRIF plan that delivers a core stream of income for day-to-day living. You may also wish to have a RRIF that provides an additional monthly amount for the four months of the year when you are spending the winter in Florida. Finally, you may want to see a specific deposit into a separate account to satisfy the quarterly instalments that you must pay to the tax department. All of these things can be accomplished with variations of the same vehicle, the RRIF.

Sometimes people feel that they will delay the transfer of their RRSPs to a RRIF and thereby not be required to remove the minimum amount each year. Remember that any portion of an RRSP can be used for this purpose and the entire account need not be converted to a RRIF at one time.

What You Should Know When Purchasing a RRIF

- What are the investment options?
- Can it be cashed out? Is there a processing fee or penalty for transfer?
- Do the investments allow you to make lump-sum withdrawals? Are there costs to process this?
- What set-up fees, administration fees, self-directed fees, transaction fees, etc., if any, are associated?
- Can changes be made to investments or income without charge? If so, how frequently? Are there any restrictions on this? What is required to make such changes happen?
- Can your spouse be designated as successor annuitant?

RRIF Income Options

Interest Only or Growth Only	Payout is equal to the interest earned, if using a GIC or bond, or set at the estimated average return (for example, 7 percent), if using a variable portfolio.
Fixed Term	This is where you may wish to have a set amount delivered over a specific time period or to a certain age. For example, you may want $5,000 each January for the next 10 years to fund your Mexican vacation.
Level Payment	You have an amount of income that you want delivered over an extended period of time, perhaps $1,000 per month.
Indexing Payment	Same as the previous option, but adjusted on an annual basis to help deal with increasing costs of living. An example of such an option would be $1,000 per month increased by 3 percent per annum.
Minimum Withdrawal	With this option, the RRIF releases only the minimum amount required by law.

There is no required withdrawal in the year that the RRIF contract is established (the minimum required withdrawal is zero). When income commences it must fulfill the 12 contractual periods in the following year if the frequency of payment is monthly. For example, if a RRIF is established in October, but monthly income does not commence until the following year, there must be 12 payments in that year with the first payment occurring in January.

Once a RRIF has started, the minimum must be paid out each year. If you decide you want to fully stop the RRIF, it can be transferred back to an RRSP as long as you are younger than age 71, and the required minimum income for that year is paid out.

This transfer is accomplished through CRA form T2030. The normal rules for RRSPs will then apply to the account.

The Calculation for Minimum Withdrawal

The account is defined as the balance in the RRIF at January 1 of each year after the RRIF is created. There is no mandatory withdrawal in the year the contract is established.

If the RRIF owner is under the age of 71, the formula for minimum withdrawal is:

1/(90 minus age) times Account Value

For age 71 and beyond, the minimum withdrawal formula is based on a percentage of the RRIF account assets:

Age	Pre-1993 "Qualified" (%)	Post-1992 "Non-Qualified" (%)	Age	Pre-1993 "Qualified" (%)	Post-1992 "Non-Qualified" (%)
70	5.00	5.00			
71	5.26	7.38	84	9.93	9.93
72	5.56	7.48	85	10.33	10.33
73	5.88	7.59	86	10.79	10.79
74	6.25	7.71	87	11.33	11.33
75	6.67	7.85	88	11.96	11.96
76	7.14	7.99	89	12.71	12.71
77	7.69	8.15	90	13.62	13.62
78	8.33	8.33	91	14.73	14.73
79	8.53	8.53	92	16.12	16.12
80	8.75	8.75	93	17.92	17.92
81	8.99	8.99	94	20.00	20.00
82	9.27	9.27	95	20.00	20.00
83	9.58	9.58	96+	20.00	20.00

For RRIFs issued in 1993 and after (non-qualified plans), there is a substantial jump in the minimum income that must be removed between age 70 and 71. The jump to 7.38 percent from 5 percent represents a substantial increase in income of 47.6 percent from one year to the next.

The minimum withdrawal calculation may be based on the age of the planholder or the age of the spouse. If the objective is to remove as little income as possible, then the date of birth of the younger spouse should be used. In the case of a spousal RRSP where the contributor is older, a RRIF based on the older contributor's age will allow more income to be paid out without triggering the three-year attribution rule. The decision of whose age to use for the minimum withdrawal formula is made when the RRIF contract is created.

RRIF Investment Strategies

As mentioned above, you are able to convert your RRSPs in whatever form of investment they are in to your RRIF account. In essence what you are doing is stopping the accumulation of assets and starting the withdrawal of income.

As an asset designed to provide retirement income over 30 or more years, the holdings within a RRIF should reflect a long-term investment strategy. Normally, the investment objective is to provide income and moderate growth. This could suggest an asset mix of 40 percent to 65 percent in equity (stocks) and the balance, 35 percent to 60 percent, in fixed income and cash. Fixed-income investments are a group of assets that will return the original invested capital if held to a future maturity date. In addition, they pay out a fixed or constant amount of income in the form of interest.

The percentage of fixed income, stocks, and cash assets in your actual portfolio should reflect your investor profile, as well as the target mix required to meet your retirement income plan objectives. There are four reasons why this is a meaningful goal.

1. The asset mix for this objective can provide lower volatility.
2. This asset usually forms a significant part of wealth transfer to the estate and should have the opportunity not only to sustain itself but grow.
3. The account will need to experience some growth if the purchasing power of withdrawals is expected to keep up with inflation.
4. Even at a minimum withdrawal level, the RRIF would need to have an investment return of 8.1 percent just to maintain the value of the initial deposit.

The comparison below shows the current "no risk" rate of return offered by the average GIC or bond (5.5 percent). If, on a $100,000 RRIF at 5.5 percent, the initial withdrawal is set at interest only, the $5,500 of interest per year works out to $458 per month. The account balance erodes over the years because:

- The required withdrawals are at a greater percentage than interest earned.
- Between age 71 and 72, the individual's required income takes a noticeable jump.

- If we look at increasing income to meet an inflation rate of 2.5 percent, we simply magnify the problem of withdrawals relative to returns.

	"Interest Only" RRIF				"Interest Only" RRIF Indexed at 2.5%		
Age	Minimum Withdrawal ($)	Income ($)	Value ($)	Age	Minimum Withdrawal ($)	Income ($)	Value ($)
65	333	458	100,000	65	333	458	100,000
70	396	458	100,000	70	391	518	97,706
71	416	458	100,000	71	407	531	96,702
72	615	615	98,120	72	595	595	94,884
75	605	605	92,086	75	585	587	89,029
80	589	589	80,430	80	663	664	74,129
85	573	573	66,249	85	456	751	49,106
90	557	557	48,808	90	204	850	10,452
Account exhausts at age 101.				Account exhausts at age 90.			

RRIF Investment Conclusions

- If the average rates of return are less than the required withdrawals, then the account will erode and eventually exhaust.
- Investment strategies should include an aspect of both growth and income in order to provide some hedge against inflation. The sole use of "no risk" investments may provide the greatest risk of running out of capital and income. Some risk-averse investors may find this scenario totally acceptable if it guarantees income for a set period of time.
- Investments should include cash positions from which income could be drawn in negative markets.
- All asset classes should be separate so that withdrawals can be targeted to a specific asset. More on this later in this chapter and in Chapter 3.

Survivor Issues

When a RRIF is established, you can choose one of two options for spousal survivor benefits.

1. RRIF payments may continue to the surviving spouse at the passing of the planholder (successor annuitant).
2. A commuted lump sum may be paid to the spouse by transfer into their RRIF/RRSP.

In a time of uncertainty and grief, there may be merit in having the plan simply continue payments to the surviving spouse. It is less complicated and assures an uninterrupted stream of income. In addition, the money within the existing RRIF may have been invested or deposited on favourable terms that would otherwise come to an end if the contract were terminated. There is still the flexibility to make changes to the plan in the future and tailor it to the survivor.

There is no tax payable at the time a RRIF is transferred to a surviving spouse as a result of the annuitant's death.

If there is no surviving spouse, it may be best to name the estate as the beneficiary. If you name specific children or other relatives, remember that the estate is ultimately responsible for the tax payable for receiving the RRIF balance. This could create a serious problem.

For example, let's say that you appoint your daughter to receive the balance of your RRIF, thinking that your son will get other assets from the estate. This needs to be approached carefully since the tax on the RRIF will need to be paid by the estate. This may not result in an equitable division of your assets. Don't treat registered assets and other assets equally. Tax considerations should always form part of the strategy in wealth transfer. We'll discuss wealth transfer in more detail in Chapter 5.

RRIF Transfers

There may be occasions where you want to transfer your RRIF account from one institution to another. To do this you will require the same transfer form as for RRSPs—a T2033.

The relinquishing institution is required to ensure that at least the minimum withdrawal amount has been paid from the account in the year of transfer. If this amount of income has not yet been paid, you will receive a lump-sum cheque for the difference before the money can be transferred. Unlike with a LIF/LRIF transfer, income from the new institution can commence immediately. Since the relinquishing institution has already paid out the annual minimum payment, no new payments must commence until the next year, but they can commence at your discretion before then.

Summary of RRIF Features

- Unlike an annuity, RRIFs have an account balance.
- There is a wide variety of investment options.
- There is no maximum income limit.
- You may own as many RRIFs as you wish.
- Lump-sum withdrawals are allowed.
- Minimum withdrawals can be based on your spouse's age.
- A RRIF can be rolled back to an RRSP by the annuitant or the beneficiary as long as the age 71 rule is not breached.
- Income qualifies for the pension income tax credit.

THE BENEFITS OF CONSOLIDATING ASSETS IN A SELF-DIRECTED PLAN

One of the best tools for consolidating registered holdings is a self-directed account. Occasionally, the term "self-directed" makes people worry that they are going to be responsible for all the decisions regarding their plan, including making the actual investments. This is an option, but quite often this type of vehicle is used in conjunction with an advisor and the majority of direction comes from your advisor working with you. A self-directed plan allows you to pull together, under one umbrella, stocks, GICs, bonds, and other investments that are scattered about in various institutions. Keep in mind that each type of registered account—RRSP, RRIF, LIRA, LIF, and LRIF—would require its own self-directed plan, as these monies cannot be mixed together. As you move toward a target retirement date, a self-directed plan allows you to begin pulling together all of your registered accounts. These accounts may be held at different institutions and only be available for transfer at different times. A self-directed plan allows you to consolidate your holdings over time.

One of the additional benefits of this is that all activity in your self-directed account, including deposits, income payments, purchases, redemptions, changes to investments, interest and dividend payments, etc. are all recorded and summarized on your investment statement. This provides you with a detailed, consolidated statement for all of your holdings within the plan.

Maximizing Investment Options

A self-directed plan affords you the freedom to seek higher returns and reduce volatility by allowing you an increased stable of investment options. It also provides you with a vehicle to hold the offerings of different financial institutions under one plan.

One investment option that you may be considering is GICs, which may reduce portfolio volatility better than bonds. With rates on bonds relatively low and basically having a flat yield curve (which means that a one-year bond has almost the same yield as a 30-year bond), the use of GICs would provide a fixed-income component with no fluctuation in asset value. As we will discuss shortly, the market value of bonds declines in a rising interest-rate environment. The stability of a GIC's market value serves to reduce the level of volatility or risk in the portfolio. Interest earned could be paid out semi-annually or annually and form part of the withdrawals.

The trade-off in this action is that, unlike a bond, GICs cannot normally be cashed in before their maturity date. But accessing lump sums on short notice is not very common, especially in a RRIF. You could set up a specific cash component to handle such situations or make sure that one of the certificates can be redeemed prior to maturity. Life insurance company certificates, which are technically deferred annuities, are one such option. They can be partially or wholly surrendered prior to the maturity date. A market value adjustment and/or administrative charge may apply.

In using GICs, the benefit of additional stability is traded for the potential capital appreciation that might be realized through owning bonds. However, with rates currently so low, and the yield curve so flat, the potential for capital appreciation in bonds is quite limited.

Holding Individual Bonds

If you wish to hold individual income or strip-coupon bonds in your registered account, you must have a self-directed plan in order to do so. Canada Savings Bonds, on the other hand, can be held individually in registered form. They do not function like government and corporate bonds, nor is it necessary to hold them in a self-directed plan.

Strip or Zero Coupon Bonds

Strip bonds are created by taking a block of high-quality government bonds and separating the individual coupons from the underlying bond residue.

When separated, each portion, the coupon and the residue, has a specific value at some point in the future.

A GIC is purchased with a stated rate of interest or yield. Bonds, on the other hand, are issued in limited quantity and are then bought and sold from an inventory, either as a new issue or from a secondary market. The income or growth of the bond, adjusted for any capital gain or loss, divided by the price, determines the *effective yield*.

Strip bonds are a meaningful consideration for RRSP and RRIF accounts. Income bonds pay out interest twice a year on a simple interest basis. Strip bonds do not deliver interest income payments like a conventional bond, but are purchased at a discount and mature at a specific value. The difference between the purchase price and the maturity value reflects the compound rate of return applied to the strip bond over the period of time from issue to maturity, which ranges from one year to 30 years.

When strip bonds are used outside of a tax-sheltered plan, growth is taxed annually as interest income. This happens even though no interest income is being received. For tax purposes, then, strip bonds are not attractive in a non-registered situation. However, in an RRSP, LIRA, RRIF, or LIF, they can be an excellent tool.

With more and more governments bringing budgets into order and incurring less debt, there already are fewer bonds in the market, and it is expected that the availability of investment-grade bonds will continue to decline. Governments are renewing some debt but also retiring large amounts. There is relatively little new debt (bonds) being issued.

At times of heavy government borrowing, one could have realized an additional 25 to 75 basis points (0.25 to 0.75 percent) of yield on a bond over a GIC. But given the law of supply and demand, and the shrinking bond inventory, the price of existing bonds has risen, and thereby lowered effective yields. Consequently, the difference in rates between GICs and bonds has become smaller.

Combining Investments Within Self-Directed Plans

A self-directed RRSP or RRIF allows us to hold several types of investments under one plan and be creative with how we can create both income and growth.

Take an example of an individual, age 57, who is three years away from retirement. Included in his or her benefits and assets is $300,000 in RRSPs.

From this source he or she wishes to have an income of $24,000 starting at age 60. This person wants to have guaranteed income for the first five years of retirement. The following scenario uses a combination of either bonds or certificates, along with equity investment funds, structured to meet the plan objectives. The assumed return for the investment funds will be 8 percent. The $300,000 could be invested as follows:

Certificate or Bond Duration	Interest Rate (%)	Deposit Amount ($)	Maturity Value ($)
3 Years	3.42	22,036	24,000
4 Years	3.70	21,123	24,000
5 Years	3.96	20,184	24,000
6 Years	4.28	19,090	24,000
7 Years	4.56	17,791	24,000

Total deposits required = $100,224
Balance to be invested in equity funds = $199,776
Fund value at the beginning of Year 8 at 8% = $342,380

The investments can be set up in an RRSP and could be converted to a RRIF in three years, at the time income is to commence. This is an example of combining investment options and having them work together, even though only some of the holdings are actually being used to create income. Any number of investment scenarios and portfolios could be considered.

As the equity portion grows, profits can be taken and new bonds can be acquired to provide additional years of guaranteed income. All of this could be done as a way of rebalancing the portfolio. Or, the equity component could be allowed to grow to the values shown above.

Individual fixed-income instruments, whether they are bonds, GICs, or deferred annuities, do have a role in portfolio structure. Mortgage funds, bond funds, or the bond component of balanced funds are also a source of fixed-income investment.

If more guarantees are desired, a nine- and 10-year bond/certificate could be created and the balance put into segregated funds with a 10-year maturity guarantee.

Commencing Income

Because GICs and bonds have maturity dates that extend into the future, it may be several years until all of your assets are finally housed under the umbrella of a self-directed registered plan.

It is possible to deliver a stream of income from the self-directed plan based on the value of all of the registered assets, even though some of them may not have been transferred yet. Assume that you have $300,000 to invest and draw RRIF income from. You want to draw income from your holdings at the rate of 7 percent per annum, or $21,000 per year. Only $200,000 is available today, $50,000 one year from now, and the other $50,000 in three years. Income can flow from the self-directed plan at the level of $21,000 per year, and the other certificates, which will grow in value until their maturity date, can simply be transferred into the self-directed RRIF as they come due.

Delivering Income

If you have several RRIFs scattered at different institutions, you must commence income from each one of these by the time you turn age 71. With the self-directed plan, the flow of income, even if it is a minimum withdrawal, only has to come from one source. This means only one cheque, not several.

The same holds true for mutual fund investments. If RRIFs are established with four different companies, that means four different deposits. If the same companies and investments are instead housed in a self-directed plan, then only one deposit is made to your bank account. Previously, we looked at the concept of consolidating assets. Simplification, less administration, and fewer cheques were some of the benefits of this course of action. The next section reviews another of the advantages: the ability to be selective in choosing which investments will be used to create your income

Controlling Withdrawals—The Cash Wedge

Self-directed plans allow you and your advisor complete control in determining the investments you wish to use to create your income. One concept that has been helpful in times of down markets is that of the "cash wedge." By consciously allocating a specific sum of money to a money market account, you can use this resource to create income if other investment values fall. Within the self-directed vehicle you can stop taking income from other investments and have all payments come from the money market account.

Similarly, you can specify particular investment funds, bonds, or GICs from which to create the income payment.

A meaningful allocation to the cash wedge is a multiple of monthly income, perhaps enough for a year or a year and a half. Granted, the inclusion of a money market fund within your portfolio will lower overall returns, but it will also reduce volatility in the account. In a negative market, this would allow other investments some time to recover and gain in value. The money market fund could be replenished by taking profits and moving them into the cash wedge. In this way, the cash wedge would be restored for the next time you feel the need to use it. Is this a form of market timing? Not really. It is, however, a system of taking profits and rebalancing your portfolio. By doing this, you can hedge against some steep declines in market value and have a market-neutral buffer from which to draw your income. This is described in additional detail on page 190.

Topping Up to Bracket

One of the goals of effectively "layering" income is to determine which assets to use to create income and which assets to defer.

Taking fully taxable income up to the first federal tax bracket is the most basic form of "topping up to bracket." This strategy may be of great value in systematically disassembling RRSPs. There may be some real inefficiency in deferring registered assets as long as possible for the purpose of "tax sheltering."

The deferral of RRSP and other registered money can lead you into a very disadvantageous tax trap as you progress into your late 60s and beyond.

Where there are larger accumulations of registered money, the concept of topping up to bracket is worthy of consideration. The concept involves taking out additional, taxable income to the top of the current tax bracket you are in. Remember that the tax rate you will pay on each dollar within the bracket is the same.

What we are suggesting is taking out additional income, paying the tax, and converting it into non-registered money. This is totally consistent with the concepts of providing flexibility, tax efficiency, and layering income. This strategy is even more effective when done in the years before age 65, when we are not eroding the age credit or OAS entitlements.

The benefits of such action include that it:

- Creates more tax-effective income in the future
- Can serve to keep the "net income" figure low
- Helps preserve government benefits and tax credits
- Provides more control over withdrawals and taxation
- Is more tax efficient for survivor or beneficiaries
- Is more estate-friendly

There are two points to take into account when considering this strategy. First, it is worth discussing with your advisor. Does this have merit for you? If planned withdrawals from fully taxable accounts will have you comfortably below the first federal tax bracket, there may not be a need to consider this option. If your RRSP accounts will require you to take larger amounts of income out in future years, then this course of action may be beneficial. The second point is that it is not only important to consider how your taxable income is created today but also how those decisions will impact your taxable income in future years.

RRSPS/RRIFS AND THE PRIME APPROACH

Our objective is to build fully taxable income from your first dollar of income to the point where we reach the first federal tax bracket. That is the juncture where fully taxable income requires us to remove $1.60 to have a dollar after tax. The previous after-tax dollar only required us to remove $1.33, since we were in the lower bracket.

After this point it becomes advantageous to use tax-preferred and/or non-taxable sources of income. This obviously requires having some non-registered holdings.

Income should be triggered from the following sources in the order shown.

- Government benefits when available
- Employer pension or locked-in assets

- Income from registered holdings (RRSPs/RRIFs)
- Taxable distributions from non-registered holdings
- Non-registered capital

Not everyone has all of the types of assets listed above. That does not change the order of withdrawal. However, there will be times when fully taxable income is taken after the first tax bracket has been reached. But, the above-detailed order and this process will make most efficient use of the assets and benefits that you have built and will deliver income in the most tax-efficient manner.

Depending on the assets you hold, it may be better to take taxable distributions from non-registered holdings before drawing any money from RRSPs/RRIFs. This decision may vary on a year-to-year basis.

Make use of the personal exemption and the first tax bracket. Keep in mind that you can withdraw roughly $20,000 of fully taxable income and pay a relatively low rate of tax—somewhere in the neighbourhood of 15 percent if you are under the age of 65. If you are over the age of 65, a $24,000 income can be taken and the average tax rate applied will be less that 15 percent.

Even if you do not need the income, it may be beneficial to withdraw the above amounts from your RRSPs/RRIFs. You will have converted fully taxable RRSP/RRIFs dollars into non-registered assets. Shortly we will discuss ways to hold these assets in a tax-effective manner. You have also given yourself flexibility and control. With RRSPs/RRIFs, you are faced with a number of rules for money that must be withdrawn, while you are not mandated in any way to use non-registered assets.

Converting RRSPs to non-registered money goes hand in hand with having tax-preferred or non-taxable resources to use in funding those things you wish to do in the earlier years of your retirement. Again, the logic and practicality of such a move will be dependent upon a number of factors specific to your situation. If your RRSP has a smaller value, there may initially appear to be little to no benefit at all. However, if you have taxable income from other sources, it may make perfect sense. If you have larger accumulations in your name, say $150,000 plus, then it is likely better to bring amounts into income gradually, in smaller amounts, than wait and be forced to make larger withdrawals at higher rates of tax.

Keep in mind that we want to watch the level of taxable income that we are creating. Early and gradual conversion of RRSPs to tax-paid holdings and tax-effective investing of the capital is one way to do this.

The first priority is to create the level of income or access to capital that is needed to fulfill your Time Hub and Money Hub objectives. The amount of income that should be drawn from your RRSP/RRIF depends on many factors, including other income streams available, how much is being paid from government benefits and pension sources, and how much is needed to satisfy the income objectives you have.

Remember, however, that at age 71 you are *required* to withdraw minimum amounts from your registered holdings. Attempting to defer income from registered assets for as long as possible may simply create greater tax problems down the road.

Are your parents using their assets and income sources in the best possible way? It is important that they be made aware of these issues. And, after all, you are the ultimate beneficiary of those assets at some point in the future. Part of the Prime Approach process deals with those issues that pertain to wealth transfer. Any inheritance to which you are entitled will be passed to you after the estate has paid taxes. There are important planning steps that should be considered and solutions implemented to make sure that the maximum value of your parents' estate flows through to you and your siblings rather than to the tax department. The most important strategy in this context is prepaying the tax liability on the transfer of registered assets—RRSPs, RRIFs LIFs, and pensions—between generations. The wealth-transfer planning stream is a key consideration in intergenerational planning, and is discussed in detail in Chapter 5.

Since, as mentioned above, assets will flow from one generation to another after the estate has paid taxes, it means that you will ultimately have non-registered or tax-paid assets in your portfolio. This use of these assets in creating retirement income is the focus of the next section.

SECTION 4:
Non-Registered (Open) Assets

When we examine the assets of those about to retire, we commonly see a lack of non-registered holdings. There are several reasons for this. Given the advantage of being able to deduct an RRSP contribution, this tends to be where most people put their retirement savings. In fact, we would contend that most individuals view the tax saving as the primary reason to make an RRSP contribution, with the objective of accumulating retirement assets being only secondary.

There may be a fairly good reason for this. Very few people actually make the maximum RRSP contributions to which they are entitled. As few as 35 percent of all eligible taxpayers make any RRSP contribution at all. If non-registered savings generally occur after RRSPs are maximized, is it any wonder these amounts are small?

Income for non-registered assets may become available on an irregular or unexpected basis. Often, non-registered assets are created as a result of an inheritance, but can also be created by borrowing money to invest (leveraging), through a share incentive program, or from the sale of a business interest or principal residence. This is positive because in order to employ many of the more tax-effective and creative income strategies, non-registered assets are required.

As you read through this section, you will find that the information and strategies put forth are an overlap between two of the Prime Approach cogs—structural planning and investment planning. As we told you in the beginning, it is normal for all of the planning channels to be interconnected. This is one of the key premises of the Prime Approach. Retirement income planning is a multidisciplinary, integrated process.

For the purposes of discussion, the terms "non-registered" and "open" will mean exactly the same thing.

HAVING CASH ON HAND
Normally, open assets are used as the cash, emergency, or liquidity accounts that every individual should establish. There are a number of reasons to have money set aside in a liquidity account.

- The knowledge and comfort that you have a cushion of money if and when you need it
- The immediate resources available in the case of an emergency
- Access to money needed to take advantage of an opportunity
- Alternative assets should you not be able to redeem certain GICs
- The ability to unwind structured investments to create the capital you want

The amounts allocated for this purpose will vary by needs and preferences. We have seen everything from six weeks to six months of expenses as a measure of how much should be put in this type of account. While it serves a purpose to have some money in a liquidity account, it is not effective to have large sums held within it. Remember, because you are dealing with short-term money in liquid accounts, your returns will usually be very low. And what little you do earn will be subject to taxation.

You do not want to have your money invested in anything that has a chance to suffer a loss or be variable, because the time horizon for this money may be very short. Typically, the best investment vehicles for an emergency fund include:

Money Market or T-Bill Accounts Issued by the government of Canada, these instruments are purchased at a discount and then mature at full face value. The change in the value is the rate of return. These are short-term vehicles with maturity dates of 91 days, 182 days, or 364 days. In an open account the growth is treated as regular income for tax purposes.

Short-Term Notes of No Longer Than 30 Days Offered by most financial institutions, these allow for a better rate of return than savings or daily interest accounts.

Canada Savings Bonds These are different from income or conventional bonds for several reasons. They are only sold during a specified time of the year. Yield is set each year at the time of sale. There is no secondary market for these bonds (buying and selling); they are simply cashed. As such, the bonds always hold their original face value no matter when they are cashed in. They are good instruments for purposes of liquidity for just this reason. They may now also be purchased directly as RRSP investments.

A Line of Credit Relying on a line of credit as a liquidity account has some merit. You don't need to hold your capital in a low yield, fully taxable account. If money is required, you can simply take it from your line of credit and pay off the loan as other funds become available. You will want to establish the line of credit with your financial institution before you ever need it.

Savings or Daily Interest Accounts The rates of interest afforded these accounts can range from 0.25 percent to 0.75 percent. These accounts are the least desirable of the liquidity options.

High Yield Savings Accounts Many institutions are now offering flexible high-yield accounts which, at the time of writing, are delivering 3.85 percent to 4.10 percent per annum. This is in line with a three- or four-year GIC without the restrictions on access and withdrawals you face with a Guaranteed Investment Certificate.

EARNING INCOME FROM NON-REGISTERED ASSETS

There are many advantages to holding non-registered or "open" assets. Unlike RRSPs, there are no contribution limits and, more importantly, you have total control over when and how these assets are used. The main benefits in a retirement income scenario come from the efficient tax treatment of these assets. We are using money that has already been taxed. A large percentage of the withdrawal, therefore, comes out on a non-taxable basis. Remember that only the growth portion of the withdrawal is taxable. The benefits of this become very evident when we are working in the middle and upper tax brackets, where fully taxable income requires $1.60 or more be removed in order to get $1.00 after tax.

Having tax-preferred and non-taxable income is a huge advantage. Unfortunately, it is difficult to accumulate non-registered investments because you are using dollars that have already been taxed to do it. One exception to this would be the concept of borrowing money to invest, or leveraging as it is called. In this process, the borrowed money (the loan is non-taxable) is invested and the amount of interest on the loan is a tax-deductible expense, assuming the investments used comply with the expectations of providing elements of taxable income in the future. Another exception is an inheritance. Any taxes payable are remitted through the estate.

For many seniors a large percentage of their retirement holdings is already in the form of non-registered assets. Why is this? There are several reasons. They did not have the amount of time, or the large contribution limits currently available, to build large RRSP holdings. Also, they lived in a time of lower taxation levels. It was more functional to build up non-registered holdings and keep a larger percentage of the interest or investment earnings subsequently earned. In addition, given the way life cycles and transitions come about, many non-registered accounts for seniors are created from the sale of their principal residence at a time when their accommodations change.

Non-registered assets provide the greatest opportunity for creative delivery of tax-effective income. However, they can also be used very ineffectively and result in higher taxes. Many individuals leave themselves exposed to taxation on the interest income of non-registered money by simply placing it into GICs or bonds. This is not a tax-effective strategy. As we've shown, easily one-third to one-half of the interest earned on non-registered holdings can be lost to taxes. To compound the matter, the inability to shelter any of this "exposed" money does not help you cope with inflation.

There are several creative alternatives to this problem. The trade-off in some cases is being exposed to increased risk in exchange for potentially higher and more tax-effective returns. In other strategies, complete guarantees are in place. Is it possible to have tax-effective results using guarantees? Yes, it is.

What we are trying to accomplish through the various strategies is to have the ability to deliver income that:

- Has tax-preferred growth, in the form of dividends and capital gains
- Has a non-taxable component
- Is complementary to other income streams
- Preserves capital asset values
- Benefits the estate at the time of wealth transfer

The following strategies, including bond ladders, systematic withdrawal plans, corporate class mutual funds and pools, and prescribed annuities, show alternative uses for non-registered assets. By employing these financial tools, you can make more effective use of your non-registered dollars.

EARNING INCOME FROM FIXED-INCOME INVESTMENTS

Fixed-income investments, including income bonds and GICs, are not risk free. Actually, there is no such thing as a risk-free investment. It is true that interest payments and renewal values are guaranteed if fixed-income instruments are held until their maturity date; however, there are other risk factors that must be addressed relative to these investments.

Inflation Risk

Bonds and GICs used to generate interest income are the least effective instruments in terms of coping with inflation. It is true that their respective interest rates will rise and fall with inflation. There is a direct correlation. However, the purchasing power of fixed-interest payments will decrease over time unless the value of the underlying capital increases. This is basically impossible to accomplish if all of the interest is being paid out and the assets are held until maturity. This is one of the key reasons for combining your fixed-income holdings with equity or stock investments.

Tax Risk

Interest is the least effective form of investment income to receive. There is no preferential treatment, and interest income attracts the highest tax rate. Any time we take the opportunity to delay or defer the payment of tax, we benefit. There is no such opportunity with interest income. The erosion of both income and wealth through taxation is a risk factor to consider.

There may be a capital gain element that applies to individual bonds or bond funds held outside of registered vehicles. Such benefits may not be realized from individual bonds when the intent is to hold them to maturity. However, bond funds may generate a certain amount of their return in the form of capital gains, especially in a falling interest-rate environment.

Renewal Risk

You purchase a bond or GIC that has a specific rate of interest for a defined term. You do not know what rate of interest you will receive at the time this investment matures. Renewal risk refers to the fact that this new rate may be lower than what was originally paid, resulting in a lower amount of income.

Maturity dates of certificates and bonds should be spaced so that every-thing is not renewing at one time. Stagger your GICs and their maturity dates into one-, three-, and five-year terms. At each renewal, roll the GIC into a five-year term and continue the process. Traditionally, five-year terms offer the highest rate of interest and all of your money will be in this form, with different amounts renewing each year and being rolled forward for another five years.

This will also serve to reduce the risk of having everything coming up for reinvestment at a time when rates may be low. The prevailing inter-est rates at the time of maturity may influence and alter the reinvestment decision and the strategy, but over time this process has produced the most beneficial and consistent results.

To illustrate renewal risk, examine what actually occurred in 1993. For the sake of this illustration, let's assume that we are dealing with $100,000 of registered money so that taxation is not an additional factor. We will further assume that this is held in a RRIF where the interest earnings are paid out every year as income. If you were a retiree who had consistently used GICs to create income, a five-year certificate in 1988 would have provided a yield of 11 percent, thereby creating an annual income of $11,000 on a $100,000 deposit.

At renewal of that GIC in 1993, the five-year rate of return had dropped to 5.75 percent, while a one-year certificate had a yield of 2.75 percent. Rates had dropped significantly over five years and represented the lowest returns in 34 years. If it was your desire to keep the $100,000 of principal intact, it meant making one of two choices. You could have first renewed the certificate for five years. This would have produced an income of $5,750 each year, a substantial drop from the $11,000 you had previously been receiving. That course of action also meant locking up the rate on that certificate for a full five years. The second option was to renew the certificate for only one year in the hope that rates would once again rise. The dilemma in this option was that an income of only $2,750 would be created for the year.

The supporting argument for the GIC strategy is that the principal within a GIC is secure and the value, assuming a non-redeemable certificate, does not go down with stock market drops or interest-rate fluctuations. As is the case with a bond, if the GIC is held to its maturity date, the value of the principal is guaranteed. However, to extend the above example another five years, if it is essential for the GIC in the RRIF to create $11,000 of income per annum, and the rate of interest paid is 5.75 percent, it will be necessary to deliberately encroach upon the principal. A quick calculation shows us that this strategy will result in a reduction of the principal to $67,004 at the end of five years.

It becomes evident that even GICs carry with them an element of risk, both in the amount of potential income that they can provide and the possibility that an individual may have to encroach upon capital to provide a level of income. No investment decision is free of some form of risk.

Is there a place, then, for GICs in a retirement portfolio? There may very well be if it is the right tool to best meet your objectives. If you are using GICs as an investment, ensure that there is some opportunity to redeem all or part of the certificate before the maturity date. Normally, a certificate with this feature will carry a lower rate of return when compared to a non-redeemable certificate, but greater flexibility may be worth that difference. Care should be taken when selecting a GIC that the offering institution allows for total or partial redemption. The availability of this option does vary by institution. Most insurance company certificates, called deferred annuities, allow for encroachment on capital before the maturity date. In any institution that permits this, there may be an administrative charge and a market value adjustment if the certificate carries a lower rate of return than current market rates.

Market Risk

A feature of bonds and GICs is the return of the original investment capital if held to maturity. Bonds can be sold prior to their maturity date at current market value. The market value may not necessarily be the maturity value of the bond, and the sale of bonds either directly or through redemption of bond fund units may result in a loss. Market risk, as it applies to bonds, is discussed in more detail in Chapter 3, The Investment Portfolio.

A closer look at two of the more common fixed-income investment tools—GICs and income bonds—follows.

GICs

One fixed-income instrument with which most people have both familiarity and experience is the guaranteed investment certificate or GIC.

Interest in a GIC can either compound or be paid out. If you hold them as non-registered assets, it makes a great deal of sense to have the interest paid to you since you will be taxed on any interest earned in the year regardless if you withdraw it or not. There are three basic ways to use GICs in income streaming.

1. GICs can pay interest to you on a monthly, quarterly, semi-annual, or annual basis. You may also set up a "ladder" to deliver payments in different months. This is complementary to the strategy of staggering your maturity dates so that you do not have all of your GICs coming due at one time. Ultimately what you would like to do is hold only certificates with five-year maturities so that the maximum return is paid to you.
2. The principal of a GIC can be used to create part of the income payment. For example, $30,000 in a five-year GIC will produce an income of $562 per month. At the end of that time, all principal and interest have been exhausted. You cannot systematically encroach on the capital of a bond in exactly the same way.
3. Smaller GIC amounts can be used to buy future income. For example, let's say that we wanted to provide a guaranteed, annual income of $20,000 using GICs, starting one year from now. Using assumed rates of return, we would place the following amounts in GICs in order to deliver this future income.

Term Ending	Rate (%)	Deposit ($)	Maturity Value ($)
1 year	2.70	19,480	20,000
2 year	3.10	18,814	20,000
3 year	3.50	18,038	20,000

This strategy is similar to buying future income with strip bonds and has great application as a buffer against negative markets. The GICs can be used or rolled forward if markets are favourable and other investments are used. Because the GICs are creating interest income without immediately using it, this concept is really best suited for situations involving registered assets.

Additional Points on GICs

Bonds and GICs are commonly used to create a stream of interest income. The benefits of this approach are that you have both a guaranteed income flow and a guaranteed value of your assets at maturity. For these reasons, every retirement portfolio should have some percentage of assets in this form.

However, due to inflation and taxes, not all of your non-registered assets should simply be sitting in interest-bearing accounts. Any interest earned in an open account will be taxable in the year that it is earned. Normally, this amount should be taken into income, rather than leaving it to compound.

For your fixed-income investments, there are several strategies that should be considered. A significant one is that to make even more effective use of your GICs and bonds, consider combining deposits into fewer holdings.

Very often, people will have a large number of smaller deposits. These are usually placed with more than one institution. These smaller amounts should be combined into fewer holdings, each of which has a larger value. This will reduce the number of ongoing decisions required at the time the deposits mature. Larger accumulations with the same institution will sometimes allow you to negotiate a better rate above the posted offerings. Some insurance companies will give a higher rate of interest to a larger deposit. This is known as "banding." And, in the case of interest income, as is the case of RRIF payments, it is more convenient and orderly to receive one cheque rather than many smaller amounts per month.

Income Bonds (Conventional Bonds)

Many people are also familiar with income bonds, also known as conventional bonds. In the case of a regular or income bond, interest is paid on a semi-annual basis. A $10,000 bond with a 6 percent coupon will therefore make interest payments of $300 every six months. Since this interest does not compound but is paid out, it is referred to as "simple interest."

Bonds may be issued by a level of government, from municipal to federal, looking to raise capital by issuing debt. They may also be issued by corporations as an alternative to or complement to stock capitalization. Both government and corporate bonds can be purchased in $1,000 units with a minimum investment of $3,000 to $5,000. They are issued, like GICs, at a fixed rate of interest and with a defined maturity date. Maturities run from one year to 30 years. Interest is paid semi-annually, differentiating them from strip bonds, which pay no income but instead compound to maturity.

Durations

Bonds are subclassified according to the length of time until they mature.

- Short term—less than three years
- Medium term—three to 10 years
- Long term—more than 10 years

The Bond Ladder

In a bond ladder, six interest-bearing bonds are purchased. Each bond has a different number of years to maturity, for example five through 10 years. The bonds are selected so that the semi-annual payments each fall on a different month. This provides monthly income. The bonds are rolled forward for a six-year term at the time they mature.

Too often, people restrict the returns they receive from guaranteed investments to those instruments that have a term to maturity of five years or less. Certificates from insurance companies and government bonds have maturities of up to 20 and 30 years, respectively, so there is room for longer term deposits and higher rates of return than five-year GICs. Deposit guarantees still apply, and both life insurance company certificates and government bonds can be partially or totally surrendered before maturity.

THE BOND LADDER
The Bond Ladder Strategy

	Coupon	Maturity	Rating	Position	Price	Semi-Annual Yield	Cost
Saskatchewan	6.250%	03-Jul-09	BBBH	$21,000	$101.40	5.93%	$21,294.49
Ontario Hydro	7.000%	03-Aug-10	AH	$23,000	$105.29	5.79%	$24,216.68
New Brunswick	7.250%	22-Mar-11	A	$24,000	$106.05	5.80%	$25,452.11
Saskatchewan	6.000%	01-Jun-12	BBBH	$23,000	$101.31	5.78%	$23,301.16
Ontario Hydro	5.500%	16-Apr-13	AH	$23,000	$ 98.25	5.75%	$22,597.50
Alberta	5.500%	05-May-14	AA	$25,000	$ 98.29	5.73%	$24,572.81

Income Analysis

	Jan./July	Feb./Aug.	Mar./Sept.	Apr./Oct.	May/Nov.	June/Dec.
Saskatchewan	$656.25	$0.00	$0.00	$0.00	$0.00	$0.00 ·
Ontario Hydro	$0.00	$805.00	$0.00	$0.00	$0.00	$0.00
New Brunswick	$0.00	$0.00	$870.00	$0.00	$0.00	$0.00
Saskatchewan	$0.00	$0.00	$0.00	$0.00	$0.00	$690.00
Ontario Hydro	$0.00	$0.00	$0.00	$632.50	$0.00	$0.00
Alberta	$0.00	$0.00	$0.00	$0.00	$687.50	$0.00

Source: *Prime Approach™ to Retirement Planning.*

Each of the six bonds shown above pays interest twice yearly, creating an income payment in each of the 12 months. One bond matures each year and is renewed as a six-year bond at then-current rates. The result is a steady income stream from guaranteed investments and a process through which there is an averaging of interest rates by having only one-sixth of the portfolio coming due each year.

Summary of Fixed-Income Features

Fixed-income instruments:

- Represent a debt owed to you in the future
- Create a stream of interest income, which is fully taxable
- Provide guaranteed return of principal
- Do not normally provide a hedge for inflation

Additional features of bonds include:

- Normally, a higher rate of return
- Maturities from one to 30 years
- Partial or total liquidity
- 100 percent guaranteed return of capital if held to maturity
- The opportunity for capital appreciation

EARNING INCOME FROM EQUITY INVESTMENTS

There is really only one of two things you can do with your money. You can loan it, by placing it in debt instruments, or you can invest it, by taking an ownership position.

There are some very distinct differences between fixed-income assets and equity assets. Throughout this material, the terms "stock," "share," and "equity" mean the same thing and are interchangeable.

Equity returns fluctuate with the underlying market cycles of the asset or business. There is a business organization behind every stock that is acquired. Companies are made of bricks and mortar, and there are people employed in these businesses. Do you know what businesses are held within the mutual funds that you own? Most people do not, although it's as easy as checking the annual report from your mutual fund company to see a listing of what is held in each of the funds that you own.

There are two types of stocks—common shares and preferred shares. While there are some universal characteristics, each type of share has several distinguishing features.

Generally speaking:

- Both types of shares can pay dividends.
- Preferred shares have a stated rate of dividend payout and as such have a more predictable income stream.
- Shares with a history of dividend payments tend to be less volatile.
- Preferred shares tend to be issued by more established, profitable companies.
- The appeal of common stocks is the potential for capital appreciation.
- Should a company declare bankruptcy, preferred shareholders rank in priority above common shareholders.
- Either common shares or preferred shares can be sold for a capital gain or loss.

Aside from the potential returns of being invested in equities, an equally significant benefit to you is the tax treatment of receiving income in the form of dividends and capital gains. Whether the income was earned from individual stocks or mutual funds, there is a distinct advantage in those forms of income over interest payments. In addition, an individual stock or investment fund unit (or share) may have an element of deferred growth in the form of unrealized capital gain. As the investor, you have greater control over if and when this deferred gain is realized.

Bonds fluctuate with changes in interest rates and have their own range of volatility. Over time, however, equity ownership has generally delivered better returns than those provided by fixed-income instruments, and as such has been a better hedge against inflation.

Dividend-Paying Shares or Funds

The opportunity to receive dividend income has some tax advantages. Before the changes made to taxation of capital gains in 1999, dividend income was the most favourable form of income to receive. As noted previously, some issues related to dividend income and the calculation of net income, and required a degree of caution.

Dividend income is most commonly received through the ownership of common and preferred shares or through the use of dividend funds. Companies with consistent dividend-paying history tend to be older, more established organizations, such as banks, insurance companies, etc. As a result, these companies do not regularly experience the type of growth in share value that younger, smaller companies may experience. Instead, they tend to be more conservative investments. These are factors that make these types of stocks, whether held individually or through an investment fund, very appropriate holdings for retirement income portfolios. Because the preferred tax benefits are not realized within registered vehicles, they are most appropriate for non-registered accounts. However, the comparatively conservative nature of dividend-paying companies still makes them appropriate choices for a portion of registered portfolios.

For most investors, dividend funds are the most appropriate way to access these stocks since a relatively large amount of investment capital would otherwise be required to adequately diversify with individual equities.

Investment Funds (Mutual Funds)

When referring to investment funds or mutual funds, the intent is to include mutual and segregated funds. The additional protection features of segregated funds and strategies for their use will be addressed in Chapter 3.

If equity investing is beneficial to retirement income, the use of investment funds is a superlative way in which to do it. The reasons for this include:

- Proper diversification for smaller amounts of capital
- Professional management of capital
- Funds can be selected by specific objective or mandate that matches your goals (e.g., dividend income)

- Retirees prefer to make fewer investment decisions as they get older
- The liquidity of units allows for income streaming, whereas a portfolio holding individual stocks and bonds would require the selling of specific assets to create cash

There's also the potential for increased returns with investment funds. During the 1980s, when interest rates were 10 percent to 12 percent for one- to five-year GICs, retirement investment planning was a straightforward process. Interest rates are obviously much lower today and, as such, the same simple strategies employed a decade ago are not going to work as effectively. In fact, they may result in depleting your retirement assets.

Keep in mind that your retirement assets cannot stop working when you do. They must be invested to provide income that will last through the 25 to 35 years you will be retired—roughly one-third to one-half of your adult life. Most people equate "time horizon" with "years to retirement." This is not correct. Your income and assets may have to endure inflation and taxes for two to three decades. It is true that your investment portfolio at retirement should continue to reflect your personal investor profile and your tolerance to risk. However, the portfolio must also reflect a structure that will allow it to achieve the target rate of return needed to fulfill your retirement plan objectives. These two approaches may not yield the same plan. So the question, as always when it comes to investing, is "What am I prepared to give up?"

Proper portfolio management will also benefit your survivors, beneficiaries, and your estate. There are only small changes required to convert assets from savings to income. This can generally be accomplished without changing the actual investments.

Systematic Withdrawal Plans (SWPs)

One of the investment concepts that is promoted for reducing volatility and improving returns is that of dollar-cost averaging. This is where a set amount of money is invested each month, and a different number of units are purchased depending on the unit price.

A Systematic Withdrawal Plan (SWP) operates on the same principles as dollar-cost averaging, only in reverse. The concept begins with the investment of a lump sum of capital. Then periodic withdrawals of income are taken. Systematic withdrawal plans can also be created from existing investments where the accumulation phase has ended and the income phase begins. The key to the mutual fund SWP process is the fact that you can surrender small amounts of your investment portfolio each month by redeeming units. You cannot do the same thing in an investment portfolio that holds individual assets.

Technically this process works the same way within a RRIF, LIF, or LRIF as it does for non-registered assets. Any time that an individual is receiving periodic income from an investment fund, whether in a RRIF, LIF, LRIF, or open account, they are taking part in a systematic withdrawal plan. In the RRIF/LIF/LRIF situation, any amounts paid from the account are fully taxable. The difference in the case of open money is the preferred tax treatment to be realized. Several mutual fund companies enhance these tax benefits to an even greater degree through something referred to as T-series units. More detail on these will follow.

Another key benefit of SWPs is that they establish some degree of discipline in how money is drawn. Implementing a specific withdrawal strategy can be vital in maintaining a balance between maximizing income and minimizing risk to capital.

There are two different approaches to the withdrawal of money through a SWP.

1. Constant Payment Strategy

In this strategy, the same amount of income is drawn out during each period, whether monthly, quarterly, semi-annually, or annually. This approach provides the most stable income stream, and with inflation adjustments it will help address the issue of maintaining your standard of living. The only disadvantage is that you would need to increase withdrawals during times of high inflation, which may also be a time when portfolio assets are decreasing in value. The combination of factors may create a serious risk to the principal.

2. Constant Percentage Strategy

This approach to income streaming helps to protect your investment capital by lowering withdrawals in years of lower or negative portfolio returns. Withdrawals are maintained at a constant percentage of the portfolio value at the previous year-end. This strategy allows for additional withdrawals during years of rising returns, thus providing the opportunity to fund enhancements to your standard of living.

SWPs usually require an initial minimum investment of $25,000, although this varies by financial institution. You establish the amount of income and the frequency of payment and can change these details at any time. There is also an option to have the income increase automatically each year by a predetermined percentage in order to deal with inflation. The withdrawal of income can be stopped and restarted at any time. In addition, you always have the flexibility to access lump sums of capital.

Although account values will vary and on occasion be below or above the amount at which you started, you are simply withdrawing a small portion of the account once a month, quarter, etc. There are two factors that make this process work.

First, markets tend to rise over time. Any long-term graphs you will see on market indexes have them moving from the bottom left to the top right, indicating an increase over time. As markets and values increase, you will be required to surrender fewer investment units to create the same dollar amount of withdrawal, even if income is being adjusted for inflation.

Second, over any meaningful period of time, there are more months with positive returns than there are months with negative returns.

FIGURE 2.3: ONE WITHDRAWAL PER MONTH

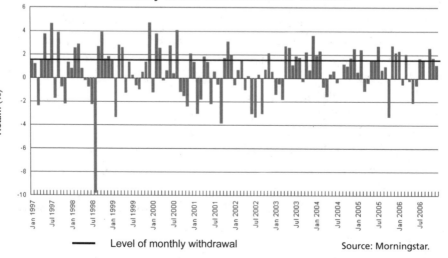

Monthly Withdrawal from Jan 07 to Dec 06

Source: Morningstar.

We are going to the well once a month to draw out a bucket. Some months there will be no rain and the water level may be lower than before. Other months will see heavy precipitation and the water level will rise. Regardless, we are not withdrawing everything at once. We are only taking out one bucket per month.

Investments chosen for use with SWPs should include some of the following criteria:

- Growth potential, such as through equity or balanced funds
- Low distributions in the form of capital gains (high tax-efficiency)
- Tax-free switches, such as through mutual fund corporations
- Tax benefits found under "T-series" units (discussed shortly)
- Fall within the overall asset allocation strategy

Tax-Advantaged Income

There are obvious advantages regarding the tax treatment of distributions in the form of capital gains and dividends. In addition, the calculation of how SWP payments are taxed provides substantial benefits, as this basic example demonstrates.

Suppose you invest $100,000 into a fund at a cost of $10 per unit or share. Assuming 8 percent growth, the account is worth $108,000 at the end of one year. You withdraw the $8,000 as income. On the surface, it may look like the entire $8,000 realized from redemption of units or shares will be taxed as a capital gain. But the actual tax treatment is much better.

With the growth of the fund, the units are now worth $10.80 rather than $10.00. At this unit price, it would be necessary to redeem 741 units to create the $8,000. The realized gain is the difference between the redemption price of $10.80 and the purchase price of $10.00, times the number of units sold. In this example, then, this works out to a taxable capital gain of $592.80 ([$10.80 minus $10.00] times 741 units). At an approximate 50 percent inclusion rate for capital gains, this means that $296.40 would be included as income. For a receipt of $8,000, the amount of tax payable would be $118.56 at a 40 percent marginal tax rate, or $77.01 at a 26 percent marginal tax rate.

Compare this to the fact that $8,000 of fully taxable income would result in tax payable of $3,200 and $2,080 at the 40 percent and 26 percent brackets, respectively.

The adjusted cost base of your original investment will become smaller each year as withdrawals are made. As a result, the amount of tax payable on the income will increase on an annual basis. However, even if the entire income amount of $8,000 becomes taxable as a capital gain, the amount of tax payable is $1,600 at a 40 percent rate and $1,040 at a 26 percent rate. This is half of the tax that is payable on fully taxable income.

Especially in the early retirement years, when taking fully taxable amounts of income from registered accounts, the SWP is a very effective complement to deliver additional income on a tax-effective basis. As illustrated in the following example, this strategy produces meaningful income but adds very little to the net income on your tax return. This is a very desirable combination.

This illustration, from Dynamic Mutual Funds, shows a tax-advantaged income in the early years, when retirees have the most flexibility and health to enjoy their retirement. Some other notable points include:

- Income can be received on a very tax-effective basis.
- There will be some taxable distributions that are in addition to the gain on the surrender of units.
- Actual returns will vary from the average, creating deficits and surpluses in the account balance at year-end. This is a reality. Also, some years will have larger taxable distributions than others.

As with all examples in this book, this example is not to suggest that assets should be deployed in one particular concept or strategy. There are many good vehicles and combinations of tools that will provide income from non-registered assets while respecting your possible desire to avoid encroachment of capital.

T-Series Investment Funds

This series of mutual funds is designed to pay out income on an even more tax-effective basis than SWPs. The enhancement with this program is that initially the majority of each payment will be return of capital. That portion of the payment that is return of capital will be non-taxable. Taxable distributions are reinvested into the fund.

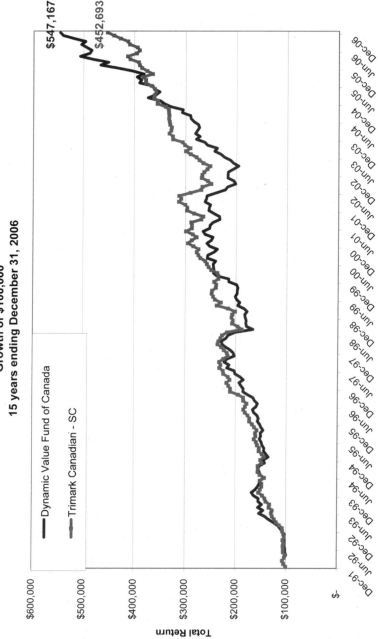
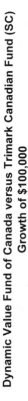

Dynamic Value Fund of Canada versus Trimark Canadian Fund (SC)
Growth of $100,000
15 years ending December 31, 2006

— Dynamic Value Fund of Canada
— Trimark Canadian - SC

$547,167

$452,693

Total Return

$600,000
$500,000
$400,000
$300,000
$200,000
$100,000
-$

Dec-91
Jun-92
Dec-92
Jun-93
Dec-93
Jun-94
Dec-94
Jun-95
Dec-95
Jun-96
Dec-96
Jun-97
Dec-97
Jun-98
Dec-98
Jun-99
Dec-99
Jun-00
Dec-00
Jun-01
Dec-01
Jun-02
Dec-02
Jun-03
Dec-03
Jun-04
Dec-04
Jun-05
Dec-05
Jun-06
Dec-06

Source: Globe HySales, Dynamic Funds

Simply described, T-series investment funds will deliver extremely tax-effective income in the early years. In most cases the payout is fixed at a rate of 8 percent per year—the anticipated future growth of these accounts over the years.

Investment growth in the form of capital gains is deferred. At the ultimate surrender of the account or when the adjusted cost base of the fund becomes zero, income or proceeds will be taxed as a capital gain. This is still a preferable way to receive income. Assume that you are receiving a base level of income that is fully taxable up to the first federal tax bracket. The use of this type of vehicle will allow for additional income to be paid, with only a small portion of it being taxable in the early years. Following the Prime Approach, you may wish to plan to do additional things in your early years of retirement and want more income during that time. These types of funds allow you to have greater income without having the same increase in your taxable income.

Bond Funds

It is essential that when you consider fixed-income investments such as bonds and bond funds, you also remember that changes in interest rates will have an impact on their value. Simply stated, when interest rates drop, the market value of existing bonds will rise. And when rates do rise, they will have a negative impact on the market value of fixed-income vehicles. Current yields on bonds and bond funds are in the 4 percent to 5.5 percent range. They serve as a balance and a safe harbour in times of volatile markets. In a retirement income portfolio, they can be a source from which withdrawals can be made should stocks decline in value.

With these products, it is important to note what overall fees you may be paying. In a managed account or packaged portfolio with a flat management fee that applies to the account as a whole, you may have a substantial portion of the bond returns eaten up by costs.

Diversified Monthly Income Funds

Diversified monthly income funds appear as a subcategory of balanced funds, since they contain a number of different asset types including cash, bonds, preferred shares, and income trusts including REITs and royalty trusts. As the name and holdings of these funds suggest, the objective of high-yield funds is to create a diversity of income streams for unitholders. The different asset categories, all with a goal to produce income, have a combined objective of higher investment returns, more-tax-efficient returns, and lower overall volatility than traditional bond and mortgage funds.

Recent returns for high-yield funds have been excellent compared with equity funds and other fixed-income offerings. If the interest-rate trend reverses as the economy starts to improve, it will have two effects. First, the inflation rate will begin to move up, and in turn will have an initially negative impact on these types of assets. Second, the falling interest rates will drive up some of the returns realized by the holdings of these funds. So, as always, some caution should be exercised in how much exposure you should have to this or any asset class. Balance is the key. When you discuss investment allocation with your advisor, you may find that it's appropriate to have fixed-income funds and/or high-yield funds form part of your portfolio.

Mortgages and Mortgage Funds

The ability to purchase fixed-income assets through mortgage funds provides a degree of diversification among holdings that would not otherwise be available to the average investor. As prevailing interest rates change, the value of mortgage funds will fluctuate in much the same manner as bonds and bond funds.

Some mortgage funds may focus on residential mortgages and some may lean toward commercial mortgages. Some funds are a blend of both of these types of loans. Mortgage fund returns over the long term are fairly close to, although slightly lower than, those of bond funds. Correspondingly, there is a lower degree of volatility with mortgage funds. One of the reasons for this is that there is a continual stream of capital repayment in a mortgage fund. As a result, mortgage funds may be viewed as a somewhat more defensive fixed-income fund.

Corporate Class Mutual Funds or Pools

When we purchase a mutual fund, or unit trust, or unit trust our investment dollars purchase "units" of the fund. In a mutual fund corporation, rather than acquiring units, investors buy different classes of "shares" within "the company." A mutual fund corporation will likely hold several different mutual funds within it as part of the corporation. One of the significant differences between this legal status and that of unit trusts is that the exchange of different classes of shares within the same corporation is not viewed as a disposition for tax purposes.

In essence, what a corporate class fund or pool does is allow investors the same type of trading and investment decisions as one would make with their RRSP, yet with no immediate taxes triggered from a trade. In this regard, the "corporation" provides the same benefits for open money as the RRSP shelter provides for registered funds.

This provides very tax-efficient flexibility. Assume that you have made a meaningful gain on some "Canadian Class" shares and wish to move some or all of these holdings to the "American Class." Unlike a regular unit trust mutual fund, there is no taxable disposition. Even if you move the entire account to the "Money Market Class" of shares, no capital gain will be realized until you have income or lump sums paid out to you. There is another factor. Any gain that you realize, even out of the Money Market Class, which would be interest income in a unit trust arrangement, will be received from the corporate class fund or pool almost exclusively as a taxable capital gain.

Exchange Traded Funds (ETFs)

Exchange Traded Funds, or ETFs, are basically open-end mutual fund trusts. They are listed on and can be traded on major stock exchanges, just like individual stocks, and as such they can be bought, sold, and traded at any time during regular market hours. This feature is most significant if you are actively trading these funds.

You can acquire units that track a specific index, market sector, or management style. All are 100 percent RRSP-eligible.

Another feature of ETFs is that they have very low management fees. However, brokerage charges will apply to purchases and transactions. Advisors who employ these investments will add their own charge for services rendered. The same holds true for F-class mutual funds.

For the do-it-yourselfer, however, ETFs may very well be a preferred, diversified investment. For those who wish to manage their own portfolio, on a passive investment basis, at the lowest possible fees, ETFs should be a consideration.

Real Estate

Some people view real estate as another form of equities. Others view real estate as a totally separate asset class.

Within the last 15 years, there have been very different patterns of performance between stocks and real estate funds. Their performance has been negatively correlated, which means that when one is performing poorly, the other is performing well. This is good for diversification and risk reduction.

Some investors believe that a tangible investment such as real estate may be more to their liking than equities and bonds. In fact, real estate prices have been on the rise, especially for cottage and leisure properties, while stocks and bonds have periods of negative returns. Remember, however, that the constant trap into which investors find themselves lured is that of trying to escape something that at the moment may not be performing well, and running to something that has attractive recent returns. It is the times when markets are declining that it may be more appropriate to be adding to stock positions rather than taking money out.

The concept of real estate as a component of an investment portfolio is different in the retirement context. If your investment objective is growth, there may be portions of non-registered capital that can be allocated for the purchase of specific properties. Unless these are rental units, there will be no income generated. If the real estate market continues to rise, though, there is a deferral opportunity. This approach may have particular merit if you have non-registered assets that are "redundant" (not required for generating income).

One of the other ways to access the real estate market but with greater diversification in terms of holdings is through some of the real estate funds offered in the marketplace. Within an income-generating investment portfolio, this can be an attractive addition and include yet another asset class for the purposes of risk reduction.

Discretionary Management

As previously discussed, there are many advantages to investing through mutual funds. Discretionary management involves the use of individual stocks and bonds rather than funds or pools. This approach has basically all of the same benefits of mutual fund investing, but also has some additional features.

- Discretionary management provides better control of taxable distributions.
- Portfolios are specifically tailored to you. You do not simply become a unitholder within a pool or a fund.
- You have the ability to purchase specific stocks when you enter the program, as opposed to participating in an existing portfolio as you do with funds.
- You know exactly what investments you own and how much you own.
- You may have the opportunity to interface with the money manager.
- Management fees can be 40 percent to 50 percent lower than mutual funds.
- They operate on a fee-only basis. There are no front- or back-end loads.
- For non-registered holdings, any fees are tax-deductible expenses.

The opportunity to enter into these arrangements is predicated by the amount of capital that you have to invest. The minimums are set for several reasons. In order to be able to properly diversify your holdings, there is a certain amount of capital required. Larger accounts allow the management company to levy a lower level of management fees. Normally, the base entry level of this type of program is a minimum of $500,000 to $1,000,000. This is determined by the investment manager and the organization involved. The amount may be an aggregate that includes registered and non-registered holdings, holdings of you and your spouse, etc. If the sum of your household investable assets meet the threshold, you may find this an interesting option to consider. Your advisor should be able to assist you with this process.

REDUNDANT ASSETS

Redundant assets are those that are not being used for any particular purpose, either to create income, for liquidity, or to prepare for an anticipated capital expenditure. These assets tend to appear most frequently in situations involving older retirees, especially single seniors, and in situations where the health of one person in a couple is failing. They are, in essence, sitting idle and adding little if anything to your portfolio.

It is important to note that at the outset of income planning, the assets in question may not actually exist in their ultimate form. For example, additional income-producing assets may come into a retirement scenario as the result of an inheritance or through the sale of a principal residence or other real estate. We find many situations where the redundant assets sit wasted, often placed in low yield, highly taxed accounts. The money ends up being taxed, even though the income generated is not even being used.

There are two important considerations concerning the use of redundant assets. As you will see, these points tie into the timing of when these assets actually become available.

First, is there any way to anticipate the arrival of this capital and build it into the Prime Approach to using income and assets at retirement? In other words, if we are confident that at some juncture there will be this introduction of capital into your situation, does that provide you with greater discretion to use income and assets in the earlier years of your retirement? We are not advocating a "spend your inheritance before it arrives" mentality. What we are seeking to know is whether you can be afforded some additional flexibility and opportunity in your initial retirement years based upon the expectation of a future injection of capital.

Second, when this capital becomes available, is there a better use for these assets that allows for more efficient realization of your goals based on your Time Hub and Money Hub priorities at that time? Is there an opportunity to make use of this capital to enhance health-risk management or wealth-transfer goals?

We have found that the answer to the above points is almost always "yes," but it takes planning and ultimately implementation to make your redundant assets work for you. You, in conjunction with your advisor, can make a big difference in how these assets are used and what they are able to accomplish for you and for future generations.

PRESCRIBED ANNUITY CONTRACTS (PACs)

An annuity is a guaranteed stream of future income payments made up of a combination of principal and interest. In a regular annuity the interest payments are much larger at the beginning than at the end. This works like a mortgage in reverse. Think about it. How much principal do you actually reduce in the first five years of a mortgage? Very little. Most of what you're paying is interest.

Prescribed annuities receive very different tax treatment than do regular annuities, which can work favourably for you. Prescribed tax treatment takes the estimated total interest payments (in the case of a life annuity) or the exact amount of total interest that will be paid (a term-certain annuity) and deems that for each year of the annuity the interest portion will be the same amount. In other words, it levels the interest amount and the tax-free return-of-capital amount for each year of payment. The end result is that there is more tax-effective income in the earlier years.

The total amount of interest to be paid over the duration of the annuity is calculated, then divided over the number of payments in the life of the contract. This would be a straightforward exercise in the case of a term-certain annuity, where the term of payment is known, but what about for a life annuity? In this case, insurers use the same mortality tables found in the CRA' s Interpretation Bulletin IT-111R2 to project a life expectancy. This number of years is deemed to be the life of the contract.

Prescribed Annuity Taxation

In order to qualify for prescribed tax treatment, the following conditions must be met.

- The original capital must be after-tax money. This could be capital from the proceeds of a life insurance contract, proceeds from the sale of a principal residence, or the value of a maturing GIC.
- The annuity can be in any form—term-certain, single life, or joint life.
- The contract must be owned by an individual, not a corporation.
- The income cannot be indexed.
- The guarantee period of a life annuity or the end of a term-certain annuity cannot exceed the primary annuitant's age 90.

Prescribed Annuity Versus a Five-Year GIC

Both a PAC and a GIC deliver guaranteed income, a welcome feature considering potential market volatility. How do these options compare? The following illustration examines this question.

ASSUMPTIONS: MALE AGE 65, FEMALE AGE 62

Non-Registered Capital: $100,000

Five-Year GIC Rate: 5.0%

Marginal Tax Rate: 40%

	GIC	Single Life* Annuity	Joint Life Annuity
Annual Income	$5,000	$7,174	$6,537
Taxable Portion	$5,000	$2,413	$2,504
Tax at 40%	2,000	965	1,001
Net Income From Taxable Portion	$3,000	$1,448	$1,503
Non-Taxable Portion	N/A	4,761	4,033
Total Net Annual Income	$3,000	$6,209	$5,536

*For the 65-year-old male.

The annuities illustrated above are life annuities with a 15-year guarantee period. By the time you read this, interest rates for five-year GICs will likely have changed. Any resulting increase or decrease in the interest rate used in the GIC example will be reflected by a corresponding increase or decrease in the amount of annuity income shown. The two numbers are directly correlated.

The net income created by the PAC is dramatically higher because we are using tax-paid capital as well as interest to form the total payment. This means that the annuity will not transfer to the estate like the GIC. If this is a concern, the strategy of using an insured prescribed annuity, or "back-to-back annuity" as it is sometimes called, can solve this problem.

Insured Prescribed Annuity

One dilemma facing retirees is the trade-off between having investments that are in the form of guarantees and the low interest rate/high tax environment that applies to those investments. How can you take non-registered capital and create a guaranteed income, provide a meaningful rate of return, make the income tax effective, and preserve the capital you have invested? The answer is the insured, prescribed annuity, also known as a back-to-back annuity. This strategy combines a prescribed annuity with a life insurance contract and returns the money used to buy the annuity to the estate at the passing of the annuitant.

In order to realize potentially higher returns than those from GICs, those individuals whose one-time idea of risk was having more than $60,000 on deposit at any one institution are turning to variable investment options. Variable investments include those holdings such as stocks and bonds where the market value of the security fluctuates. The trade-off for pursuing these higher returns is the reality that the principal invested is no longer guaranteed.

As discussed earlier, SWPs provide not only the potential for higher long-term returns but also the tax benefits of receiving income in a combination of capital gains, dividends, and tax-paid principal. They do not, however, guarantee your investment's principal. The downturn and turbulence in world stock markets has led some retirees to feel uneasy about SWPs and variable investments in general. While there is still tremendous merit and benefit to the long-term use of these strategies and vehicles, there is an opportunity for you to create a guaranteed income stream using an insured prescribed annuity.

For the sake of our illustration, we have assumed that John and Diane are clients. John is 65 years of age and Diane is 62. Given government benefits and their respective employment pension income, they find that they are each in a 40 percent marginal tax bracket. They jointly hold a sum of $100,000 of non-registered capital. They wish to safely invest this money, preserve the capital, and receive income. The following description and the table below show two options they can consider to meet these objectives.

If they place the money in a conventional GIC with an effective payout rate of 5.0 percent, the annual income will be $5,000, all of which will be taxable. At their tax rate this would create tax payable of $2,000, leaving $3,000 as a net income.

If they purchase a joint life annuity combined with a joint last-to-die life insurance contract, the net income changes very favourably, even after the premium for the insurance coverage is removed. The concept is very straightforward. A joint life annuity is purchased so that a guaranteed income of $6,590 is payable on an annual basis for as long as either John or Diane are alive. In order to create the highest possible income, we have chosen an annuity with no guarantee period. What this means is that at the second passing of John and Diane, there is no benefit to the estate and the heirs. This is why we have acquired a joint last-to-die life insurance contract. The annual premium would be $1,344. At the passing of the second client, a tax-free benefit will be paid to named beneficiaries or the estate, thereby replacing the original capital. The estate is in exactly the same position as if the other investment option, a GIC, had been purchased. The major benefits are realized in the after-tax income that John and Diane will receive for as long as either of them is alive.

ASSUMPTIONS: MALE AGE 65, FEMALE AGE 62, BOTH NON-SMOKERS

Open Capital: $100,000

Five-Year GIC Rate: 5.0%

Marginal Tax Rate: 40%

	GIC	Single Life* Annuity	Joint Life Annuity
Annual Income	$5,000	$7,602	$6,590
Taxable Portion	$5,000	$2,421	$2,508
Tax at 40%	2,000	968	1,003
Net Income From Taxable Portion	$3,000	$1,453	$1,505
Non-Taxable Portion	N/A	5,181	4,072
Total Net Annual Income	$3,000	$6,634	$5,577

*For the 65-year-old male.

In the joint life scenario, even after removing the amount required to fund the insurance they still have a guaranteed net income of $4,233. This is $1,233 more each year, on an after-tax basis, than current interest rates would provide from a bond or a GIC. This represents an increase in their spendable income of 41.1 percent. Stated another way, they would have to own a GIC or bond paying an interest rate of 7 percent to deliver the same after-tax income as the joint life annuity.

The illustration above used an insurance contract where premiums are payable until the second death, which is also when the benefit would be paid to the estate. Another option in this strategy is the use of insurance where the death benefit is still paid at the second passing, but the premium stops at the first death. The difference in premium would be $235 per year. If this strategy was used, the total insurance premium would be $1,579 per year instead of $1,344. However, at the time the first death occurred there would be no more premiums payable. This means that the net income to the survivor would be $5,577 each year for the rest of his or her life. This is $2,577 or 85.9 percent higher than the after-tax income that would be paid by the GIC. A GIC or bond would need to pay an interest rate of 9.25 percent to create the same after-tax return. And, like the other options, the $100,000 comes back to the estate tax-free when the survivor passes away.

In attempting to implement this strategy, John and Diane must know that the insurance coverage can, in fact, be acquired. This is the obvious first step. Since the coverage is based on a second-to-die strategy, underwriting has some degree of flexibility. If John or Diane has some problems with standard issue of the coverage, there may not be the option of having the premiums stop at the first passing. This would negate the increased, spendable income shown earlier, because premiums would continue until the second passing. However, if the premium was required to continue until the second passing, it would be $1,493 per annum, far less than the $1,727 shown above.

It makes sense to apply for the coverage with several carriers since underwriting decisions can vary greatly. Having shopped the market in this manner, John and Diane can obtain the coverage on the most favourable terms. Companies that wish to impose a rating on the insurance, or decline to issue the coverage, are then among the best candidates for the annuity purchase. This is because they feel that the individual or couple involved has a shorter-than-average life expectancy. As a result, the life annuity income that could be obtained from these insurers is likely to be higher.

Ultimately, our clients will have received more after-tax income from the insured annuity than they would from the GIC. At the second passing, the estate receives $100,000 tax-free from the insurance, preserving the capital. An added benefit is that the insurance proceeds will flow into the estate directly, circumventing the will, and therefore be exempt from probate.

The one trade-off in this whole arrangement is that these clients will not have access to the principal if it has been used to purchase an annuity. However, this is not a large issue if the prime focus is to satisfy the guaranteed investment and income objectives stated earlier.

Note that this is a concept that you may apply to either a portion or the whole of your non-registered holdings. Again, total planning is the key.

There is, however, usually sufficient merit in the analysis of the numbers to consider this as an option for part of your income strategy.

TAX-DEFERRED ANNUITIES

The insured prescribed annuity put forth a strategy that uses more than one financial tool in order to achieve the objectives of the retiree in the best manner, but there are other examples where the combination of financial tools works very efficiently to pursue a desired result. In the following example, we look to create guaranteed income with tax-deferred growth over a 10-year period.

This example compares a five-year GIC at 5 percent to a combination of a 10-year-certain prescribed annuity and growth funds within a corporate class fund or pool.

Amount to Invest: $100,000

Five-Year GIC Rate: 5%

Term for Annuity Certain: 10 Years

Net Rate for Growth Funds: 7.5%

Marginal Tax Rate: 40%

Purchase GICs		Purchase Annuity Certain	Invest in Growth Fund
$100,000	Amount Invested	$27,205	$72,795
$5,000	Annual Income	$3,195	$0
$0	Tax-Free Amount	$2,715	$0
$5,000	Taxable Amount	$480	$0
$2,000	Tax Payable	$192	$0
$3,000	Total Net Income (Annual Income Minus Tax Payable)	$3,003	$0
$100,000	Value at End of Annuity	$0	$150,032
	Fund Break-Even Rate	3.91%	$100,000
$3,000	Net Income After Annuity Ends		$9,001

We have used a prescribed annuity contract for a 10-year-certain period to deliver the same after-tax income that would result from a GIC at 5 percent. The annuity costs us $27,205 and the difference, $72,795, is invested in growth funds in a tax-efficient investment including corporate class funds or pools We do not expect much, if any, taxation along the way, but we have adjusted the net rate of return to 7.5 percent to accommodate the impact of any tax.

The use of mutual fund corporate class funds or pools allows us to defer the tax, and the resulting value of the investments at the end of 10 years is $150,032. For the sake of simplicity we have assumed that income withdrawn on this amount at a rate of 7.5 percent would be fully taxable as a capital gain. If this were the case, the net income at a 40 percent marginal tax bracket would be $9,001.92 ($150,032 times 7.5 percent equals $11,252 at a 50 percent inclusion rate and 40 percent marginal tax rate). This is basically three times the net income delivered by the GIC.

The break-even rate is the compound growth the account would have to realize in order to be worth $100,000, *net of taxation*, by the end of 10 years.

Of course, you could use as much money as you wanted to create the annuity. You may wish, for example, to have a net income equal to 150 percent of what the GIC would deliver. This would take more of the investment money up front, leaving less for the investment funds. There are many different ways this could be set up. Once again, the combination of financial tools can create multiple benefits for you.

CHARITABLE ANNUITIES

Various charities and qualifying organizations are offering their own form of annuity. This charitable annuity is a form of giving on your part, and in exchange you receive tax-favoured income. Basically, you give an amount of capital to a charity and in return you receive a guaranteed income. The income will be in the form of an annuity, either term-certain or for life. However, in order for your donation to qualify as a gift and for you to subsequently receive the annuity payments tax free, the total amount of income to be received by you cannot exceed the value of the original gift. This "acid test" is prescribed by the CRA.

For example, let's look at a male age 63 who gifts a charity with $50,000. In return he will receive an income of $3,000 per year. The CRA's mortality tables (the same ones used in calculations for prescribed annuity contracts) show that the life expectancy of a male age 63 is 21 years. Since the income ($3,000) times the number of years of expected payments (21) exceeds the value of the original donation, it is deemed that no gift was made.

Now let's look at a situation that meets CRA's acid test. An 80-year-old male acquires an immediate annuity of $5,000 per annum, payable for life, in exchange for a donation of $60,000 to a registered charity. He has a life expectancy of nine years and as such can expect to receive a total of $45,000 ($5,000 times nine years). The difference between the $60,000 donation and the $45,000 in expected income means that he will receive a donation credit of $15,000. In addition, the resulting annual income of $5,000 would be received tax free as it is deemed to be a return of tax-paid capital. Should the individual live longer than the stated life expectancy used in the original calculations, the income will continue to be received, and on a tax-free basis.

The use of a charitable annuity does not necessarily mean an enhancement to your income. Yes, the use of a prescribed annuity in the above example would have the effect of delivering more annual income. However, it is a method whereby gifting can be done while the individual is alive and at the same time receive a tax-effective income in return. Before this avenue is pursued, other options for charitable donations should be examined. Of course, the merits of any particular action will depend upon all of the factors involved in a given situation.

PRINCIPAL RESIDENCE

One of the decisions to be made when you retire is where you are going to live. There is a two-part answer to this consideration. First, is it your intention to remain in the city, province, or country in which you now live? If all of your children have moved to a different location, you may feel compelled to be closer. (Suggestion: you may wish to check with the kids first on this one.)

Second, if you are not going to move away, is it your intention to stay in the house you currently are in? If you choose to do so and your house is free of a mortgage, then you are able to live rent free. On the other hand, if you don't need all of the room you once did when you were raising a family, you could sell your home and acquire more modest accommodations. If you make such a decision, there is the potential to create some non-registered assets if the new purchase price is lower than the proceeds of sale from your old home. In Canada, if you sell your principal residence for an amount that is greater than the purchase price, there is no tax on the gain. There can only be one principal residence designated per family. It need not be the residence throughout the year, but it must be owned, and inhabited by you for at least part of the year, in order to qualify.

Another option that might be considered is to sell your home and invest the proceeds. For many Canadians, the equity in their principal residence is one of their largest non-registered assets, but not one that generates any income. Retirees may consider selling their home, investing the proceeds of the sale and using the investment returns to pay the rent on their new residence. Usually their goal is to keep the investment capital intact. The problem with their calculations in most cases is that they forget about the taxation on their investment returns. Rent is paid in after-tax dollars, and is not a deductible expense.

The Reverse Mortgage

One option for creating income from your home while remaining in it is the reverse mortgage. The concept of obtaining a loan from the equity in your principal residence has been used in France for more than 100 years, and in British and U.S. markets for more than 30 years. The primary source for these loans in Canada is CHIP, the Canadian Home Income Plan, which has been operating since 1985.

Under this arrangement, homeowners take out a loan against the equity in their residence. There are three basic repayment programs in CHIP. First, no payments are made while you live in your house. The loan is repaid at the time the house is sold. Second, you can pay the interest charges on an annual basis, which avoids eroding the equity of your home. Third, you can repay the loan entirely after three years, without penalty.

The rules regarding the program are as follows:

- The home must be mortgage free or the remaining loan must first be cleared with the proceeds of the CHIP loan.
- The home must be in an urban area. Farm properties will not qualify.
- Borrowers must be at least age 62. Because of the capitalized interest, the plan works more efficiently when the retiree is older.
- Individuals can borrow between 10 and 40 percent of the appraised value of their home depending on the borrower's age, their marital status, and the prevailing interest rates.

- The loan proceeds can be taken as a lump sum, an annuity, or a combination of both. Without going through the mechanics, we'll tell you that loan amounts and annuity payments are received on a tax-free basis.
- Title of the home always remains in the borrower's name even if the value of the property drops.
- If real estate prices rise, the homeowner, not CHIP, benefits. If real estate prices drop, then the amount left over for the homeowner after paying CHIP will be less.

The decision to enter into a reverse mortgage should not be made lightly. The step should be taken only after other income-generating avenues have been explored and then only as an action that is necessary to provide additional cash flow. The average borrower pays back CHIP at the end of 12 years and keeps 50 percent of the home's sale price. If this occurs, options for the homeowner in terms of other housing choices from that point forward may be limited due to reduced proceeds of the sale. This would also greatly reduce potential wealth transfer. For these and other reasons, the CHIP program requires that a potential participant receive independent legal counsel and encourages active discussion with other family members. It is appropriate to take both of these actions before entering into this arrangement. The concept should also be a point of discussion between you and your advisor. You can obtain more information about the program by calling 1-866-522-2447, emailing info@chip.ca, or visiting www.chip.ca.

NON-REGISTERED STRATEGIES AND THE PRIME APPROACH

As shown by the previous examples, financial tools can be combined to effectively accomplish your objectives. The first issue, as always, is defining what it is you wish to accomplish. The use of non-registered assets within the Prime Approach strategy is predicated on the creation of additional income in the most tax-effective manner.

For example, let's assume that you have fully taxable income up to the first federal tax bracket. It is an advantage to receive any additional income from that point forward in the form of either tax-preferred or non-taxable amounts. Remember the two key reasons for this.

First, the next dollar you receive over the first federal tax bracket will be at roughly a 38 percent to 40 percent marginal tax rate. This means you need to withdraw $1.61 to have $1.00 to spend. This will not be the case with tax-preferred or non-taxable dollars. The less strain you can put on your assets to create the income you want, the longer the assets will last.

Second, in order to maximize tax credits that are available to you, your net income calculation should be kept low. The use of non-registered assets can assist you to increase your total income but keep your taxable income at a lower amount.

Taxable distributions include the interest paid from bonds and GICs, the dividends paid from owning shares of corporations, and the capital gains realized by selling capital property, shares, or units of mutual and segregated investment funds. They also include your proportionate share of interest, dividends, and capital gains from non-registered investment funds that you own, even if you are not redeeming units. By law, any amounts of interest, dividends, and capital gains realized by the investment fund are passed through and taxable to us.

Have taxable distributions from your non-registered holdings paid to you as income. Don't compound interest on GICs or reinvest mutual fund distributions. You will be taxed on these amounts in the year that they are earned, so use the money as income. If you are running into large amounts of distributions, your advisor should be able to assist you with how to invest these amounts once the tax bill has been reconciled.

Discuss with your advisor GICs, mutual funds, and some of the other income options you have seen in this section. Some people state that they do not like annuities or believe in life insurance, yet the combination of these two tools can create greatly enhanced, guaranteed income while preserving estate values. Don't be concerned with what a financial tool is called. Be aware of what it can do for you in helping you to reach your objectives.

How can the concepts and strategies identified in this section be constructively applied to your parent(s)? Remember that what may benefit their income situation now may ultimately provide a greater wealth transfer to you at some point in the future. Have you had the opportunity to discuss these issues with your parents? Do you know what their objectives and priorities are? The chapter on health-risk management includes the topic of "The Talk You MUST Have With Your Parents." Handling assets and income are all part of this dialogue.

During the prime retirement years you have the opportunity to enjoy the fruits of what you have spent an entire lifetime working toward. The Time Hub motivators are those of purpose and self-actualization. And, as long as your health allows you to do so, doing what it is you wish to do will also make you feel fulfilled.

We still make the mistake of saying to clients on a Friday, "Have a nice weekend." We then pause and say, quite correctly, "Oh, I guess for you it's *all* weekend."

SUMMARY OF THE STRUCTURAL PLANNING CHANNEL AND THE PRIME APPROACH

The majority of the material we have covered to this point pertains to the structural planning channel. It is the most significant area in integrated retirement income planning. Its purpose is to create your desired income stream by triggering assets and benefits in the most efficient manner. This involves determining the order in which income sources will be used and the amounts that will be withdrawn. Normally this involves combining income from a number of different sources. Our bias is to first engage those assets that have limited flexibility and low tax-efficiency.

Discussion points and objectives for you and your advisor within the structural planning channel should include:

- Assessing where you are currently
- Determining your objective and priorities
   Lifestyle or Time Hub objectives
   Money Hub priorities
   Income targets
   Survivor income issues
   Critical dates
   Asset use
- Gathering necessary information
   Your investor profile
   Inventory of assets and benefits
   All documentation requested in the data forms found at the back
of this book

- Creating a written plan complete with the steps and timing of implementation

    Remember that the structural plan is only one of four channels to be addressed. The integrated planning process behind the Prime Approach means that objectives and action taken within the other three planning channels must also be considered as part of the structural plan. This will have the direct result of increasing the amount of discretion and flexibility you have with your income-producing assets. With this in mind, we now proceed to discuss the other planning channels. The next channel is the investment portfolio.

CHAPTER THREE

The Investment Portfolio

Our second gear, the next planning channel, is that of the investment port-folio. This chapter is designed to describe some strategic and procedural concepts that can be of benefit to you and your advisor in investing your retirement assets. In some areas we will refer back to the previous chapter on structural planning. There is a large overlap between these first two planning channels and appropriate alignment is required. This is why the two key documents in the integrated approach are your written plan and your investment policy statement. Often, in first meetings with potential clients we find that they have neither of these critical documents, even though they have been working with a "financial planner."

There is a very large difference in investment strategy between accu-mulating assets and taking care of assets. During the accumulation years, amounts are being added at different times to build your portfolio. At the point when you are drawing income, amounts are being removed and little if any new assets are coming into the portfolio on a regular basis. The strategies that follow recognize this important difference.

THE PURPOSE OF YOUR CAPITAL

Basically there are three potential functions of your retirement assets—liq-uidity, income, and growth. Each has the underlying objective of capital preservation or safety. Each of these functions has its own:

- Specific purpose
- Unique investor objectives
- Distinct strategies
- Appropriate investment vehicles for implementation

In the process of determining what type of investor you are, you must assess what it is you want your capital to do. For example, for your retirement assets, what percentage weighting would you allocate to the following objectives?

Growth___ Liquidity_____ Safety___ Income_____ = 100%

Asset allocation is simply the investment mix that is appropriate for you given a number of factors, including your situation, objectives, risk tolerance, and requirements from your income plan. What do we mean by "investment mix"? It is the percentage of your assets you should have in cash, fixed-income holdings, and equities.

Through the use of an investor profile your advisor can determine your risk tolerance and ultimately tailor the asset allocation of your portfolio to you. There are a number of factors that comprise the questions asked in any investor profile. Most, however, deal with Money Hub priorities rather than Time Hub priorities. This does not flaw nor diminish the process. Rather, it suggests that the structured retirement income plan, which is the first planning channel, is a necessary component in establishing the final asset mix that is most appropriate for you in order to achieve your retirement goals. That is why we contend that the planning channels must work in tandem, in an integrated approach, in order for you to derive the best results.

It is very appropriate to look at your entire situation when dealing with asset allocation. For example, government benefits and pensions in the form of annuities are part of the equation and should be considered for what they are—fixed-income assets. This does not suggest that all other holdings go into equities, but it is valid to look at all of the income sources when establishing your asset mix. This process is just as much income allocation as asset allocation.

For larger investment portfolios, it may be appropriate to break down holdings into pools of capital, each of which addresses a specific objective.

This strategy allows for distinct investment choices that are most appropriate for the purpose of the particular pool.

It is difficult to suggest that there is a minimum asset level at which the pool strategy is appropriate. The decision will depend on several factors, including what percentage of your assets is registered versus open, and your income requirements relative to the value of your assets.

Three key considerations in the use of your retirement capital are

- Preservation of capital
- Tax efficiency
- Costs of investing

Addressing these considerations will be the underlying focus of what is discussed in this chapter. As part of the complete retirement income plan, considerations for those assets that are providing your income are also critical. In this context, an element that is common to all of the above steps is risk management.

RISK MANAGEMENT

Consider that once you have completed your lifelong endeavour of building your assets and benefits, the primary consideration in using them is to have them last, in order to create income streams, enhance lifestyle, and/or provide an inheritance/legacy to future generations.

Limiting the potential for loss or reduction of capital assets is the focus of risk management. There is, after all, a direct relationship between the income stream from a capital asset and the resulting impact on, or "health" of, that asset.

It goes without saying that protection and preservation of your capital assets are key to perpetuating income and to realizing other objectives. Risk management as it pertains to the preservation of capital must address the following areas:

- Capital loss (running out of money)
- Investment loss
- Purchasing power loss
- Loss to survivor
- Health-risk loss
- Tax loss, to both income and estate

The focal point of this chapter will be to examine capital preservation issues as they relate to capital loss and investment loss. Purchasing power loss and loss due to income tax were covered in Chapter 2. Loss to survivor refers to those income streams that would either reduce or disappear for the surviving spouse in the event of the passing of the partner. It is necessary, in overall planning, to be aware of these potential or eventual reductions in household income. Health-risk loss and the estate aspects of tax loss will be examined while addressing the third and fourth planning channels, health-risk management and wealth transfer, in Chapters 4 and 5. Obviously there will be some overlap among these areas. The fact that there is this relationship is the main reason that all of these issues must be addressed to achieve complete planning.

In dealing with the capital loss and investment loss areas of risk management, we will cover a broad array of planning concepts. As was stated at the outset, it is not the objective of this book to be the comprehensive authority on each planning channel. No book can be the definitive source in dealing with such a diverse range of strategies. Similarly, with this section, the intent is to identify the risk-management issues pertaining to the investment of income-producing assets and provide some general suggestions and solutions in these areas.

CAPITAL LOSS

Loss of capital results when you encroach upon assets to deliver the income needed. Sometimes this is intentionally done, and other times assets have been invested in such a way that they cannot consistently produce a rate of return that is equal to or greater than the rate at which income is being withdrawn. In either case, the value of capital assets declines.

In discussing this issue with clients we find, not unexpectedly, that their most common desire is to stream out income without altering the original amount of the investment. In other words, they want to keep their principal intact. Some people want to actually grow the value of their holdings while still withdrawing income. Others would like us to time it so that the cheque to the undertaker bounces. And, of course, there is everything in between. It is important for you and your advisor to determine how you feel about this issue.

The Longevity of Your Investments

The rate at which we are drawing upon an asset and the rate at which it is growing will determine what happens to the value of the asset. The table below shows the number of years that an asset will last if there is a certain level of withdrawal and a certain rate of return.

For example, assume that we withdraw from our assets at the rate of 8 percent ($200,000 provides an income of $16,000 per annum).

- If the account earns a return of **8 percent**, we will never exhaust the asset.
- If the account earns a return of **10 percent**, we will have an increasing account value plus an increasing income.
- If the account earns a return of only **7 percent**, we will exhaust the asset in 30 years.
- If the account earns a return of only **6 percent**, we will exhaust the asset in 23 years.

How Long Will Your Investments Last?

Withdrawal Rate	Rate of Return 5%	6%	7%	8%	9%	10%	11%	12%
6%	37 yrs	*	*	*	*	*	*	*
7%	25 yrs	33 yrs	*	*	*	*	*	*
8%	20 yrs	23 yrs	30 yrs	*	*	*	*	*
9%	16 yrs	18 yrs	22 yrs	29 yrs	*	*	*	*
10%	14 yrs	15 yrs	17 yrs	27 yrs	*	*	*	*

Source: *Prime Approach™ to Retirement Planning.*

If we increase the desired income each year by 2.5 percent to cope with inflation, the following numbers result:

How Long Will Your Investments Last?
Withdrawals adjusted for inflation at 2.5%

Withdrawal Rate	Rate of Return 5%	6%	7%	8%	9%	10%	11%	12%
6%	21 yrs	24 yrs	29 yrs	40 yrs	*	*	*	*
7%	17 yrs	19 yrs	22 yrs	26 yrs	35 yrs	*	*	*
8%	15 yrs	16 yrs	18 yrs	20 yrs	25 yrs	31 yrs	*	*
9%	13 yrs	14 yrs	15 yrs	16 yrs	18 yrs	22 yrs	27 yrs	*
10%	11 yrs	12 yrs	13 yrs	14 yrs	15 yrs	17 yrs	20 yrs	25 yrs

Source: *Prime Approach™ to Retirement Planning.*

A difference of 1 percent or 2 percent in investment return over an extended period of time has a dramatic impact on the capital value of an asset from which income is being drawn. The longevity of an asset can be extended from 25 percent to infinity by increasing returns by just 1 percent. Clearly, the rate of return you receive on your assets after retirement is just as important as it was during the accumulation years.

Investment Returns

Any illustrations showing future income streams are going to assume an average rate of return that follows a linear path. For example, a 7 percent average return is illustrated as 7 percent per year. This is true if you are using a bond or GIC that has a consistent flow of guaranteed income at a guaranteed rate with a guaranteed maturity value. The issue here is that most people today have at least some of their income-producing assets in a variable portfolio, and the return, year over year, is an unknown quantity. It's important to realize that variable portfolio investment returns are anything but linear or consistent.

Also important is how money is withdrawn relative to how growth occurs or interest is credited. For a simple example, let's use a $100,000 investment at a withdrawal rate of 7 percent to create $7,000 of income. Using these numbers, the assumption is that the income will be paid and the capital will stay intact. This would be true if:

- The income was drawn at the end of the year in one lump sum after the 7 percent, or $7,000, was credited to the account.
- The growth was credited evenly on a monthly basis and withdrawn at the same amount.
- The $7,000 was credited to the account at the beginning of the year and the income was subsequently drawn.

However, in an investment portfolio with any degree of variability, none of the above applies. The result is that the capital value of the account at year-end will either be greater or lesser than the amount initially invested.

The other mistaken assumption often made by investors and advisors alike is that the amount you will withdraw each month is $7,000 divided by 12. This would work out to $583.33 per month. If this is done you will see slight erosion of the original capital over time. You would actually need a return of 7.29 percent factored evenly on a monthly basis in order to keep the initial principal intact.

Returns and Fees

Using the same example as above, the following numbers show that even a small decline in the rate of return, such as through investment fees, will have a substantially negative effect on your investment capital over an extended period of time. Drawing income at a rate of 7 percent on an initial investment of $100,000 will deliver $562 per month. If the rate of return over time is less than 7 percent, the capital will erode to some degree.

Rate of Return	6.75%	6.50%	6.25%	6.00%
5 Years	$98,637	$97,272	$95,920	$94,581
10 Years	$96,749	$93,534	$90,395	$87,338
15 Years	$94,130	$88,413	$82,914	$77,626
20 Years	$90,591	$81,396	$72,784	$64,641
25 Years	$85,469	$71,783	$59,067	$47,263
Years to exhaust capital	23	22	21	20

This illustration shows how significant even a nominal difference in the rate of return can affect your investment capital when you are withdrawing income. Fees should therefore be an important consideration in your investment decisions. In this context, you should be aware that certain in-house investment products, wrap accounts, managed programs, subadvisor funds, and segregated funds can add from 0.25 percent to 1.50 percent (25 to 150 basis points) to the regular management fee of the underlying fund or funds. When the rate of return for an investment fund is published, it must, by law, always be stated net of any fees.

The costs of investing are a consideration because they reduce the return that is credited to your holdings. They also have a direct impact on how long your income-producing assets may last. But, and this is a very important but, when investing in equity funds, you cannot simply look at management fees and determine whether an investment is a good or bad one. We have no difficulty with comparing fees on fixed-income funds, since the range of returns is relatively small. However, there are too many factors that come into play with equity or stock funds to suggest basing your investment decisions on fees alone.

Understand the Impact of Fees

As stated above, basically all variable investment products have a management fee. It is how revenues are generated in the investment industry. This fee is a cost you pay for the investment and potentially other services including, in most cases, advisor compensation.

In most cases this fee is not transparent in that you do not see it deducted from your gross returns. It is common for an investor to see only their returns after fees have already been deducted. This is totally in line with the manner in which the securities regulators require they be quoted. I use the word "pay" because although you likely don't write a cheque, these fees are deducted from your account and your returns.

The range of fees on variable investments can run anywhere from about ¼ of 1% per annum to nearly 4% per annum depending on the investment option and advisor compensation. As stated above, these amounts are deducted from your overall returns.

Commonly, one of components in the fee structure is what is referred to as "imbedded compensation." This is an amount paid to your advisor or the institution with whom you work. As a consumer what you need to know is

1. What is the total management fee I am paying?
2. What amount of the fee is for additional benefits or features of this investment?
3. How much of this fee is for service and advice?
4. What am I receiving from my advisor or institution for the fee I am paying?

This "cost to benefit" relationship relative to fees and advice/service is more transparent if your institution or advisor is actually adding a fee to an investment option where compensation is not imbedded. This is the usual practice where ETFs, pools, or F-Class mutual funds are used as the investment options by your advisor or institution.

During the years when you are investing to build your retirement assets, investment fees will reduce your overall returns. When the time comes to draw income from your investments, the fees you pay will have an impact on the yield of your portfolio, as illustrated in the following table.

The Yield Challenge

This table shows different asset combinations and the potential average yields that could be generated, before fees. It then shows what the actual investor return or yield would be given different fees levels. Obviously, the higher the fees, the lower the return or yield to you. Not as obvious is the fact that the vast majority of investors don't know how this impacts them because they don't know the level of fees they are paying on their portfolio.

Assumptions	(Pre fee) annual returns	Equity	10%	Bonds	5%	
Equity / Bonds 40% / 60%	Fees	1.5%	2.0%	2.5%	3.0%	3.5%
Yield 50% / 50%	7.0%	5.5%	5.0%	4.5%	4.0%	3.5%
Yield 60% / 40%	7.5%	6.0%	5.5%	5.0%	4.5%	4.0%
Yield 80% / 20%	8.0%	6.5%	6.0%	5.5%	5.0%	4.5%
Yield	9.0%	7.5%	7.0%	6.5%	6.0%	5.5%

Return or yield to the investor

Investment Mathematics

"Success in investing is a function of time, not timing." This adage has been around the investment community for decades. It goes hand in hand with the concept of long-term investing. There is, however, one significant timing consideration when it comes to investing for retirement income: if income is being drawn from variable investments, the investment returns in the initial years are critical in preserving capital.

If you accumulate assets and experience negative returns and a resulting loss in value, you are going to require some substantial returns to break even, as shown below. The cumulative return needed is higher because we are working with a small amount of principal.

Amount of Portfolio Decline	Cumulative Return Needed to Compensate
10%	12%
15%	18%
20%	25%
25%	33%
30%	43%
40%	67%
50%	100%

Suppose that during this period of decline illustrated above, you had the opportunity to invest more money when markets were low, thereby lowering your average cost of holdings and benefiting when returns improved. This would be ideal. However, in retirement you will most likely be withdrawing money at these times, not adding it.

During times of declining markets, there is a big difference between accumulating assets and drawing income from them. If your investment of $100,000 experienced a loss of 7 percent two years in a row, you would have an account balance of $86,490 at the end of the second year. It would take 2.2 years at a positive 7 percent return for your account to break even.

If you were also withdrawing a monthly income of $500, the results would be quite different. Your account balance at the end of two years would be $74,490. At a 7 percent return, the account would never break even, since the $500 monthly withdrawal would continue to reduce capital. The account would exhaust in 26.8 years. If income was reduced to $375 monthly, the account would break even in 21.5 years.

As shown below, the same investment returns realized in a different order have no effect on the value of your account while assets are accumulating or growing.

The first row of numbers represents investment returns that fall out on a consistent or linear basis. That is not, however, how variable investment returns are realized. We have taken the variable returns of an actual balanced portfolio and listed them in row two. Row three takes the same numbers that were used in row two and reverses the order in which they occur, to show that there is no effect on either the annualized return or the accumulation balance. That is a basic law of mathematics. In multiplication, the order of factors does not affect the resulting product.

ACCUMULATION

Year 1	Year 2	Year 3	Year 4	Year 5	Year 6	Year 7	Year 8	Year 9	Year 10	Averate Return	Annual Balance
7%	7%	7%	7%	7%	7%	7%	7%	7%	7%	7%	$196,715
9.4%	14%	13%	23%	-4%	10%	-1%	21%	-4%	-7%	7%	$196,715
-7%	-4%	21%	-1%	10%	-4%	23%	13%	14%	9.4%	7%	$196,715

If, however, withdrawals are being made, the order of investment returns has a significant impact on your assets.

WITHDRAWAL, WITH INCOME AT 7% ($7,000) PER YEAR

Year 1	Year 2	Year 3	Year 4	Year 5	Year 6	Year 7	Year 8	Year 9	Year 10	Averate Return	Annual Balance
7%	7%	7%	7%	7%	7%	7%	7%	7%	7%	7%	$100,000
9.4%	14%	13%	23%	-4%	10%	-1%	21%	-4%	-7%	7%	$117,986
-7%	-4%	21%	-1%	10%	-4%	23%	13%	14%	9.4%	7%	$83,150

The difference between the second and third scenarios, which have the same annual returns but in reverse order, is $34,836 or 42 percent.

The key to risk management in any investment portfolio is diversity and balance. Make sure you have several years' worth of income in cash or fixed-income positions. This does not prevent markets from declining, nor does it negate the reality that your total assets will likely decline in times of falling markets. However, it will reduce the necessity of having to collapse investments that are down in value in order to deliver income, and more importantly it allows those declining investments the opportunity to heal over time.

Remember that when income is being drawn from assets, we start the year knowing that we have a negative rate of return equal to the percentage of income being withdrawn. For example, $21,000 of income from a $300,000 portfolio is equal to an investment loss of 7 percent. Our realized investment returns will be applied to our portfolio, and at the end of the year our account balance will be ahead, behind, or even.

Withdrawals and Deferred Sales Charges (DSCs)

If you are drawing income from variable investments, any year following a year of negative returns could add an additional frustration. You may be in a situation where you incur sales charges as a result of withdrawing your retirement income. To encounter this expense at a time when portfolio values are being pummelled is just one more aggravation to deal with.

Many advisors place invested mutual fund and segregated fund money on a deferred sales charge (DSC) basis. (The other option is on a front-end basis, whereby you pay a negotiated sales fee on the amount you're investing.) When this is done, all of your money is invested without there being an initial cost to you. The advisor is paid, up front, by the fund company, not out of your initial investment capital. The trade-off here is that you have a scale of redemption charges that applies to withdrawals over a five- to nine-year period, depending on the institution. A simple redemption schedule is illustrated below.

Redemption in	Charge
Year 1	5.5%
Year 2	5.0%
Year 3	4.0%
Year 4	3.0%
Year 5	2.0%
Year 6	1.0%
Year 7 and Later	0.0%

The charges decline as the years go by, and ultimately reduce to zero. This is because each year the fund company recoups a portion of what they paid out on your behalf from the annual management fees that are charged to your investments. They just need you to leave your holdings with them long enough to allow them to break even.

The general rule is that you are allowed to withdraw up to 10 percent of either the dollar value or number of units that you hold as of January 1 of each year. Exceed this amount and DSC charges will apply.

If you are drawing income at a set dollar amount and your investment portfolio has fallen, you could be exceeding the 10 percent free withdrawal amount that you are permitted. For example, on a $100,000 deposit, 10 percent is $10,000. This could be withdrawn without fees. If the investment return was zero for the year, the account would sit at $90,000 on January 1. You could only remove $9,000 (10 percent of $90,000) without DSC charges. If you chose to maintain your $10,000 income, you would incur a redemption charge on the additional $1,000. The percentage of charge applied would be determined by your respective DSC schedule, and in this example may represent $10 to $50.

Dealing with DSC Fees

The first step in dealing with DSC fees is to speak with your advisor to see if your money was invested on a DSC basis. You can also look at your investment statement to see if the letters DSC appear next to your holdings.

If your holdings are invested on a DSC basis, check with your advisor or your investment's prospectus to see what the DSC schedule is. Determine how long these investments have been in place. In other words, where are you on the schedule? If you are not sure, ask your advisor or the financial institution with which you work.

Make sure that the 10 percent allowed withdrawal is fully realized for this year, even if it is just converted within your account to a front-end zero-load version of the same fund. You cannot carry it over and accumulate it except for specific segregated fund arrangements, and with one investment fund company that will permit a carryforward of three years (30 percent).

Reduce the amount of your withdrawal to match the amount you can remove without fees. If you must withdraw more from your account than the 10 percent free withdrawal amount, you'll have to bite the bullet and pay the fees.

A small amount of investigation and planning, in conjunction with assistance from your advisor, can enable you to address this issue in advance and deal with it appropriately.

Low Load and F-Class Options

Your advisor may place your investments into a "low load" option that has a two- or three-year schedule rather than seven, and may or may not permit withdrawals without a cost. Here's the point: Your advisor should be setting this up on a basis where you are not going to be charged for what you want to do. There is no need for you to incur costs for withdrawals if your objectives are defined at the outset. To this end you may wish to discuss the use of "No Load" investment options. With this structure, there are no charges at the time of purchase or when amounts are redeemed. With nearly all fund companies, regardless of the load option chosen, the actual net return to the investor is the same. Where there can be a positive difference in favour of the investor is in a structure known as "F Class."

Every investment fund or pool has a management fee. Add in other items such as additional costs, marketing, taxes, and imbedded advisor compensation and you have the Management Expense Ratio or MER. An F-Class version of a fund or pool has stripped out many of the MER costs (including advisor compensation). Normally, a negotiated fee for services is added by the advisor, but even with that, the resulting total cost to the investor will be meaningfully lower. That means more return in your account. As well, the portion of the fee negotiated for the advisor is usually considered a deductible cost on non-registered (open) investments. These same mechanics would also apply to exchange traded funds (ETFs). By having the opportunity to disclose, discuss, and agree upon the level of advisor compensation, meaningful savings and efficiencies can be realized in terms of investment costs. This is particularly true as account size increases.

INVESTMENT LOSS

Investment loss is the reduction in your portfolio's value as a result of a decline in your assets' market value. Variable investments are just that—variable in terms of their returns. On average, bonds outperform stocks in three out of every 10 years. The stock market experiences negative returns in one of every four years.

What follows are some of the issues and solutions to pursuing potentially higher returns and minimizing the downside risk that variable investing entails.

Risk and Return

Regardless of what investment you choose, there are two factors that work in tandem—risk and return. Simply stated, higher returns historically have been delivered by those investments that also have the characteristics of higher risk (volatility). These are also the investments where the growth receives preferred tax treatment. The investments that have lower risk or volatility have historically also been ones with lower returns and less tax efficiency.

Investment *return* is quite an easy concept to understand; however, most people do not know what is meant by investment *risk*. Investment risk is the chance or possibility of loss. All investments carry some form of risk. Even those instruments with guaranteed returns and maturity values are subject to tax risk, inflation risk, and renewal risk.

Risk means different things to different people. To some the greatest risk (and fear) is the possibility of losing their investment principal. To others it is the risk or danger of outliving their capital and, as a result, their income. It is ironic that too conservative an investment portfolio in retirement may result in a depletion of capital. What the risk-averse investor fears the most—loss of capital—is the actual end result of their use of strictly guaranteed investments in a low interest-rate environment. What this ends up being is, in fact, a conscious encroachment upon capital.

Risk, as it pertains to a structured portfolio, does not mean losing all of your money. What is does suggest is that the value of your holdings will fluctuate. Variable investments do not have a maturity date and you can collapse or surrender them any time. Unfortunately, people often do so at a time when performance is flat or negative, which is not normally a beneficial practice. Obviously, if this is done at a time when the portfolio or particular holdings within it are down, a loss will result.

During the accumulation years, most people are less concerned about risk and more concerned about the return they are receiving. In the retirement years, risk becomes the primary issue, while return, although still important, becomes a secondary issue.

In the accumulation years, if the risk and allocation profiles are low, and a subsequently lower rate of return is expected, then people have several choices. They can:

- Work longer since they will be able to accumulate more capital over a longer period of time. Similarly, they will need more capital to provide a certain level of income in the retirement years if the investment return is lower.
- Save more money.
- Reduce the level of income they want in retirement.
- Adjust their asset mix to target a higher rate of return.

If, at retirement, the risk profile suggests a lower expected rate of return than is required to meet the objectives of the income plan, then the retiree is again faced with choices. They can:

- Lower the amount of income they are withdrawing.
- Anticipate the erosion of capital from withdrawals (capital loss).
- Adjust the asset mix to target a higher rate of return.

In both the accumulation and income stages, there are two measurements in asset allocation that need to balance with each other. First, what is the risk tolerance profile that you are comfortable with? Second, what is the risk tolerance that needs to be assumed in order for the asset allocation to achieve the objectives within your financial plan? A discussion with your advisor should help you determine what the most appropriate mix is, given these factors.

The investment of your retirement-income-producing assets is a very different process from accumulation. We do not subscribe to the theory that there are defined asset allocation models predicated solely upon the investor's age. Even though age is one consideration, ultimately the asset mix for any individual or couple is going to be determined through a number of factors that will vary for each situation.

Asset Allocation and the Efficient Frontier

In 1990, the Nobel Memorial Prize in Economic Sciences was awarded to Harry Markowitz, Merton Miller, and William Sharpe for their pioneering work in the theory of financial economics. In plain English, what they did was create the blueprint for asset allocation, also called model portfolio theory. The process involved combining asset classes to create a portfolio that would deliver the best possible return for an acceptable amount of volatility or risk. Stated another way, using historical data and the prize-winners' theory, you could estimate the expected return on a portfolio for which the asset mix was determined by the amount of volatility acceptable to the investor. This relationship of asset mix and return to volatility is what is determined by the investor profile, and no investing should be undertaken until this is completed and documented.

Whether it is an individual investment or an investment portfolio, the risk/return relationship will fall on or under the curve of the efficient frontier. For any investment, you will need at least three years of historical data to be able to meaningfully plot its position on the risk/return grid.

FIGURE 3.1

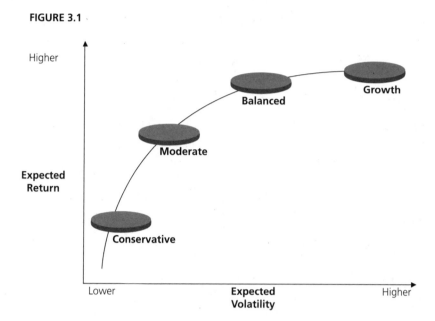

Source: *Primve Approach™ Retirement Planning.*

So where do we, as investors, want to be on this efficient frontier? We want to be in the upper left-hand corner of the chart. We want to get the highest rate of return for the least amount of risk. As the efficient frontier tells us, however, no such investment exists. So, in the world of trade-offs that is investing, the very first question that you as an investor have to ask yourself is this: "If I cannot get what I want, then what is it that I am prepared to give up? Low or no volatility carries with it a lower rate of return and higher taxation. Am I willing to forgo higher potential returns and tax efficiency, or am I prepared to tolerate fluctuations in the value of my holdings?" That's the trade-off.

We cannot control interest rates, individual equities, stock markets, global events, or inflation, but we can control the investment allocation in our portfolio. This is the one element of investment-risk management over which we have at least some control. This is by no means an exact science, but over time this process does have merit. As the saying goes, "It is better to be approximately right than precisely wrong."

By combining asset classes in specific combinations we can achieve the best of investment objectives—we can increase the returns and lower the volatility we would experience if we left our investments in only one asset class. Asset allocation within your portfolio, tailored to you and your objectives, is investing, not speculating or gambling.

An Efficient Portfolio

Optimization of a portfolio suggests that the asset mix can deliver the best rate of return for an acceptable amount of volatility. Alternatively, optimization proposes to deliver the current rate of return that a portfolio experiences, or targets, for the lowest amount of volatility.

FIGURE 3.2: THE RISK TO RETURN RELATIONSHIP

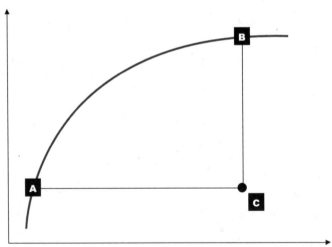

Source: *Prime Approach™ Retirement Planning.*

Your current portfolio should be assessed in order to determine if you could reposition your investments to:

- Obtain the same return with less risk, or
- Realize a higher return for the same level of risk

The structural plan serves as the blueprint for the delivery of income from your assets and benefits based on your Time Hub priorities and objectives. The plan will have used an asset mix that is tied to the target rate of return needed in order for your objectives to be met. This may or may not be consistent with the asset mix that is suggested by your investor profile. If your plan requires a higher rate of return than your personal profile suggests, then you are back to the issue of trade-offs. Do you lower your income or do you increase the amount of equities in your portfolio in order to increase your investment return over time? Obviously, the increased weighting in stocks will result in greater fluctuations in portfolio value. Is this something you can tolerate in order for your asset mix to have a better opportunity to reach its target rate of return?

REDUCING RISK

One of the effective strategies for reducing overall risk in a portfolio is to diversify by asset class. Keep in mind that we say reducing, not completely removing. There are risk factors involved with every asset class. The following examines the different risk factors affecting bonds and stocks by looking at these two asset classes separately.

Tactics to Reduce Bond Risk

Investment-grade bonds may be sold on the open market prior to the maturity date. The proceeds of such a sale may be more or less than the amount originally paid for the security, depending on four key factors:

1. The credit rating of the bond
2. The term to maturity
3. The coupon rate of the bond
4. Prevailing interest rates

The following example illustrates how the market value fluctuations occur, using approximate values. Assume you have a bond with a coupon rate of 6 percent that matures 10 years from now. With this duration to maturity, interest-rate swings will have a more dramatic effect on the market price of the bond.

A new-issue bond maturing in 10 years is then bought at par with a face value of $100,000 at 6 percent interest. This means that every six months there will be an interest payment of $3,000. This is a total of $6,000 of interest paid every year and a guaranteed value at maturity of $100,000.

If interest rates rise to 8 percent, an investor taking a new-issue bond at par will only need to buy a $75,000 bond to generate the same income of $6,000 per year. If the 6 percent bond goes on the secondary market to be sold, it will have a value closer to $75,000 than to $100,000. It is said to be selling at, or being purchased at, a "discount." Even though it was purchased for $75,000, the bond still pays $6,000 per year in interest and matures for $100,000 in 20 years. The additional principal realized would enhance the yield to maturity.

Conversely, if interest rates drop to 5 percent, the market value of the bond will appreciate. If you recalculate, you will find that at 5 percent it takes $120,000 to generate $6,000 of interest. So the bond will have a market value well above the par value at which it was issued. But, it will still only mature for $100,000 in 20 years, and the yield to maturity would be less than the current yield as a result.

The above numbers illustrate the shifts in the bond's market value if the interest-rate changes happened close to the issuance of the new bond with a long maturity. As stated previously, the term to maturity is one factor affecting the price of bonds. If you were to buy or sell the bond closer to its maturity date, the effects of interest rate changes on the value of the bond would not be as substantial as those shown above.

Bonds can be volatile, although fluctuation ranges are not as dramatic as they are for equity investments. In Canada, on a calendar year basis from 1951 to 2001, there were as many years of negative returns for bonds as there were for stocks.

In early 1994, this fact really hit home. People who had put money into GICs five years earlier at 11 percent were facing renewal rates of 2.75 percent for one year and 5.75 percent for five years. This difference in return was not simply a drop in rates. For retirees, it was a drop in income. The $100,000 that created $11,000 in annual income would now only generate between $2,750 and $5,750 per year. These were the lowest rates in 34 years and presented people with some very difficult decisions in terms of how they should reinvest.

Bonds and mortgage funds over that same five-year period saw positive double-digit returns. The returns on those funds were substantial because of the recent, progressive drop in interest rates. As falling interest rates caused the market value of bonds to increase, the underlying assets had risen in value, positively affecting returns. During this period, some bond funds posted returns of over 20 percent, while mortgage funds had returns in the mid-teens.

People ventured into these funds to try and catch the returns they saw posted. After all, how risky could bond and mortgage funds be when they held no stocks? Unfortunately, for those who put money into these funds, interest rates started to rise substantially through the rest of 1994 and 1995. What this meant was that the underlying value of the bonds and mortgages actually dropped. These novice investors, many of whom had not been in variable funds of any kind previously, received statements at the end of 1994 showing a decline in value from their original invest- ment. They panicked.

If they had stayed in the investments, they would have recovered the loss in value and earned a respectable return through 1996 and 1997 when rates once again subsided. But many did not stay invested, believing that it was better to incur a loss and get out than to see their holdings ultimately disappear. As bewildered as they were to this point, they were even more bewildered to see that on top of everything else, there was a taxable ele- ment from the interest earnings that had to be taken into income. How could there possibly be a taxable receipt when the account was showing a loss at the end of the year? Well, the interest was paid on the bonds and mortgages even though the market value of the underlying holdings declined. This amount had to be distributed to unitholders and declared as taxable income.

This is a classic example of people making choices without having all of the relevant information and basing investment decision on recent performance.

It is very important to note that with any bond, income, or strip, the value at maturity is guaranteed. The only time a gain or loss is incurred is if the bond is sold before maturity. The fluctuation in your account is reflected in how assets are valued by the market at the end of a trading day. Whether or not it is your intent to hold the bond until maturity, the actual market value of the bond must be reported.

It is important to note that there is one exception to the above points on bond market values relative to changes in interest rates—a separate class of bonds known as Real Return Bonds (RRBs). They have a fixed coupon rate that is adjusted upward for the inflation rate. Speak to your advisor about these. This is one bond investment that is best acquired through a fund rather than individually. The performance of RRBs correlates negatively to income bonds and bond funds, which makes such bonds a good inclusion for the fixed-income portion of your portfolio.

Tactics to Reduce Equity Risk

Reduce Specific Risk and Market Risk

Generally speaking, there are two types of risk associated with investing— specific risk and market risk. Although it is impossible to eliminate risk, there are proven ways to minimize the downside exposure we may have to either one of these elements.

SPECIFIC RISK

Specific risk is that which is unique to a particular stock. For example, the value of a stock in a particular company may be affected by such things as:

- Capability of management
- Change in management
- Labour problems
- Product appeal
- Merger or acquisition
- Consumer preferences
- Government interference
- Financial health
- Market desire or dislike for the security
- Investor sentiment

It is suggested that specific risk can be "squeezed out" if a portfolio holds 30 or more stocks. For the average investor, this would require a relatively large amount of capital. One of the reasons that managed money in the form of mutual funds, segregated funds, wrap accounts, and pooled funds is efficient is it allows for substantial diversification for an investor with smaller amounts of capital. It is common to see 30 to 60 stocks within these types of accounts.

MARKET RISK

Market risk reflects what is happening in a market or markets as a whole. World markets may be affected by such issues as:

- Business or economic cycles
- Inflation
- Interest rates
- Geopolitical events
- General market conditions
- Investor sentiment

There is no way to totally eliminate market risk, but it can be substantially reduced by using a combination of asset classes that perform differently at any given time. There are basically three asset classes—cash, bonds, and equities—and many subclasses within each of these. As mentioned previously, income-generating real estate and income trusts may also be viewed as separate asset classes. For example, subclasses of bonds can be government or corporate, domestic or foreign, and vary by duration or by term to maturity. Stocks have even more subclassifications, including growth or value, domestic or foreign, large, mid, or small cap, conservative or aggressive, etc. With so many different asset subclasses, it is sad for us to see clients who come in with little diversification but much duplication in their portfolio. It is not beneficial to have four different equity funds in your portfolio if they are all large-cap, global growth funds. If they are performing and moving in a similar pattern, your portfolio has duplication, not diversification.

FIGURE 3.3

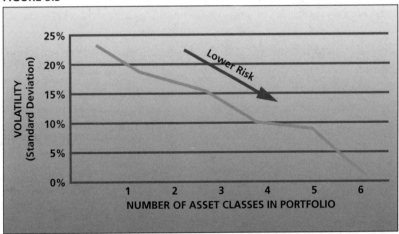

Source: Franklin Templeton Investments. Reprinted with permission.

The objective of diversification is to combine asset classes that do not move or perform in exactly the same manner. Combining those asset classes and/or investments that are negatively correlated serves to reduce the overall volatility of the portfolio and "smooth out the ride" as the returns are being realized. The chart below illustrates how volatility is reduced as more asset classes are included in a portfolio.

The major purpose of asset allocation is to control risk, not to maximize returns.

Use Investment Style

Although there are several types and hybrids of money management styles, the two predominant and distinctly different methods are value and growth.

VALUE

This process involves searching out those companies whose share values are trading below what is believed to be the fair market value or intrinsic price. When the manager sees something truly undervalued and feels it will come back to its potential market value, they will acquire it. It may in fact take years for this to happen, but the belief is that undervalued stock of a good company is a wise purchase not only for purposes of returns but also for purposes of risk management. There is a margin of safety in buying something that is already trading at a discount. Unfortunately, what everyone really wants to do is buy those things that are rising in value. The desire to purchase what has done well lately is only human nature. But it is not only imprudent investing but also laden with risk (think about Nortel).

Value managers do not simply acquire a stock because it is cheap. The reason it's cheap may be because it is a bad company or the earnings prospects are simply not there. But when value managers see good value and a future catalyst to make the share value rise, they make purchases. When the value of the shares reaches what the managers believe is fair value or even slightly beyond, they will sell them, having realized the gains they wanted from that company.

GROWTH

If the value style of management is slow, plodding, and boring, the growth style of management can be described as the life of the party. This is not to say that fundamental analysis is ignored, but growth managers are more concerned with riding the wave of rising stock prices as earnings momentum moves upward. Popularity of a stock and the number of people buying are the reassurance and safety factors for growth investors.

Growth managers usually buy in after value managers have made their moves, and also tend to hold onto their stocks longer than their value counterparts. What attracts investors to the growth style is the exciting momentum of stocks on the rise. Growth managers get most of the attention when markets are rolling upward and that is the time most investors like to "hop on board."

THE BEST STYLE

Performance differences between the two styles can produce dramatically different results over short time periods. For example, in the late 1990s, when technology stocks were skyrocketing, value managers were having flat to negative returns in their funds. Everyone wanted the 30-percent-plus returns that they heard their neighbours were getting and no money was going to value managers. Growth mangers ruled! Since the end of the first quarter of 2000, though, value managers have buried their growth counterparts in terms of performance comparisons. This is why proper asset allocation dictates that some of each style be included in a diversified portfolio.

However, over the long term, one style is not necessarily better than the other. For example, this is how the annualized returns break down for the 10-year period ended December 31, 2006.

Broad-based index	**9.3%**
Growth-based index	**9.2%**
Value-based index	**10.5%**

When it comes to selecting the "best" management style, it is not solely the level of returns that are the important comparison, but the path that was taken to earn them. Growth managers and investors traditionally will have gone through a more volatile experience over the last 10 years than will have the value proponents. Over the same 10-year period examined above, the cumulative return for both styles is shown below.

	Value Fund	Growth Fund
10-Year Annualized Return	10.5%	9.2%
Cumulative Return	162.0%	140.2%

Two considerations for reducing risk by using investment strategy regarding style are as follows.

GO THE VALUE ROUTE

It may make perfect sense to have all, or at least the majority (75 percent), of your equity investments managed in the value style. After all, in retirement we are not out to try and double our money but rather to obtain an investment return that is meaningfully above guaranteed rates with low volatility. This sounds like a perfect job description for a value manager to me. There are going to be periods of time, however, where this style is not in favour and returns will be flat or negative. You are also going to have lower performance at a time when the growth positions are taking off and your neighbours are once again bragging about their returns. Why are they never as eager to talk to you about their losses?

For the purposes of creating retirement income, the value approach may provide you with less volatility along the way. Since slow and steady is a preferred course with retirement assets, a larger proportion of your holdings could be placed with money managers who employ this style. You may find it preferential to have all of your holdings managed this way. Remember, though, that the trade-off will be likely missing some of the big returns associated with growth managers. This may be acceptable for avoiding the traditionally larger losses incurred in growth investing.

When you are making periodic contributions to a savings plan, higher volatility actually serves to increase your investment returns. However, when you are making periodic withdrawals, higher volatility is a disadvantage. This is yet another fundamental difference between the accumulation years and the income years.

SELL HIGH AND BUY LOW—THE CASH WEDGE

This strategy incorporates a number of income and investment concepts within it, some of which have already been mentioned in other sections. It is not complicated and makes use of the variance in performance between asset classes.

This all begins by using what we refer to as the cash wedge. It consists of a defined amount of capital that is allocated to a money market account within the portfolio. It is from this segment that the actual income amounts are paid out of the portfolio. The amount is established by you and your advisor and is a multiple of the income you will receive. In the sample shown below we have allocated one year's worth of income payments in this way (12 times $1,500 equals $18,000).

FIGURE 3.4: THE CASH WEDGE

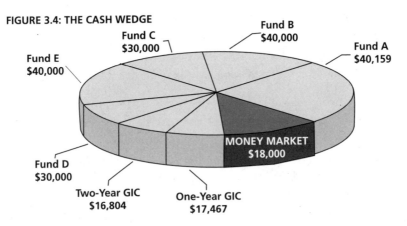

In this example we have also set up income for the second and third years by putting $17,476 into a one-year GIC at 3 percent. This will be worth $18,000 at the start of the second year. It will then be used to replenish the money market fund as income continues to be drawn. We replicate the process with $16,804 in a two-year GIC at 3.5 percent. If we have initial investment returns from the other selections that will allow us to take profits and replenish the cash wedge, we may end up renewing the GICs or bonds.

The objective is to maintain the original value of the cash wedge by taking profits where and when appropriate. We want to maintain the cash wedge but not have too much money in this form. Any profits realized that need not be used to restore our cash wedge can therefore be used to acquire additional units or positions in the investments that are flat or negative. If you have proper diversification in your investments, you should *expect* to have one or more of your asset classes/investments in a flat or negative position at all times. They should not all be performing in the same manner.

This is a sell high, buy low process that will likely, although not guaranteed, result in higher returns. It will create a portfolio that will, over time, experience a lower degree of volatility. It is important to note that all of this is done with an eye to maintaining the appropriate assets mix that was established at the outset.

We believe that it is valid to employ a buy and hold strategy, but remember:

- The portfolio should reflect the appropriate asset allocation.
- Profits are taken or rebalancing occurs on a predetermined and defined basis.
- We are not attempting to outsmart the managers we have selected.

Many people saw a large increase in the value of their investments through the late 1990s. If they did not take the profits off of the table, they saw the same accounts come down to a value lower than their initial investment. We are not suggesting that you divest of good investments, but that you should have a process through which you take profits and maintain them.

An exceptional planner, friend, and business associate of mine often reminds me that taking profits and/or rebalancing is very important when you are investing a lump sum of money. There are no external additions of capital after the fact. Taking profits on a defined and systematic basis, and buying more of those positions in your portfolio that are low, will produce better returns and reduce the amount of volatility over time. It is an important factor of portfolio management, especially when you are dealing with the investment of large, lump sums of capital as you are at retirement.

These are among many different approaches that you can discuss with your advisor. Your advisor will also be able to identify value and growth managers that would fit into your portfolio and the extent to which each should be used. Some money managers use a blend of styles. We have just touched on the two most distinct and familiar approaches by discussing value and growth.

Ultimately, the path that you may wish to follow will be in conjunction with how you and your advisor craft your Investment Policy Statement (IPS), the governing document in how your money will be managed. This will be discussed in more detail later.

CORRELATION

An often overlooked yet essential aspect of diversification is correlation, or how the various funds and holdings within your portfolio move in relation to each other. In truly efficient diversification you do not want to have separate investment positions that track closely to each other in terms of how they move. Otherwise, you will have everything moving up in value at the same time (that's the fun part) but you will also have everything moving down at the same time. If you have pairings of funds or pools with high correlation, they will basically be moving in tandem. You will have duplication rather than diversification, and that is simply not efficient. Low correlation is an essential factor to the sell high, buy low strategy described above. Your advisor can assist you in determining the correlation of your holdings through the diagnostic tools at their disposal.

Add Fixed-Income Assets

There should be some fixed-income holdings in every portfolio. The trade-off is that any money diverted to fixed-income instruments will carry the prevailing returns. Currently they are low, which means that in exchange for a more secure or less volatile portfolio that includes higher amounts of fixed-income holdings, the remaining investments (those not used for fixed-income or cash placements) need to work that much harder to deliver the average return required on the original amount of capital.

The following shows the equity returns necessary to create a portfolio return of 7 percent, assuming fixed-income returns of 5 percent:

Asset Mix

Fixed Income	Stocks	Stocks Must Return
70 %	30%	11.66%
60 %	40%	10.00%
50 %	50%	9.00%
40 %	60%	8.33%

Conventional income bonds could be used if we are dealing with short time frames of two to three years, but remember that the interest on income bonds does not compound. We need to keep in mind that if we are dealing with non-registered accounts and we are creating future annual income by using bonds or GICs, all interest amounts will be taxable on an annual basis.

An important thing to note as it relates to non-registered, interest-bearing investments and the new rules on pension splitting for those age 65 and over: The interest generated from a bond or a guaranteed investment certificate (GIC) is not eligible as income for pension splitting. However, if the interest is generated through a deposit with an insurance company in a Guaranteed Investment Annuity (GIA) it *does* qualify for income splitting. Technically, the deposit is a deferred annuity and the interest component of that is eligible for the pension amount and for income splitting for those over the age of 65.

Invest for the Long Term

Retirement is an extended phase of life requiring a long-term approach to investing. As the amount of time that an investment has to work increases, investments that fluctuate in value become more stable and their risk decreases. In other words, investing over the long term reduces both short-term gains and losses as the averages apply.

Guaranteed investments with lower yields become more risky over time as inflation decreases purchasing power and taxation eats into real returns. Remember that retirement assets may have to create income over a 25- to 35-year period. This is a long-term investment horizon.

Let your assets work for you over time and don't think you can "time the market" and decide when you should be in and out of investments. In our database of 4,500 investment funds there is no fund called the "Market Timing Fund," and that's for a reason. Market timing simply does not work over time. Performance is going to be different each year, and you should expect that there are going to be years of negative returns. This is not the exception—it is the reality.

Withdraw Income Smartly

We can reduce risk to a portfolio if we are drawing income from those positions where investment returns are favourable and leaving alone those that are currently flat or negative in performance.

To this end it is preferable, in retirement income planning, to be able to choose the investments from which we will be making withdrawals. The specific investments within the cash wedge can be identified.

Whether we are stripping profits or drawing directly from the investment, we do not want to be drawing down on any holdings that have fallen in value. Much use is made of balanced funds and structured portfolios during the accumulation years. At the time we are creating income, these vehicles are not as efficient, unless we are dealing with a smaller account size. For example, we cannot direct the fund company to pay the income needed out of the bond portion of a balanced fund. This will simply involve a surrender of units, which in turn reflects the proportionate composition of that fund or portfolio. Separate investments, funds, or pools are a preferable structure so that the specific source of withdrawals can be more clinically determined.

Consider Using Segregated Funds

In the investment planning process, you and your advisor will determine what is the most appropriate asset allocation and ultimately the best placements for you. This may be in mutual funds, wrap programs, pools, ETFs (Exchange Traded Funds), or discretionary management. One other option may be the use of segregated funds.

Segregated funds are basically mutual funds with an insurance company wrapper around them. They function very much like regular mutual funds, but the big difference is that they come with guarantees and features not found in regular mutual funds.

MATURITY GUARANTEE
A maturity guarantee provides that a minimum amount of capital is guaranteed to be in the account at the "maturity" of the contract and/or at different "checkpoints" in the life of the contract. The maturity date is 10 years after the deposit is made. The amount of guarantee can be 75 percent to 100 percent of the original deposit. The higher the guarantee, the higher the management fee charged to your account. The value of your account at the end of 10 years is the greater of the investment balance or the guarantee. In either case, you will not be below the amount originally invested. It is important to note that if any withdrawals are made, this reduces the guarantee.

DEATH BENEFIT GUARANTEE

The death benefit guarantee states that a minimum of all deposits, minus any withdrawals, will be paid to the estate/beneficiary at the time the planholder passes away. If the investment value is higher at the time of death, the greater of the two values is paid.

Some restrictions on the guarantees may exist based on the age of the investor at the time he or she enters into the contract. Provisions, guarantee limits, and features vary by issuer.

CREDITOR PROTECTION

Your investment capital may be protected from creditors in the event of personal financial distress or liability. There is an application for those who are in business or professions where they are personally at risk.

PROBATE FEE AVOIDANCE

If you have listed a named beneficiary, the proceeds are payable directly to that person, thereby avoiding probate fees that would otherwise apply.

THE TRADE-OFF

If this chapter has taught you anything, it is that there are always trade-offs when it comes to investing. In order to cover the costs of reserves that need to be established for the purposes of providing guarantees, pay submanagers and advisors, and still make a profit, the management fees on segregated funds tend to be 0.50 to 1.50 percent higher than that of regular mutual funds. It is therefore common to see segregated funds with management fees from 2.50 percent to more than 4 percent. That is a pretty hefty bite out of your investment returns.

Earlier in this chapter, the issues of fees and the impact of small differences in the rates of return you earn were closely examined. If the guarantees are important to you, then the costs may be worth it. This is ultimately a decision you and your advisor must discuss.

It's also important that you know that the previously described guarantees, which are the major attraction of segregated funds, are reduced when withdrawals are made. This is done on either a proportionate basis or a dollar-for-dollar basis, depending on the insurance company involved. As an example, if you are withdrawing at the rate of 7 percent per year, you are reducing your guarantees by a similar or the same amount. Year over year, that will really erode the value of those guarantees unless death occurs early in the process. And yet, even though the guarantees are reducing, the higher management fees stay intact. As stated above, whether segregated funds are right for you depends on what type of guarantees you are looking for in your investments and every situation is different. But, if the guarantees reduce with every income payment and the costs stay the same, I question the value of using segregated funds in a withdrawal scenario.

Don't misunderstand—there is definitely a use for and a place for segregated funds, but like any other investment vehicle, they are not the best or only solution for everything. If your advisor recommends segregated funds because he or she is not licensed to offer you other investment alternatives, it may be in your best interest to get another opinion.

CONTINUED PRODUCT EVOLUTION FOR RETIRING BABY BOOMERS
Variable Annuities with Guaranteed Income
Late in 2006, Manulife Financial introduced Canadians to an income delivery vehicle that has been extremely popular in the United States since 2002: a variable annuity with a guaranteed minimum withdrawal benefit (GMWB). It would take a few pages to describe this product in detail, but here is an overview of this product which, at the time of writing, has also been offered by other insurance and fund companies and continues to have enhanced features introduced to the offering. At the time of writing, here is what the offering entails.

This product is really a portfolio of segregated funds that provides a stream of guaranteed income for a life. (Originally it was only for a 20 year period and this still applies if income starts before age 65.) The amount of income paid for each year is equal to 5 percent of the original deposit if income commences immediately. It is not a guaranteed investment return of 5 percent, but a guaranteed return of your original capital equal to five percent annually.

What these products (and income-producing Principal Protected Notes detailed below) are designed to do is eliminate the danger of depleting principal when withdrawals and negative investment returns occur at the same time early in retirement (see Investment Mathematics, page 173). The percentage of guaranteed withdrawal can increase from 5 percent if the original deposit is made in advance of the time that income commences.

For example, if you make your original investment today and start income 10 years from now, there is an enhancement to the 5 percent GMWB of 5 percent (of the 5 percent) per year. In plain English, if there were a full 10 years between the initial investment in this vehicle and the time income commenced, the GMWB would be 7.5 percent instead of 5 percent. You can prorate this enhancement for any period of time less than 10 years between the initial deposit and the start of income.

In addition to this protection, they allow for "resets" every three years if your investments have performed well and your account balance has increased over and above the original deposit. This may not only serve to increase your annual income, but also to extend the payment period, if you commenced income before age 65 and have the 20-year minimum benefit period. The resets are allowed every three years. The United States version of this product provides for resets every year.

On non-registered portfolios, income will initially be taxed as a refund of premiums. This means that there will be no taxation on income until such time as the sum of payments exceeds the adjusted cost base. This "return of principal" is very tax-efficient as an income stream and in line with the principles of "layering income" that we have discussed.

The point of scrutiny that you need to exercise is the cost of these guarantees. Some of the portfolios I have seen run about 3.4 percent per year in management fees. That is pretty hefty and more costly than most regular segregated funds, which are expensive to begin with. All of the marketing illustrations show you how your portfolio and income can increase if the investment return is in excess of the 5 percent withdrawal. Well, inasmuch as that is true, that investment return must not only exceed the 5 percent withdrawal but also the 3.4 percent management fee, which is taken off your returns with adds up to 8.4 percent.

Like all financial tools, there is application for this vehicle in the proper context, where features meet needs and deliver an efficient result. And there are trade-offs. My advice is that you understand how this product meets your objectives and compares to other alternatives. Understand how pricing affects the likelihood of resets that are in your favour. In the end, I prefer this offering to a GIC or extremely conservative portfolio, but I still believe that it is in your best interest to compare what it can do for you with other options that are available in the marketplace, many of which are discussed in this book. An informed choice is always the best choice.

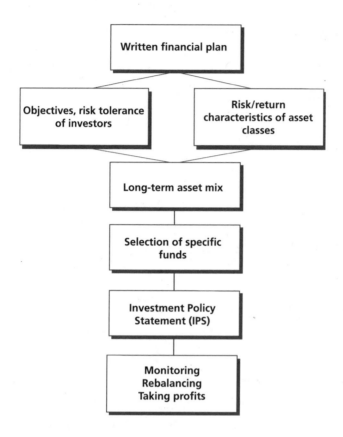

Principal Protected Notes (PPNs)

Principal Protected Notes (PPNs) are issued in different forms with various features, but the bottom line for these products is still the same. They allow people to invest while protecting their downside exposure by guaranteeing the amount of capital that was originally invested. Some notes are designed for the accumulation years, while others are specifically issued for those people seeking income. The variety of notes available is increasing both in terms of investment options and features. You may want to investigate these offering or discuss them with your advisor to see if there is a fit for what you want and what they can deliver as part of your portfolio.

Avoid Common and Costly Investment Mistakes

There are two factors that determine investment results—investment re-turns and investor behaviour. Commonly the latter serves to undermine the former. The following are some of the more common and costly mistakes that investors make. Work through your Investment Policy Statement with your advisor to minimize these problems.

- Not defining investment objectives
- More time spent picking investments than on asset allocation
- Extrapolating short-term investment result (e.g., "This will go up forever," or "Will the market ever stop falling?")
- Having unrealistic expectations
- Trying to time the market
- Lack of discipline and patience (realize that not making changes to your portfolio is actually an action)
- Chasing returns; buying high and selling low
- Expecting all investments to perform positively at the same time
- Expecting a manager's investment approach and style to work all of the time
- Not having enough proper diversification
- No Investment Policy Statement
- Not using an advisor

Any human decision is 80 percent emotion and 20 percent logic, so emotion weighs heavily on investment actions. Fear is a much more powerful motivator than greed. Often investors act on the desire to feel "safe" in the short term to the detriment of long-term investment returns.

Some people initially like to be involved in managing some of their retirement investments. What we have found is that eventually this too is a responsibility that they would like to delegate. The main reasons for this change in investor thinking are as follows:

- They become concerned that the ability to make clear and rational decisions is declining as they age.
- They become tired of the responsibility and don't wish to do it anymore.
- They realize that if something should happen to them, their spouse is not in a position to be making the same kinds of investment decisions.

Use an Investment Policy Statement (IPS)

The Investment Policy Statement (IPS) is a document written with input from you and your advisor that provides understanding and direction to the entire investment process. It also serves to create a more systematic and disciplined approach to ongoing decision-making. The use of an IPS, in conjunction with a detailed, written financial plan, enhances the potential success in meeting investment objectives. Just as important, it plays a significant role in limiting investor mistakes and quantifying expectations.

Your IPS should include the following:

- Review of your objectives, circumstances, and investment tolerances
- Objectives of the asset mix and target rate of return
- Details of the asset allocation mix and specific investments
- Guidelines for portfolio/manager evaluation
- Triggers for action, including rebalancing, taking profits, and replacing managers
- Disclosure of the fees associated with the investments chosen
- Expectations/commitments for service

It should serve as a communication tool between you and your advisor and should be the basis for discussion at review meetings.

Understand that Investing Is a Process

Investing for retirement income is not a singular event. It is an ongoing process that requires review and change. Remember that the Time Hub and Money Hub priorities, which change from time to time, will drive much of the decision-making. As a result, the structural income plan and the IPS should be the tools that are used to determine your investment actions. These two written tools are the blueprints for managing your income-producing assets.

YOUR PARENTS' INVESTMENTS

A common benchmark measure for someone in retirement is the five-year GIC. The S&P/TSX Composite Index and the Dow Jones Industrial Average may be among the accepted index measures for the industry, but for retirees and seniors the five-year GIC is normally the benchmark against which investment performance is measured. This is the return they could have received with taking, in their mind, absolutely no risk. That is true in terms of asset value volatility and future value, but not, as has been discussed, in terms of risk in other forms. During periods of low or negative investment returns, many advisors have heard clients express the fact that they would have been better off to have left their money in a GIC.

As we have illustrated throughout this section, while there is a place for guaranteed investments, they do have their limits and disadvantages. Remember that there is a relationship between the rate of withdrawal from retirement assets and the value of that asset. Dependence upon lower yielding GICs may mean using capital to create the income required or lowering your lifestyle to match the income. In many cases, we see fully taxable interest income serving no purpose other than to create needlessly high taxation and a clawback of government entitlements. Obviously there is great merit to establishing an investment portfolio that is built around specific objectives and preferences. Often we see that this has not been considered when it comes to the parents of the boomers. The following are questions that you may wish to use in examining your own situation and that of your parents.

- Have you and/or your parents gone through a planning process?
- Is the tax department getting too much revenue from your/their income?
- Are there redundant assets that could be deployed in a different way to better realize objectives such as health-risk management and wealth transfer? Remember that proper planning in this area benefits you.
- Are beneficiary designations and ownership registrations consistent with what the will says (assuming that there is a current will)?
- Do you have an IPS? Do your parents?

SUMMARY OF THE INVESTMENT PORTFOLIO CHANNEL AND THE PRIME APPROACH

The purpose of this area of planning is to establish tailored investment portfolios based on your investor profile, tolerances, and the rate-of-return objectives driven by your written financial plan. The bias here is a view to risk management. Points to cover include:

- Assessing risk tolerance
- Consolidating your assets
- Determining optimum portfolio asset mix
- Selecting appropriate investments and/or investment managers
- Identifying investments or pools from which income will be drawn

- Considering tax efficiency
- Establishing service and communications expectations
- Establishing guidelines for:
  * Rebalancing the portfolio
  * Taking profits
  * Overall management
- Creating an IPS

A key concept within the investment portfolio channel of the Prime Approach involves consolidating all of your income-producing assets and benefits under one planning umbrella. You may have assets scattered among various financial institutions, at work, and among various advisors. To have this process work most efficiently for you, you need to choose one person to pull it all together. This may be an independent advisor or it may be at your preferred financial institution.

The benefits of doing this will be better planning, less confusion from conflicting advice, and less administration in terms of reporting and the number of cheques you will receive. The investment advantages include better asset allocation and portfolios, control over the amounts and sources of income, and an opportunity for better tax efficiency. The objective, where possible, is to create the amount of income that is needed, but keep taxable income low. The improvements in the wealth transfer channel is greater expediency, less cost and tax, and much easier transition for your beneficiaries and estate.

The other investment consideration that connects to the structural plan is looking for those investment opportunities that are most tax efficient. A properly diversified portfolio that contains different asset classes is the best way to defend your assets against the saboteurs of inflation and taxation. Equities or stocks have traditionally done the best job in this regard.

There are many investment options in the marketplace today and you can expect that even more creative vehicles will evolve to address the needs and wants of the baby boomer generation. With any investment vehicle, there are features that are attractive and some that are not. As is the case with so many decisions in the financial world, it is not so much a question of "what would you like?"; it is a question of "what are you prepared to give up?" It is very important to make an informed choice on any investment vehicle and is always constructive to assess options. Any variable invest-ment products that come with guarantees will also come with higher fees attached. This erodes your investment returns. Yet some products, like the variable annuities with guaranteed minimum withdrawal benefits and Principal Protected Notes, may be very superior to GICs in terms of potential returns and tax efficiency over your retirement years. Know the details before you enter into what is supposed to be a long-term invest-ment strategy. Remember that there is often great merit in investigating how a combination of investments and investment vehicles can produce the result you are looking for in the most efficient manner.

Under the Prime Approach, assets and income streams are used to provide the funding required to realize the Time Hub objectives. The investment portfolio is a key part of this process. The operative word here is "process." It is necessary for you to buy into the structural plan and the investment process. Your commitment to this will allow you, in conjunc-tion with your advisor, to deal with fluctuations in investment returns over the years. You cannot abandon your plan and your process in years of turbulent or negative investment results. Work through the plan and the IPS with your advisor to keep on track. Use these tools as the focal points of discussion in reviewing your situation.

Remember that the projections prepared for you in your retirement plan will likely use average rates of return and show this return as a constant, year after year. In reality, it would be a fluke for a variable investment port-folio to have the same returns two years in a row, let alone 30. As such, be prepared to have account balances in your portfolios show either a surplus or a deficit when compared to your financial plan projections. Do not let the changes in your asset value draw you off course or make you hit the panic button. Average rates of return are just that—average.

You will find that of the returns provided by the assets in your portfolio, some will be flat and still others will be negative. Expect this to happen. Any well-diversified portfolio will have certain asset classes or holdings that at any point in time will show investment returns that are flat or negative relative to other positions that you hold. This does not necessarily mean that you have poor investments. It likely means that you have investments that are negatively correlated, meaning that they perform in a different and complementary manner to each other. That is what you want. You do not want to have everything performing or behaving in the same way. That would be duplication, not diversification. Although it may be fun when markets are on the way up, it is a disaster when markets fall.

This chapter examined various strategies that address investment-risk management and capital preservation. Similarly, the financial costs associated with incurring and surviving a critical illness, or needing home-care services or long-term care, are considerations that should be addressed and planned for in order to preserve your assets. The Prime Approach encourages the planned use of assets and income during the years of retirement when you are enjoying your best health. Many people will suggest that it is your health, and not the value of your assets, that is truly the measure of your wealth.

You can anticipate that at some point in time during your retirement years, as you and/or your spouse face changes and challenges with your health, you will require assistance in your day-to-day living. There may also be a time where a critical illness, such as cancer, stroke, or heart attack, impacts your life unexpectedly. This is not intended to be morbid but to express the reality. You would be the exception if one of these things did not happen to you or your spouse. The following chapter will address the issues of health-risk management and present solutions that you can discuss with your advisor.

CHAPTER FOUR

Health-Risk Management

The next planning channel is that of health-risk management. Your personal health is your greatest asset. It also represents one of the greatest risks to the "health" of your income-producing assets. Most people mistakenly believe that the government will look after them as they become older and require care. However, the segment of the Canadian population over age 80 will double in the next 20 years and triple in the next 40 years according to Statistics Canada, putting unbearable strain on an already overburdened, understaffed, and underequipped health-care system. In Canada, the average cost per year for health care for those age 65 to 74 is just over $4,200, for those age 74 to 84 is just over $8,000, and for those over age 85 is approximately $16,000, according to the Canadian Institute for Health Information.

There comes a time when one's state of health holds steady at best and then declines. This is a time after which there is no improvement. After this point our health is on a path of deterioration. This is not a pleasant point to reach, but it is significant to issues related to the Time Hub. At what moment do we stop thinking about and planning for our own future? When do the dominant thoughts of the future start to focus on the future of those whom we care about rather than on ourselves?

As discussed in the previous chapter on investment planning, one of the key goals of retirement income planning is capital preservation. This can be more intelligently dealt with once you have established your objectives and priorities in the area of health-risk management and determined how this liability will be funded. There are some key issues here that need to be addressed. The more we work with our retiring and retired clients, the more conviction we have about the importance of preparing for and managing health risks and the associated costs. There are several reasons for this.

A person can lose his or her health either through a critical illness (defined later in this section) or by simply reaching a point where ongoing care is required. There are both emotional and financial costs associated with this for the individual afflicted, the spouse, and the family.

Shorter hospital stays mean longer at-home recovery and higher financial, physical, and emotional costs. When you or your partner suffers a critical loss of health, the golden years turn to the olden years. That period of time between the last child leaving home and the first elder needing care is the time of greatest independence. We have defined the prime retirement years in the same manner—that point when retirement commences until the first elder needs care. This applies to either spouse in the example of a retired couple. As a boomer, you or your spouse may already be in the role of caregiver to your parent(s).

People needing long-term care are not going to go without it, but as the boomers reach this point, the level, quantity, and quality of care they receive will largely depend on their ability to pay for it.

Disability insurance or "income replacement" is a benefit few people would think of doing without while in their working years. If you are unable to work due to an accident or illness, this coverage provides you with an income. When you retire, this coverage stops. You don't need disability insurance when you are retired. You no longer have an income that needs to be insured. But you should have "asset insurance" in the form of Critical Illness (CI) coverage and ultimately Long-Term Care (LTC) coverage. After all, it is your retirement assets that are now providing income, and they need to be protected. Coping with the costs of a critical illness or long-term care could severely reduce or even deplete your retirement assets. This source of income should be protected and there are ways to do it.

DEFINE YOUR OBJECTIVES

Medical advances and drug therapy are enabling people to live considerably longer than ever before. People are more likely to survive conditions that, in the past, would have led to death. To address health risk we need to look at the implications of incurring a critical illness or requiring long-term care. This is a very sensitive issue but a very important planning channel within the Prime Approach to retirement income planning.

We'll assume that you *do* want to:

- Continue to enjoy a certain quality of lifestyle
- Ensure your spouse can enjoy retirement
- Be able to make choices
- Be able to have access to the amount of care and the type of care that you will need
- Maintain you independence and dignity

We'll also assume that you *don't* want to:

- Be forced to accept the lowest form of care and/or facility
- Have to go on long waiting lists
- Reduce or exhaust your retirement assets by paying for your long-term care
- Be a burden to your spouse or your family
- See the inheritance for your children and grandchildren reduced
- Create emotional and financial hardship for your spouse or family

Ironically, as you examine these issues in more detail, your tendency may be to assume that these issues will never face you, when in fact, you would be the rare exception if they did not. For many reasons, CI and LTC issues should be addressed in advance. Proper planning can provide a course of action to follow and a mechanism for funding should this type of care be required.

CRITICAL ILLNESS (CI)

A critical illness is defined as the diagnosis of or the onset of heart attack, life-threatening cancer, stroke, coronary-artery bypass surgery, multiple sclerosis, Alzheimer's, Parkinson's, the need for major organ transplant, kidney failure, paralysis, coma, blindness, deafness, or loss of speech. Today, heart disease, life-threatening cancer, and stroke account for 80 percent of the deaths in Canada, up from 14 percent in 1900.

The Chances
At 40 years of age:

Out of 100 healthy males, 30 will have a critical illness by age 65

Out of 100 healthy females, 27 will have a critical illness by age 65

Between age 40 and 65, your chance of incurring or being diagnosed with a critical illness is 10 times greater than your chance of dying.

Dealing With the Costs of Critical Illness
While the incidence of critical illnesses has increased dramatically, so has the survival rate. The costs incurred by the survivors of these illnesses can be substantial. Although the costs of basic treatment are currently covered through provincial health plans, the major costs of dealing with illness and surviving illness are borne by you and may cover such things as:

- More immediate medical treatment
- The best physicians and facilities to treat your illness
- Experimental or alternative treatments
- Adapting your residence for special needs
- Private care at home or for a care facility "per diem"
- Costs of extended travel or relocation
- Costs of drugs and treatments not covered by provincial programs

The above expenses can have a seriously negative impact on your retirement assets and income. For example, the Canadian Cancer Society has estimated that two-thirds of the costs related to cancer treatment are indirect expenses not covered by provincial health-care plans.

To cover such expenses personally, your only choices may be to:

- Use retirement assets (RRSPs, savings, etc.)
- Sell fixed assets (house, cottage, valuables)
- Settle for what treatment is available, when it is available
- Impact other family members emotionally and financially
- Reduce the retirement lifestyle of you and your spouse

These are your options unless you have the ability to use discounted dollars.

Using Discounted Dollars

Using discounted dollars is another way of saying "using insurance." The concept behind insurance is very simple. You and others like you make small contributions to a pool in exchange for protection from a particular disaster. This may be fire, auto coverage, life insurance, or heath-risk coverage. Premiums for any of these forms of insurance are not deductible from income, but proceeds from a claim are not taxable when received. The term "discounted dollars" applies since what you pay in premiums is a mere fraction of the benefit you would receive from a claim.

Rather than using your retirement assets to pay for the costs of a critical illness or for long-term care, use discounted dollars or insurance. As you will recall, the concept of discounted dollars (paying pennies to get one dollar of benefit) is the fourth D of effective tax planning. Within this chapter, we will look in detail at using insurance vehicles for both CI and LTC costs, as well as some funding options for both of these.

Assume that you have a $200,000 home and $200,000 sitting in a bank account. In the morning mail, you receive the renewal for your fire insurance. The policy's premium is $1,000. You could turn to your spouse and say, "You know the premium is $1,000 and we've never had a fire in our home. In fact, there has never even been a fire in this neighbourhood. Let's not spend the $1,000 on insurance. If the house burns down, we'll just replace it by taking the $200,000 we have in the bank account and building a new one." That evening as you are watching TV, you see smoke coming out of the kitchen. We assure you that if this happened you would be running down to the insurance company with the $1,000 cheque in hand.

It's not logical or financially practical to put at risk $200,000 when $1,000 per year would cover that risk. Why is it any different with loss issues related to critical illness, long-term care, or life insurance? As it pertains to our health, at age 65 and beyond, there is smoke in our kitchen. This is the time that health-related risks are the greatest, and it is also a time when we find people not insuring those risks. Use your retirement assets to do the things you want to do during your retirement. Do not use them to self-insure.

There is a distinct difference between longer life expectancy and years of good health. Remember that medical science may have enabled us to live longer, but that does not mean that all of those years are spent in good health.

Critical Illness (CI) Insurance

This is one insurance product that was not designed by an actuary or an insurance company. The concept was that of Dr. Marius Barnard, brother of Dr. Christian Barnard, a noted South African heart surgeon. Marius saw the financial difficulties incurred by those who had survived a critical illness and recognized the need for some form of coverage that would protect them from this hardship.

CI insurance is not life insurance or disability coverage. It pays a lump-sum, tax-free benefit to you if you either incur a critical illness or are diagnosed with one. The benefit is payable only after you have survived 31 days after incidence or diagnosis. If death should occur, your estate or beneficiary would be entitled to a refund of the premiums that had been paid.

There is also a refund-of-premium (ROP) option that repays to you, your survivors, or your estate, at set points in time, the sum of annual premiums paid into the plan if no previous claim is made. Coverage can extend for as long as you live or for a defined period of time.

The payment of benefits allows you to make more choices regarding your treatment. One of those choices may be to seek services outside of Canada. In the case of seeking more immediate treatment with specialized physicians, equipment, and facilities, it may very well mean going to the United States. For example, if you are diagnosed with a serious life-threatening illness, you may wish to seek treatment that is not available to you locally. If you go to the U.S. for treatment, the costs are not covered by provincial health plans. For most people, the largest cashable asset they have is their RRSP. Anything removed from your RRSP is taxable as income. For the amounts required, you need to draw out two dollars to get one dollar after tax.

If you do survive the illness and the treatment, what kind of retirement lifestyle have you left yourself, with that severe a depletion of your assets? Whether you survive or not, what kind of retirement have you left for your spouse?

If, for a cost of $3 or $4 per day, you could have access to the U.S. health-care system, would you be interested? This, among many other things, is what CI insurance can do for you.

Providing You with Choices

The benefit you would receive from a CI claim can assist in many other ways. For example, the tax-free lump sum could be used to:

- Clear off debt
- Allow for a longer convalescence period before returning to work
- Permit you to return to work part-time
- Allow you to retire sooner
- Allow you to retire immediately

The greatest cause of illness is stress. All of the options listed above would be actions that would reduce stress. In addition, this coverage helps protect the retirement lifestyle of you and your spouse by protecting your income-producing assets. Try the following exercise.

- Think of three people you know who are within five years of your current age and have had either heart disease, bypass surgery, cancer, or stroke, and survived.
- What were some of the worries these people had to face?
- Would a tax-free sum of money have assisted them in terms of faster treatment, faster recovery, less worry, less stress, and greater peace of mind?

If you are retiring early and have left your health benefits with your employer, this becomes an even more important issue. You should at least cover off the time until the younger of either you or your spouse reach age 65. The financial impact of a critical illness is magnified greatly if it occurs in your earlier retirement years.

LONG-TERM CARE (LTC)

Long-term care (LTC) generally deals with providing non-acute nursing assistance to those who are restricted or prevented from being able to live independently due to an ongoing (or chronic) condition or conditions or cognitive impairment. Long-term care may take place in the home or in a care facility.

Long-term care is different from traditional care in that it is designed to maintain a level of independent living, not to provide a cure or improvement in the condition.

The incidence of LTC needs is increasing for two main reasons. First, people are living longer. Advances in medical treatment and drug therapy have extended our life expectancy. More and more people are able to survive serious illnesses and add years to their life. The second reason deals with the fact that hospital stays are now generally very short and the care that used to be delivered in the hospital must now be received in the home or in a care facility.

The New England Journal of Medicine stated in 1994 that 43 percent of people age 65 and older will spend some time in a long-term-care facility. The average length of stay is 2.5 years. About 10 percent of those individuals will stay five years or longer.

In Canada, there is a dangerous belief that the government will look after all of the costs of such needs. This is not the case. The burden of long-term care is being shifted to individuals. In the summer of 1999, Alan Rock (then health minister) told a home-care forum in Toronto that one in five adult women is now looking after someone in the home who is either chronically ill or disabled. Those women spend an average of 28 hours a week in that caregiving role. Family members provide 90 percent of eldercare in Canada and 60 percent of those caregivers are women.

For the caregiver, assuming a spouse, there is the emotional and financial cost of dealing with substantial health-care expenses, plus the need to look after their own personal living costs. There is still more to this issue than the monetary considerations of providing care. There is also a human cost in terms of the personal wear on the caregiver: the impact on his or her lifestyle and ultimate financial well-being. Who, in turn, looks after the caregiver should he or she eventually need care?

Government Services

The range of long-term-care services and facilities provided by government programs varies widely between provinces. Some of the restrictions for users include:

- Qualifying for benefits by condition
- Qualifying for benefits by income (means test)
- Availability of services or facility
- Limited choices and options
- Limits on amount of assistance (maximums)

Several types of covered care fall under two main categories—home care and facility care.

Home Care

The home has become today's recovery room. Shorter hospital stays, day-surgery procedures, and limited hospital space all have contributed to this trend.

Home care is a program of care delivered to a person in his or her home as recommended by a physician, and provided by a licensed nurse or an authorized employee of a health-care agency. This benefit could be triggered by an injury or sickness, the inability to perform two or more Activities of Daily Living (ADLs), cognitive impairment, or medical necessity caused by chronic illness.

ADLs include eating, bathing, transferring (moving in and out of bed), dressing, and toileting.

The objective of most retirees facing the need for care is to remain in their home for as long as possible. If care can be delivered in this setting, it will allow people the choice to maintain the additional degree of independence that being in their home affords them.

HOME-CARE COSTS
In-Home Visits

- $25 to $35 per hour (registered nurses or auxiliary nurses)
    * 1 one-hour visit each day = $1,000 per month
- $12 to $15 per hour (medical services aid)
- 24-Hour In-Home Nursing
    * $112,000 per year (Licensed Practical Nurse)

Facility Care

The facility-care benefit is triggered by the same impairments as described above under "Home Care," but when health- or personal-care services are required on a long-term basis in a long-term-care facility at the order of a physician.

FACILITY-CARE COSTS
- Government Facilities
  - * Occupancy is 100%
  - * Waiting lists are in the 1,000s
- Certified Facilities (Government Subsidy)
  - * $1,600 to $2,200 per month (after subsidy)
- Private Retirement Homes
  - * $2,500 to $6,000 and more per month

In the case of facility care, in addition to qualifying for care by your condition, a financial or means test is applied to determine the level of funding for which you are responsible. Means testing for benefits is normally a function of taxable income from the previous year. This is the same means test that is applied to qualify for other government entitlements. There may also be an asset test that is used to determine the availability of or level of assistance. Most provinces in Canada have at least one means test to determine eligibility for benefits.

What *You* Pay—the Per Diem

"Per diem" is Latin for "for each day." A per diem is basically the levy that is charged to you as the cost of being in a long-term-care facility. It is an amount assessed over and above that which is already paid for by government. The amounts are charged on an ability-to-pay basis, and the measure to determine how much you are able to pay is based upon your net income from the previous year, less total tax payable. There is a different yet corresponding schedule that applies if the person receiving care is single or married. In the married context the combined net income of the household is used, minus combined total tax payable. Each province has its own table of a per diem payable relative to net income. As net income increases, in approximately $50 increments, the amount of per diem required increases. The following table provides a rough example using selected net income amounts.

Single	Married	Per Diem
$15,240	$36,463	$35.90
$20,023	$41,209	$49.00
$23,783+	$44,906+	$59.00

Long-term-care costs do qualify in the calculation of the medical tax credit if a licensed practitioner has referred the patient to a licensed facility. The credit can serve to reduce taxable income, but not net income.

There are some ways to lower or avoid a per diem, including reducing your net income. This goes hand in hand with tax planning, which was discussed previously. Practically, your net income would have to be very low to avoid a per diem. A tactic some retirees use, in their later years, is to move assets into the hands of their adult children. Any income or growth is taxed to the children, and the arrangement is that after tax is reconciled there is a division of the interest or growth earned. This may be a bit cumbersome in terms of how it affects the children's tax bracket but to some people it is worth the effort to avoid using their own assets to pay for care. In the calculation of what should be paid personally, there is nothing to stop governments from one day conducting a means test on the children.

Even after an individual qualifies, it is essential to realize that each province sets limits on the benefits to be provided. Home care may be provided, but the number of hours and the number of visits may be limited. Access to government-subsidized long-term-care facilities is also regulated, and since this is the lowest cost alternative, long waiting lists exist in many provinces.

The costs of these services, over and above any government assistance, will have to come from your income or assets. One option to help fund these costs is long-term-care insurance.

Long-Term Care (LTC) Insurance

The main reason Canadians have a difficult time wrapping their heads around the concept of providing an external source of funding for their long-term care is that they believe that government and the current medical system will look after their needs. But they may be very mistaken in their assumptions.

With the demographic realities of this nation, combined with the extended longevity we will continue to experience, we will simply have more people requiring these services. At the risk of sounding callous, the facilities will be better and more readily available to those with the money to pay for them. For the rest of us it will be a matter of accepting what is available, when it is available. Those who prepare ahead for this eventuality will have a more dignified and enjoyable experience at this point in their life.

The difficulty advisors have in conveying this message effectively is that most people believe that either the government will look after them or that it will simply not matter what type of care they receive when the time comes. What is often neglected is the impact on other family members, including one's spouse and children.

If, 10 years ago, advisors had begun telling people about long waiting lists for treatment, doctor and nursing shortages, and other challenges we are facing in the Canadian medical system, their clients would have dismissed it as hype. Today, these realities are upon us. Unfortunately, even today the messages advisors are sending us about long-term care are similarly being ignored. The trend, however, is evident, and the sooner individuals start to take the necessary steps to address this need, the better they and their families will be served.

Acquiring LTC coverage does not mean being sent to a nursing home. What it does mean is that there will be money available to allow people to maintain their independence, freedom of choice, quality of life, and dignity.

In addition, you are protecting:

- Your retirement assets
- Your spouse's retirement/care
- Your children's/grandchildren's inheritance
- Opportunity for charitable giving

Premiums are paid into an LTC plan for a defined period of time, even though coverage lasts for life. This premium period is determined by the client's age at the time the coverage is purchased. There are also policy options such as inflation protection and return-of-premium (ROP) riders.

All benefits are received on a tax-free basis and are paid directly to the insured or their designated power of attorney (POA).

There are no physical examinations to go through; you must only complete a basic questionnaire. Issue ages are from 40 to 80.

Currently, there are limited upgrade options in terms of facilities available, although this is expected to change over time and varies from province to province. Facility-care payments can be viewed, at this point, as primarily being a cost-efficient and tax-efficient way to pay the per diem that is required based on your taxable income.

Building Your Coverage

The following are some considerations when building your LTC coverage.

AMOUNT OF COVERAGE

The amount of LTC benefit is available in daily units of $10. The premiums for such coverage are calculated by multiplying the unit rate by the number of units. For example, a person wanting $50 of daily home-care benefit will purchase five $10 units.

Some insurers allow you to choose a different amount of coverage for home care and facility care. There is a daily maximum amount that can be acquired.

ELIMINATION PERIOD

In addition to choosing the amount of coverage, you can also choose the length of the elimination period. This is the amount of time that must pass from the point when a policyholder would qualify for benefits until the first payment is made. This may be anywhere from zero to 90 days. A longer elimination period will result in a lower premium.

The Benefit Period

What is the duration of time that a benefit would be payable? The options are for one year, two years, five years, or your lifetime. A longer elimination period or shorter benefit period will reduce your premium amount. The average stay in a facility-care home is two and a half years; however, Alzheimer's patients spend an average of nine years in a care facility. A higher premium for lifetime coverage is very worthy of consideration. Examine the differences in premium for the various benefit periods, and discuss these options with your advisor.

On average, the additional cost for a private-care room over and above the amount paid by government is $1,800. This monthly cost is roughly equal to an annual premium for a policy providing long-term facility care coverage for a male age 65.

In looking at the annual premium, calculate the total cost of this coverage as a percentage of your net worth. In the end, this is what this coverage is allowing you to protect. It does provide cash flow to cover the costs of care, but in essence you are really buying protection for your assets. For example, if both you and your spouse are age 65, the total cost for a $50 daily benefit with a 60-day elimination period would be $4,246 per year for unlimited benefits and an ROP option. If the value of your pensions, RRSPs, non-registered assets, and home total $600,000, then the premium for this coverage is roughly 1.5 percent per year of your net worth. Remember that this coverage includes an ROP option that can be activated if the coverage is not used. There will be more on this feature later in this chapter.

You and your advisor will want to carefully assess the various providers of products and determine which features are most important to you. Definitions and requirements for claim eligibility vary among providers. There are also differences between contracts in the definitions of what makes any particular care facility eligible for you to trigger a benefit. All LTC contracts that we have seen allow the insurer to increase premiums after the contract is issued. Some contracts contain a premium cap that guarantees future increases cannot exceed 25 percent of the original premium. Some contracts pay out on a reimbursement of costs basis, while others simply pay the contractual amount at claim and allow you to determine how it is spent.

Note that a $100-per-day benefit is equal to $36,500 per year, tax-free for this purpose. How long would your retirement assets be able to pay out this amount before they were severely reduced or exhausted? You now see the true value of LTC coverage.

Refund-of-Premium (ROP) Option

Both critical illness and long-term care coverage have a refund-of-premium (ROP) option that allows for the refund of premiums paid should death occur without a claim having been made against the policy. Certain CI contracts also have the ROP option built in after the contract has been in place for 10 years or 20 years, or at a certain age.

ROP is an optional rider that can be added to the base contract. The inclusion of this rider can increase the basic premium by 50 percent to 100 percent. So, is it worth it? From the calculations we have seen, you would need to realize an after-tax investment return of roughly 22 percent on the amount equal to the cost of the rider in order to break even with what it provides in the contract. Yes, it is worth it if the cash flow or assets are there to cover the premium. Remember that it is not necessary to include the ROP option. It is better to have CI or LTC coverage without it than to not have any protection at all. Bottom line? Having the resources to pay for your own care creates better access to the health-care system. Long-term-care insurance is the most cost-efficient way to cover these costs.

The ROP in LTC coverage applies to the facility-care portion only and not the premium paid for home care. Facility care represents about 80 percent or more of the overall premium. Plus, even if benefits are payable under the home-care portion, the refund of premium for facility care will still be in effect if there is no payment of facility benefits.

Asset Exchange and Redundant Capital

The previous chapter made reference to what we call redundant capital. This is any asset that is not being used to satisfy an income or liquidity need. Usually there are much better ways to employ these assets. One is to conduct what we refer to as an "asset exchange." In an asset exchange, money is moved from redundant assets to cover premiums for health-risk and wealth-transfer tools that can accomplish certain objectives much more effectively. This may be done as an outflow of earnings or by withdrawing small lump sums. What makes this so efficient is the following.

First, if you ever incur a claim, you have benefited from having the coverage in place. There is no question about that. Second, let's suppose that you suddenly pass away. There was no claim on your CI or LTC contract and a refund of premium is payable. All of the payments made into the plan are paid back to the estate.

Ultimately, what the coverage has cost is the net, after-tax investment return that would have been realized if you had not had to pay for this coverage. Aside from providing an injection of capital or cash flow for long-term care, the other objective in having this insurance was to protect your assets. Given these points, the bottom-line question is this: Is it better to have a lower overall return on your investments because money was used for insurance premiums, or to have a reduction in your capital assets because you had to pay for care?

Whether premiums come from cash flow or redundant assets, it is much easier for your assets to carry the cost of insurance than to carry the cost of care—especially when the insurance premiums can be refunded if there is no claim.

The Talk You *Must* Have with Your Parents

Children who offer to have parents live with them have absolutely no idea of the mental, physical, emotional, monetary, and time demands to which they will potentially be subjected. At the same time, there is most often a level of care required that children, despite the best of intentions, are not qualified to provide.

There is a large improvement in your peace of mind when you know that your parents are being looked after. There is also the issue of the time you would otherwise have to spend looking after them. You may already be looking after a parent or a spouse as you read this. If so, you know the demands it places on you. If you are able to plan for and put instruments in place to address the care of your parents or your spouse, you are actually buying time for your own retirement.

This type of planning does not mean that you do not care about your parents. It means that you can realize your retirement goals while knowing that things are looked after. You will know that your parents are receiving the kind of qualified care that they need. This allows the time that you share with your parents to be spent on the emotional and spiritual caring they need, rather than the physical or medical care that they require and that you are not qualified to deliver.

Add to the above fact that you may not live in the same city as your parents at the time when this care is required. Often, the caregiving duties fall upon the shoulders of one of the children in the family. This may be as a result of proximity or preference, or driven by gender. Care may become an obligation that is unequally shared. This unequal and often overwhelming distribution of duties can be lessened to a great extent through planning and by implementing some tools to address costing issues. For example, children could purchase LTC coverage in order to protect their inheritance and alleviate their feelings of obligation. Care for parents is a planning issue that should involve all family members.

The baby boomers are the first generation that will have to deal with aging parents who have such an extended life expectancy. There needs to be some intergenerational planning. It is not the easiest discussion to have, but from an emotional and stressful perspective it is far better to deal with these issues *before* care is needed rather than after the fact. And, it is far more efficient.

You may find it a tremendous advantage to have an advisor involved in family meetings. This will lessen the chance of misunderstanding in the discussions, and the advisor can act either as a resource, a facilitator, or both.

In addition to coverage for their parents, boomers should also be looking at this type of insurance for themselves. By acquiring this coverage earlier, boomers can obtain more benefit for a lower premium. Look at buying $300 of care per day now and having premiums stop by age 65, rather than waiting until age 65 and paying the same premiums throughout retirement for a $100-per-day benefit. Premiums are, of course, subject to change. Some people and advisors prefer those contracts that include a cap for maximum increases in premium. We may one day find that there is a point where guaranteed premiums are no longer offered by insurers.

SUMMARY OF THE HEALTH-RISK-MANAGEMENT CHANNEL AND THE PRIME APPROACH

There are two distinct purposes for the health-risk-management planning channel. First, it is designed to reduce or eliminate the use of your personal assets and income in covering the costs of health-related risks, including critical illness and long-term care. Second, it helps to ensure that your standard of living is protected for both the individual afflicted and the caregiver so that both of you can maintain your lifestyle and your dignity. Steps in this planning channel include:

- Identifying risk issues
- Relating to lifestyle (Time Hub) goals
- Assessing available program and funding options
- Establishing a course of action for contingencies
- Addressing power of attorney and health-care directives

So how many assets do you need to make health-risk planning come together? How can you provide the income you want, while at the same time fund CI/LTC and life insurance premiums? The answer varies. It may require a minimum amount of investable assets of $300,000 or $500,000, depending on how these assets are split between you and your spouse and on the percentage of holdings that are non-registered.

How do you use your accumulated retirement assets and benefits in the most effective manner? How do you maximize the enjoyment of your best retirement years? How do you prepare for health costs and ultimately transfer wealth to future generations? How can you do all of these things?

By understanding the relationship between your retirement income, your assets, and risk-management issues, you can enhance your best retirement years and still plan for future contingencies dealing with your future well-being and lifestyle. Your income and assets can be used for your retirement lifestyle, while insurance can cover off the risk contingencies for the least cost and greatest tax-efficiency.

One thing about human nature that I do not understand is this: Why are people eager to insure those things where there is a possibility of loss, but reluctant to insure against those events that are certainties?

Remember that it is the Time Hub priorities that drive our monetary decisions. To a large extent, health is the primary factor in establishing the other Time Hub priorities. You may enjoy your best retirement years by defining what it is you really want to do and then going about actually doing it. As you grow older and your health begins to deteriorate, other Time Hub priorities will become the major drivers of decisions and objectives, but health issues for you and your spouse will still be a large factor. Your focus may not be on planning the trip you want to take, so much as making sure you don't trip and hurt yourself.

From a Time Hub perspective, the boomers will have to deal with the issue of their aging parents and the care they need. This may involve a substantial number of years. The difficulty for the boomers is that they are used to fixing things. Declining health of a parent (or spouse) is something that does not have a fix to it. It must be managed. This may likely encroach upon that most precious of commodities for the boomers—their time—unless plans and financing alternatives are put in place before they're needed.

You may recall that two of the Time Hub priorities are safety and accommodations. As our health begins to fade, we may find greater comfort and safety provided by the familiar surroundings of our own home. The ability to receive home care will allow us the opportunity to remain in our house longer than would otherwise have been the case. By the same token, a single retiree living alone may not feel safe and secure in his or her own house and may wish to change residences. Priorities change as we go through the various stages of retirement. Our state of health may be one factor that causes us to feel unsafe and dictate that some changes are necessary in order that we may have the security we need.

At the beginning of this book, we used an example that we would like to revisit. The scenario was that of an 83-year-old retiree who just lost her partner of 55 years. We asked you to consider what her view of the future might be, how her Time Hub and Money Hub priorities may have changed, and how her priorities might continue to change as she loses her health. It is at this point that the future of her family and the generations to follow may matter more to her than her own. This leads us to the next planning channel, which deals with the transfer of wealth from one generation to another.

Wealth Transfer

The fourth planning channel deals with wealth transfer, also referred to as estate planning. If you are the beneficiary, this is your inheritance. If you are the person moving assets to future generations, this is your legacy. As we will discuss, the transfer of wealth can happen while the person is living or by direction of the will. By using an integrated planning model, both the lifestyle of the retiree and the ultimate estate to be transferred to heirs can be enhanced. This is one of the end results of the Prime Approach to retirement income planning.

Like any other section, this could be a book unto itself and there are many excellent books dedicated to this topic. It is not our intent to go into great detail on issues such as estate freezes, succession planning for your private business, etc., since this book is aimed at the average Canadian retirement situation. Certainly the wealth-transfer issues discussed here will apply to those in business or professional practices, just as will all of the principles and concepts in this book. Our hope is that the material contained within this chapter and the other parts of this book serve to create constructive discussions between client and advisor. Obviously every situation has its own unique needs and circumstances. The general issues discussed in this chapter are designed to foster further conversation on the key issues involved in this fourth planning channel.

We stated previously that there are three main reasons why people do not spend their money. First, they worry about running out of income. Second, they are concerned about funding health-care costs. Third, they want to leave a legacy. Integrated planning can provide solutions to these concerns and create more freedom for the retiree.

THE COMPOSITION OF YOUR ESTATE

Your estate is composed of all tangible assets owned by you or in which you have an interest:

- House/cottage
- Rental or other real estate
- Automobiles
- Jewellery and other personal possessions
- Art and other collectibles
- Antiques and other furnishings

It also includes all intangible assets owned by you or in which you have an interest:

- Bank accounts
- GICs/treasury bills
- Stocks/bonds/mutual funds
- Deferred annuities
- Business interests
- RRSP/RRIF/pension benefits
- Life insurance
- Tax-deferred investments

STAGES OF TRANSFER

Wealth transfer can actually happen in stages. You may make gifts of some of your assets while you are alive, and there is, of course, the ultimate transfer that occurs at passing. In the case of a married couple, there is a transfer of wealth at the first passing. Normally, everything transfers to the surviving spouse, although there may also be some special provisions in the will to move assets to other individuals.

Survivor Income Issues

As it relates to a couple in retirement, it is very important that you and your advisor know what will change with respect to income streams or assets at the passing of either partner.

- What specific changes will occur to household income and benefits at the passing of either spouse?
- Are there any sources of income that will disappear immediately?
- Are there any sources of income that will disappear over time? If so, when? By how much?
- Is asset ownership set up to allow simple and immediate transfer? Is this appropriate given other estate plans?
- Do registered assets have appropriate beneficiary designations?
- For a surviving spouse, should the estate or a charity be the beneficiary?
- Do RRIFs, LIFs, or LRIFs provide for continued payments or a lump-sum transfer to the surviving spouse?
- Are there any locked-in vehicles that can be transferred in non-locked form?
- What effect will this have on taxation now that income is only in the name of one person?

At the time one of the married partners passes away, Time Hub and Money Hub priorities change. This requires a review of overall planning and a redefinition of goals from this point forward. For reference in this chapter we refer to the point where one of two people passes away as the "disposition" stage of retirement planning. When the second of two people passes away we are in the "distribution" or wealth-transfer phase.

PLANNING FOR WEALTH TRANSFER
The general objectives of wealth transfer are listed below. Like any other aspect of dealing with your assets, your desired outcomes are more likely to be realized if planning is done in advance and the necessary action steps are implemented.

The general objectives of wealth transfer are to:

- Transfer assets to intended beneficiaries in an orderly and expedient manner
- Minimize taxes
- Reduce expenses and administration costs
- Maintain confidentiality

There are also more specific planning issues that serve as reasons for transfer. The resulting actions may be triggered while those transferring wealth are living, by direction of the will at death, or both.

Transfer During Lifetime (Inter Vivos)

There are many reasons why individuals or couples seek to gift or transfer assets out of their names while they are still living. Some of the reasons why this action may be taken include to:

- Transfer authority to maintain assets in event of incapacitation
- Potentially avoid appointment of a committee
- Reduce the number of financial decisions
- Control transition of ownership to the next generation
- Reduce taxes
- Lower income to reduce or eliminate the clawback of benefits
- Provide funding in the event of unforeseen disability
- Provide peace of mind by having things in order
- Provide money to heirs earlier (or fill a need on the heirs' part)

Transfer at Death (Testamentary)

The will becomes the master document for the transfer of assets at death. It becomes important that asset ownership and beneficiary designations are consistent with the intent and direction given in the will. Planning for orderly wealth transfer through the will accomplishes the following goals:

- Controls who administers the estate and how
- Controls disposition of assets
    * To whom
    * How much
    * When
- Minimizes taxes
- Creates legal structures, such as trusts
- Reduces estate expenses
- Designates a preferred guardian for underage children
- Provides for contingencies

METHODS FOR TRANSFERRING YOUR ASSETS

There are several ways in which assets can be moved out of your name and into the hands of others.

Sell

During your lifetime, you may transfer an asset for consideration. Whatever you may *actually* receive, the tax rules assume that you have received "fair market value" and may require you to pay tax on the sale of that asset accordingly.

Gift

Instead of selling, you may choose to gift an asset. There are no limitations on the gifts you may make. Again, for tax purposes, you are presumed to have received fair market value for the asset you have gifted. Suppose, for example, that you had an investment that had grown from $50,000 to $75,000 and decided to gift it to an adult child. You are deemed to have transferred it at fair market value ($75,000). You are therefore liable for the taxes payable on the $25,000 gain.

If you *give* an income-producing asset to a spouse or minor child, or to a trust for either (trusts will be discussed shortly), although the recipient actually receives the income, such income will be attributed to you for tax purposes. In any discussion of inter vivos gifting, we are referring to non-registered or open assets. You cannot gift registered vehicles without first de-registering them and paying the taxes. This defeats the purpose. Within the section on taxation some detail was spent on splitting income that does not involve gifting. Before making such gifts, you should get proper advice.

Charitable Giving

Charitable giving can produce significant tax saving benefits while you are alive and for your estate at your passing. There are many ways to make gifts to charitable causes. It is not the mandate of this section to detail all of them. Rather, we will focus on the tax issues related to such actions.

Charitable contributions are not a deduction from taxable income. They are calculated as a non-refundable tax credit in the following manner:

Amount of gift	$1,000
Credit for first $200 ($200 x 15.25%)	$ 32
Amount over $200 ($800 x 29%)	232
Federal tax credit	$ 264
(plus your provincial credit)	

Remember that a tax credit is a dollar-for-dollar offset of tax payable. You are allowed to combine or pool your charitable contributions with your spouse and claim them under one name. This saves having to satisfy the lower $200 threshold twice. The end result to you is a larger tax credit for the higher-income earner.

While living you are allowed to claim a maximum of 75 percent of your net income as a charitable donation. You can also choose *when* to actually claim the credit and determine *how much* you wish to use. You have a carryforward for up to five years.

If the gift is made at death or through the will, the maximum amount moves to 100 percent of net income for the year. Since there is obviously no opportunity for carryforward if this is the final tax return, application can be made to apply any unused donation to your tax return for the year preceding the year of death, to a maximum of 100 percent of net income.

We have seen situations when a retiree would like to make a contribution to a charitable cause and provides direction in their will to do so. Normally, it will state in the will that a specific amount is to be paid from the estate to the charity involved. With recent changes in legislation, it is now possible to designate charities as the direct beneficiaries of registered assets (RRSPs, RRIFs, LIFs, LRIFs, etc.). This allows money to flow directly to the charity and avoid passing through the estate. The value of registered money is fully taxable to the estate as income in the year of passing (we are assuming no spousal rollover here). You are allowed to make charitable gifts up to 100 percent of net income in the year of passing and the previous year. There are many options to explore for charitable giving, and these can be investigated with your advisor.

Recent changes to the gifting rules, by completely eliminating the tax on any accrued capital gains, now encourage the donation of publicly traded securities (including mutual funds and segregated funds) to charities. This creates an even greater win for both the receiving charitable organization and the estate of the donor.

Note: Although deductions for gifts to charities are generally restricted to 75 percent of net income in any year, gifts may be fully deductible under special provincial statutes, like donations of certified works of art under the Cultural Property Export and Import Act (Canada). Gifts made by individuals in the year of their death and the preceding year (including bequests or legacies) may be equal to 100 percent of net income.

Trusts

You may prefer to transfer an asset, during your lifetime or on your death, to a trust for someone rather than directly to the person. A trust is an ownership structure whereby a trustee or trustees hold title to an asset that you have contributed for the benefit of some other person. Frequently a trust is created to:

- Maintain control of how assets are spent or disposed of
- Pay funds out over time
- Protect assets for someone who is a minor
- Effect an estate freeze to reduce taxes
- Protect assets and provide income for someone who is otherwise incapacitated
- Provide for the management of your estate, while living, if you feel you can no longer take care of it yourself

These objectives can be accomplished while still allowing considerable flexibility or discretion to the trustees. If the intended beneficiary of the trust is receiving government assistance, it is particularly important that the benefit to that person be available only at the discretion of the trustees. Because many factors should be addressed in establishing a trust for handicapped or other assisted persons, you should seek professional advice first.

Since June of 2001, individuals and couples over the age of 65 have been able to use a form of trust known as an Alter Ego/Joint Partner trust. This is a form of inter vivos trust that may work in tandem with or as a complement to other estate-planning tools you are using to achieve your objectives. Whether this or any trust vehicle is appropriate is a discussion for you, your advisor, and your lawyer.

Taxation of Trusts

In establishing a trust, the assets transferred into an inter vivos trust will trigger a deemed disposition. The same applies to a testamentary trust when it is not a spousal trust. In a testamentary spousal trust the rollover provisions apply and there is no required deemed disposition on the growth of transferred assets.

Trusts are required to file a separate tax return by March 31 if they have a December 31 year-end. For inter vivos trusts, any income earned is taxed at the highest marginal rate. Income earned in a testamentary trust is taxed at the same graduated rates as the income of an individual taxpayer. Neither of these trusts has the benefit of either personal exemptions or non-refundable credits.

In this regard, setting up a spousal trust serves the purpose of ultimately lowering the tax that will be paid on income-producing assets. For example, if half of your estate is left to your spouse and half to a spousal trust, the end result is income split between two taxpayers. This will likely result in some meaningful tax savings. The merits of this will depend upon the amount of money involved and the ongoing costs of maintaining the trust. Any process, however, that has the potential to save taxes is worth investigating.

Note: Any consideration of establishing a trust should include discussions with appropriate legal and tax specialists.

WEALTH TRANSFER AT DEATH

Transfer by "Operation of Law"

Some assets may transfer directly to another person on your death, not passing through the estate. This is called a transfer by operation of law. The main benefits of this are that there are no probate or administration costs that would otherwise be applicable if the assets first passed through the estate. There are two primary strategies to use to undertake a transfer by operation of law.

Joint Tenancy

Joint tenancy occurs when property is held in the name of more than one person. On the passing of one of the owners, it automatically passes to the survivor. The law provides that in the case of a common disaster where both owners are killed, and it is impossible to determine which person died first, the younger of the two is deemed to have survived the older. As such, the ultimate estate distribution would be as per the will of the younger person.

Joint with Rights of Survivor

If assets are owned "joint with rights of survivor," then the deceased's interest in the property will transfer to the surviving owner. This is done automatically without going through the will, the estate, or probate. Care needs to be taken in all ownership registration if the ultimate objective is to have some of the deceased's assets go into a testamentary trust.

Named Beneficiaries

A person can designate a named beneficiary for life insurance, RRSPs/RRIFs, or other pension benefits. At the person's death, such proceeds or benefits will be paid directly to the named beneficiary if he/she survives the person. Non-registered assets do not have the same opportunity to name a beneficiary and allow for this type of transfer. The exception to this is for an asset held with an insurance company. In the case of non-registered segregated funds and deferred annuities (insurance company GICs), a beneficiary can be named and a transfer by operation of law can occur. This is because these assets are governed by the Insurance Act, which makes provision for the naming of a beneficiary on non-registered holdings.

The advantage of transfer by operation of law is that in either situations of joint tenancy or joint with rights of survivor, property is deemed to have passed outside of the estate. This will reduce probate fees, legal fees, and executor's fees, and transfer should happen without delay. Some assets passing outside of the estate are secure from claims of the deceased's creditors.

Be careful with beneficiary designations on RRSP/RRIF and pension benefits if they are not being transferred to a surviving spouse. It may result in substantial income attributed to you at your passing, even though the proceeds are actually paid elsewhere. The resulting taxes may significantly reduce your estate available to other beneficiaries. An example may be where you have named a favourite niece as the beneficiary of your RRSPs, while leaving other estate assets to your children. Your niece will receive the value of your RRSP, but the tax liability will fall to you as income in the year of your passing. The tax bill will then be settled from the values in your estate, not by your niece. This will serve to reduce the inheritance to your children and likely not make them very fond of their cousin.

Transfer by Probate

Probate refers to the transfer of one's assets on death through one's estate. A person may die without a will (intestate) or with a will (testate).

Without a Will (Intestate)

If you die without a will, those assets subject to probate will be distributed according to provincial laws. The range of intestacy laws varies from province to province. Some examples follow. These figures change frequently and are believed to be current at the time of writing.

Province	Lump Sum to Spouse	Remainder to Spouse	Remainder to Children
British Columbia	$65,000	one-third	two-thirds
Alberta	$40,000	one-third	two-thirds
Saskatchewan	$100,000	one-third	two-thirds
Manitoba	$50,000	one-half	one-half
Ontario	$200,000	one-third	two-thirds
Quebec	——	one-third	two-thirds
New Brunswick	——	one-third	two-thirds
Nova Scotia	$50,000	one-third	two-thirds
P.E.I.	$50,000	one-third	two-thirds
Newfoundland and Labrador	——	one-third	two-thirds

Intestacy laws do not take into account the sentimental value of your belongings, non-spouse or non-child relationships, or other emotional factors. They do not consider any special needs situations or implications of such things as second marriages and families.

With a Will (Testate)

A will allows you to direct who will administer your estate, to whom it will be distributed, when and what amounts will be distributed, or under what circumstances the distribution(s) will take place. If you have a will, probate simply executes the instructions you have given in the will.

Advantages of having a properly drawn and current will include:

- Choice of personal representative
- Stated preference of guardian for minor children
- Ability to select the powers/flexibility of executor
- Ability to provide for situations when a beneficiary predeceases the individual, or other potential contingencies
- Opportunity for gifts to charities and non-blood relatives
- Ability to address assets in other jurisdictions
- Ability to distribute assets exactly as you wished
- Direction for creation of testamentary trust(s)
- Reduction of tax payable from properly transferred assets
- Fewer costs of estate administration than if you die intestate

The will is the most basic yet important financial tool. It is essential that you maintain a current and valid will that defines exactly what it is you wish to do with your assets. The cost of having a basic will properly and correctly drafted is minimal ($150 to $250). The costs for not having a will are substantial. We know there are will kits and signed napkins, etc. Go to a lawyer and have this done properly. It is worth the effort.

COSTS OF PROBATING A WILL

The following information is subject to change and believed to be current at the time of writing.

	Estate Value	Cost
British Columbia	First $10,000	No fee
	$10,001 to $25,000	$208
	$25,001 to $50,000	0.60%
	Over $50,000	1.40%
Alberta	Under $10,000	$25
	$10,001 to $249,999	Progressive to $300
	Over $250,000	$400 maximum

	Estate Value	Cost
Saskatchewan	All estates	0.70%
Manitoba	First $10,000	$50
	Over $10,000	$50 + 0.60%
Ontario	First $50,000	0.50%
	Over $50,000	1.50%
Quebec	Notarial wills	No fee
	Holograph/witnessed	$80
New Brunswick	First $5,000	$25
	$5,001 to $20,000	Progressive to $100
	Over $20,000	0.50%
Nova Scotia	First $10,000	$75
	$10,001 to $200,000	Progressive to $800
	Each $1,000 thereafter	$5
P.E.I.	First $10,000	$50
	$10,001 to $100,000	Progressive to $400
	Over $100,000	$400 + 0.40%
Newfoundland and Labrador	All estates	$75 + 0.50%

Problems with Probate

When estates go through probate, survivors/beneficiaries may have to wait 6 to 12 months or longer to gain access to most of the property. Probate fees, in addition to court fees, lawyer's fees, accounting fees, and executor's fees, can average from 3 percent to 7 percent of the value of the estate. In addition, the public has access to probate files.

TAXATION ON ESTATES

You may have definite plans on how you would like to see your assets transferred. However, you have a third party who also has great interest in the transfer of your wealth. That is the tax department or Canada Revenue Agency (CRA), as it is now known.

Income taxes are due and payable with the filing of the final tax return of the deceased. The return is due six months after the date of death, or April 30 of the following year, whichever is later. Amounts owing will be a combination of taxes payable from income and the resulting tax realized upon transfer of assets.

Deemed Disposition at Death

You are deemed to have sold all assets immediately prior to your death for fair market value, even though this may not, in fact, have occurred. Any tax liability is calculated by subtracting the adjusted cost base from the deemed fair market value and adding back in any recaptured depreciation if applicable. Spousal rollover provisions may defer this taxation, but only until the passing of the second spouse.

The taxable amount is added to any other income received during the year of death.

Lifetime Capital Gains Exemption

The amount of tax liability may be reduced if the source of this tax is from the deemed disposition of shares of a Canadian-controlled private corporation or a family farm corporation. The exemption applies to $500,000 of capital gains from these sources. Various restrictions and conditions apply. This can be a cumulative claim occurring over several transactions throughout your lifetime.

Spousal Rollover Provisions

There is no deemed disposition if the assets are bequeathed to a spouse or spousal trust. This is only a deferral and ultimately there will be a disposition at a future date. The tax liability will be even greater at that time if the assets have grown in value. The rollover can be waived and an election can be made to have the deemed disposition triggered at the time of transfer if so desired.

Taxation of Registered Money

As previously discussed in Chapter 2, registered plans allow money within them to accrue and grow on a tax-deferred basis. During the contribution phase, you are allowed to deduct, from your taxable income, the amount contributed. Plans that act as accumulation vehicles for registered money include:

- Registered retirement savings plans (RRSPs)
- Registered pension plans (RPPs)
- Deferred profit sharing plans (DPSPs)
- Individual pension plans (IPPs)

When the time comes to draw regular, periodic income from these plans, they are converted to one of the following forms:

- Registered retirement income funds (RRIFs)
- Annuities certain to age 90
- Life annuity*
- Life income funds (LIFs)*
- Locked-in retirement funds (LRIFs)*—in some provinces
  *The only options for pension or locked-in funds.

All of the above vehicles carry with them one distinct feature. They all house money that has been deducted from income and has been allowed to grow on a tax-deferred basis. With this, there comes a time when a substantial amount of tax may be payable if this money is suddenly de-registered into the estate.

As we have seen, there is a provision for all registered accounts to be rolled over to a spouse, if named as the beneficiary, without triggering a taxable disposition. However, at the passing of the last spouse, the entire balance of all registered accounts is treated as income in the year of passing and the amounts are taxed accordingly in the final tax return. Substantial amounts of tax may then be realized.

USING DISCOUNTED DOLLARS TO FUND THE TAX LIABILITY

The previous chapter examined the concept of using discounted dollars—having insurance cover off contingencies and liabilities for pennies on the dollar. For purposes of paying taxes in an estate, the use of insurance becomes a very practical consideration. The following example is an application of this concept. The use of life insurance in wealth-transfer strategies will be discussed in more detail later in this chapter.

Let's use an example of a married couple that has a total of $250,000 as a balance in their registered accounts at the time of the second passing. This would result in taxes payable of approximately $125,000 when included as income in the final tax return. The good news is that the tax can be paid from the $250,000 that comes into the estate. The bad news is that the $125,000 in tax is money your children and grandchildren will not inherit.

We find that many people are not aware of how taxation is applied to registered money when it flows to the estate. The thought of that much money and that percentage of your estate being lost to tax is quite unsettling to many people. Yet, you are not being treated in an unfair way by government. Because you are able to deduct RRSP contributions and because the growth on registered accounts is deferred, you have not been taxed on this money. When this capital flows through the estate, the tax department is paid what is due to them. There are several ways to address this issue.

Insure the Tax Liability

You could put in place a joint life insurance contract with benefit payable on second passing that is equal to the estimated amount of the tax liability. The premium outlay will be substantially less than $125,000. The following examples show the annual premiums required to deliver $125,000 tax-free to the estate at the second passing. Why do we want a benefit to be paid at the second passing? Because that is when the tax liability occurs.

Age of Couple	Annual Premium to Second Passing
72 & 70	$2,664
65 & 63	$1,566
55 & 53	$787

By putting this in place, you are letting the insurance company pay the tax bill and passing the full value of your estate to your heirs. For an increase in premium of approximately 15 percent per year, the plan could be structured so that premiums ceased at first death, with the benefit payable at the second passing. Obviously, the earlier a couple enters into this strategy, the lower the premium amounts. Forms of limited pay life and universal life contracts will allow for the coverage to be fully paid within a defined period of time, thereby negating the obligation of an ongoing premium.

Insure the Inheritance

If the objective is to have your registered assets form part of the wealth transfer, there is another way to look at this issue. The only reason that a large tax liability exists in the previous example is that there was still $250,000 of RRSP/RRIF money. If no action had been taken to insure the tax liability, the heirs would receive $125,000 after tax. If you're not interested in insuring the tax liability, consider this approach.

1. Buy insurance equal to the amount that would be left over after tax. In this example, that's $125,000. Since the life insurance benefit is tax free, your children are in exactly the same financial position as if you had the $250,000 RRSP/RRIF intact.
2. Since you have structured the inheritance, spend your RRSP/RRIF money.

This follows along the concept of the Prime Approach. Cover off objectives of health-risk management and wealth transfer with the most cost-efficient, tax-efficient tools, and use your own assets to help you do those things you wish to do in your retirement years. You may even wish to gift some of your assets while you are still living, knowing that there is an inheritance that will be delivered. This planning approach provides you with more freedom in how you choose to use your assets.

Don't use your own assets for health-risk management or wealth transfer if you don't need to. Use your assets for you.

USING LIFE INSURANCE

Life insurance is one of the most cost-efficient and tax-efficient tools we have to work with. We have already detailed the concept of using discounted dollars. Life insurance may be used to pay taxes on a discounted basis or to provide an inheritance. In either capacity, it serves to enhance the value of other estate assets. There are many reasons why we initially purchase life insurance.

- Create an estate
- Replace income
- Protect family lifestyle
- Eliminate debts and expenses at death
- Cover taxes at death
- Fulfill business purposes
- Maximize pension
- Tax-shelter the accumulation of capital

Often, retirees will question why they would need to or want to have any life insurance. After all, there is likely no mortgage or debt to service. Their children have made their own lives (hopefully). They have already built an estate with the assets they have accumulated and there is no earned income to replace.

However, there are many reasons to keep and acquire life insurance after you are retired. The following are some of the more important considerations.

- Your group life insurance usually discontinues or reduces. You will find that one of the options you have when you leave your employer is to convert some or all of your group life insurance coverage without qualifying medically. This can be a great benefit if your health does not permit you to buy coverage or you cannot qualify for insurance without the addition of a premium rating. However, if your health is good, you should see what kind of life coverage you can obtain on your own. The reason for this is that non-medical issue, which is the coverage provided in group conversions, is priced higher than standard issue coverage. Check with your advisor to see what can be done independently before electing to convert your group coverage. You usually have 31 days within which to convert your group insurance. It would be wise to explore this possibility well in advance of leaving your employer.
- You may wish to have insurance in place to cover the costs of final expenses. This would be used to cover off funeral costs, as well as estate settlement and administrative costs. The offerings on television, with no medical to pass and no agent to call, are fine if you cannot otherwise acquire coverage. But, you should check to

see what you could qualify for through your advisor. You do not get
something for nothing from the insurance industry, and non-medical,
guaranteed-issue coverage is extremely expensive when compared
to standard-issue coverage. You may also wish to know that there
are options to non-medical, guaranteed-issue insurance other than
the company that advertises on television. Your advisor can help you
investigate all of the options related to life insurance.

- Having insurance in place or acquiring it could give you more
flexibility in choosing your pension income option if you are
purchasing an annuity. The concept of pension maximization was
discussed in Chapter 2.
- Insurance serves as a method of using discounted dollars to pay
taxes either on capital property or registered assets. Rather than use
$100.00 to pay for a future obligation, pay $0.01 or $0.02 a year for
the insurance needed to pay the obligation.
- Some people use cash-value life insurance as a mechanism to shelter
non-registered money. Although this is one use for some contracts,
there are other options available to accomplish this that don't have
a cost of insurance involved. There is also the issue of how cash
withdrawals are treated for tax purposes when withdrawn from
the contract. If your objective is to increase estate values and the
ultimate wealth transfer, insurance may be your best choice. As with
other financial decisions, consider all the options only after you have
determined exactly what it is you wish to accomplish.
- Insurance can be used to provide an ultimate gift to a charity. This
may be done through acquiring new coverage or by naming the
charity as a beneficiary on an existing contract.
- If life insurance is in place to cover off estate tax liabilities, it allows
you to have more freedom in using your income-producing assets.
- Life insurance may be used to balance or equalize inheritance values.
- Insurance may be used to increase or multiply the value of an estate.
Once again, if there are redundant assets, it is worth investigating the
use of those assets to fund the premium on a life insurance contract.
This will serve, on a very tax-effective basis, to enhance estate values.
- Life insurance may be used to replace assets used to cover health-
risk costs if critical illness or long-term-care coverage is not in place.

Obviously there need to be assets available to cover such medical costs. Life insurance, at the passing of the planholder, would inject a tax-free sum into the estate to replace those assets that were used.

Premiums

Insurance may be the best financial tool to use for covering costs associated with critical illness or long-term care, or to cover estate taxes. Money is required for premiums, but this expenditure is a way of reducing ultimate costs and preserving assets. The premiums can be financed in several ways.

- Cash flow of the retirees
- Redundant assets—asset exchange, taking assets from non-registered holdings
- Children could contribute some or all of the premiums

Insurance coverage properly used in planning should not be viewed as an expense. It should serve as a way to free up your other assets for you to use in your retirement.

REDUCING TAXES AND OTHER ESTATE EXPENSES

Whether you die with or without a will, your estate may be liable for probate filing fees, legal and accounting expenses, and fees for personal representative(s) administering the estate. As shown previously, probate fees are a percentage of the assets transferred through your estate on your passing. You may wish to consider the following to help reduce such expenses:

- Consider gifting or transferring your assets during your lifetime.
- Create a trust to hold some or all of your assets.
- Designate a named beneficiary to allow insurance, RRSP, RRIF, and pension benefits to pass outside of your estate.

In order to reduce taxes payable on death:

- Use available rollovers to spouse or to children, or spousal trusts.
- Maximize use of remaining capital gains exemptions.
- Bring about an estate freeze in your lifetime to reduce the value of assets held on death.

- Consider gifts to foundations or charities, including gifts of cultural property (see the Charitable Giving section, pages 231-233).

ADDITIONAL ESTATE-PLANNING TOOLS

A written will is not the only estate-planning document of importance. The two instruments listed below allow you to give specific direction according to your wishes should you be alive but unable to communicate or act competently on your own behalf. Much like your will, these need to be established well in advance, while you are able to act competently. Changes can be made to these documents as time goes on, but again only if you are deemed competent to do so.

Financial Power of Attorney

Proper estate planning includes a power of attorney, signed while you are well, designating another person to look after your assets while you are alive. Such an attorney might do your banking, manage your investments, and file your tax returns in the event that you are incapacitated, absent from the country, or otherwise unable to attend to such matters yourself.

Should you become incapacitated without having appointed an attorney, an Application to Court will be required, at considerable time and expense, to name a committee to look after your affairs. In some circumstances, the public trustee may take on that role. By signing a power of attorney now, you may avoid such complications.

Living Will (Health-Care Directive)

This instrument gives advance written instructions on medical treatment you would or wouldn't want, should a time come when you become unable to make decisions or communicate. It also lets you name someone to make medical decisions on your behalf if you become incapable.

In this way you have peace of mind in knowing that your wishes will be carried out, even if you are unable to convey them. It also relieves others from the stress of having to guess what your wishes might be. You should be aware that there are certain differences in format between provinces.

It is recommended that you review your living will on an annual basis. Having done so, you should initial and date it so that your doctor is confident that these are your current wishes. It would be appropriate for your doctor to have a copy of your directive in his or her file. For details on establishing a health-care directive, contact your doctor.

SUMMARY OF THE WEALTH-TRANSFER CHANNEL AND THE PRIME APPROACH

The topic of moving money forward to future generations involves a great deal of emotion and a very substantial range of objectives. There may be a desire at the outset of planning to move wealth forward to children and grandchildren with specific objectives in mind. This may be driven by the fact that certain children in a family situation were given special assistance earlier in life when they needed it most. In these cases, there is usually a desire to balance the ledger and treat everyone equally. Other times, there may be an objective to equalize a family inheritance as a result of certain children receiving non-divisible property such as a cottage, family business, or farm.

The purpose of the wealth-transfer segment is to plan for the ultimate transfer and disposition of your assets in an orderly manner, consistent with your objectives and with a bias to minimizing estate taxes. Elements of this planning channel include:

- Listing your assets and your spouse's assets, if applicable, held individually or jointly
- Determining your tax liability
- Determining your obligations to your spouse or other dependants
- Defining your objectives (who gets how much, when) if:
    * you predecease your spouse
    * your spouse predeceases you
    * you die together
    * any intended beneficiary dies before receiving his or her share of your estate
- Assessing your options for transferring assets
  During your lifetime:
    * transfers for value
    * trusts
    * gifts
    * gifts to charities
    * power of attorney

> * estate freeze or other orderly transfer of business

Upon death:

> * what goes to whom, and when
> * rollovers to spouse or spousal trust
> * trust for minors or other testamentary trusts
> * trusts for special needs beneficiaries
> * gifts to charities or foundations
> * estate equalization
> * reduction of exposure of assets to probate

- Reconsidering your tax liability
- Satisfying your tax liability (if any)
  > * life insurance
  > * reserve or sinking fund
  > * sale of estate assets
- Documenting the plan
  > * ensuring your will is current and consistent with your objectives
  > * establishing a power of attorney
  > * considering a living will
  > * listing location and description of assets, important papers, and names of advisors, and advising heirs where these are located

The Time Hub priorities drive the Money Hub decisions. Although initially many clients decide not to worry about leaving a legacy, we quite often see a change in attitude as these same clients grow older. There does become a desire to "leave something behind" in order to be remembered. This is not to suggest that people will be forgotten if they do not leave something of monetary value. However, the ability to send wealth forward seems to enhance the belief that there will be an even stronger memory that will live on after they are gone. It is the one thing that people can do in an attempt to leave a legacy. Consider that providing an inheritance has an ongoing effect on those who receive the money. This ongoing benefit to the heirs or recipients, in the form of assets and/or wealth, is a way of living on after they have departed.

The desire to do something for which they will be remembered gets stronger as individuals get older and closer to a time when they may not be here much longer. This is a Time Hub priority often driven by a combination of love and self-actualization. This act of perpetuating their presence through providing an inheritance becomes a personal goal. It may also be done out of a desire to continue the memory of a partner who has already passed away.

Tax planning also drives a great number of wealth-transfer decisions. Why not see your family and heirs receive as many of the benefits of your life's work as possible? It is a case of "better them than the government." Or at least we would hope that is the case.

Why should there be some consideration for leaving an inheritance? Often retirees will say that their kids are better off today than they ever were. The children may have higher paying jobs or careers and larger houses, but they also have more debt, and current retirees had certain advantages that benefited them greatly. They:

- Received huge benefits from the Canada Pension Plan relative to contributions
- Benefited from soaring home values through the 1970s and 1980s
- Received the best of the health-care system
- Experienced lower levels of taxation throughout their lives
- Forwarded a gigantic national debt
- Did not have to deal with the pressures of global competitiveness

We do not say this to insult those who are in their 70s, 80s, and beyond, nor do we begrudge them those benefits received. Current retirees worked hard to be where they are, fought wars, and went through the Great Depression. But as Chief Seattle said at the beginning of the last century: "We do not inherit the world from our ancestors; we borrow it from our children."

And the world going forward is going to be even more demanding for the children and grandchildren of current retirees than it was for them. Asian and European cultures emphasize passing wealth forward as a function of giving future generations a better opportunity to deal with a more competitive world economy. Should it be any different here?

PART THREE

Putting the Prime Approach to Work

CHAPTER SIX

Conclusion

IN SUMMARY

The introduction of this book referred to three key components that need to come together in order for this book to work for you and make your retirement more fulfilling.

1. Gain Awareness of the Process—and Yourself

The process is really quite straightforward. It begins with defining your Time Hub and Money Hub priorities. Identifying what is important to you and determining when and how to go about realizing your objectives are essential if you wish to make the best use of your assets and your time. Do you really know yourself? Do you really know what you want to do? The data forms that follow in the back of this book are designed to assist you and your advisor in setting the Time Hub and Money Hub priorities that are the essence of the Prime Approach.

Once this is done, the next step is having an integrated plan designed specifically for you. Your priorities in both of the hubs will change over time as you go through different stages of retirement, and your plan will need to be adjusted. When you look at your plan, you'll quickly realize that the use of your income and assets for lifestyle becomes a more practical possibility when health-risk cost issues and wealth-transfer objectives are satisfied in ways that do not involve using your retirement capital.

2. Align Yourself with an Advisor

The value of an advisor is an often-underestimated factor in the success of your financial objectives. However, very few advisors specialize in retirement *income* planning. You should know how much time your advisor or prospective advisor works in this area. It is also important that you work with someone who can assist you either directly or through his or her team with all four of the planning channels.

Fee-for-service, commission-based, and fee-based planners all have common professional designations and must abide by the same code of ethics. There are excellent advisors working in each of these compensation models.

The data forms provided after this section serve as additional tools and discussion points when working with your advisor. If your advisor has introduced this book and this concept to you, work through this material with him or her. The forms and checklists are a key component in the planning and communication process between you and your advisor. That is why they are part of this book.

3. Put the Plan into Action

You may have defined the Time Hub and Money Hub priorities in conjunction with your advisor, and you may have in your possession a comprehensive, integrated written plan that has been prepared as a blueprint just for you. If you are not prepared to implement those steps that are necessary to put the plan into effect, then all you have done has been an exercise in wishful thinking.

There is some effort that must go into getting meaningful results. We don't know of very many human endeavours where this is not the case. Whether you are a boomer or a parent of a boomer, there are no doubt significant planning points, concepts, and strategies in this book that have merit for you. You have spent an entire lifetime accumulating assets to use when you retire, but the capital assets and income streams you possess do not come with an owner's manual. Hopefully this book has, to some degree, served in this capacity. But, this knowledge should be used to enhance your understanding of the process and the working relationship and interaction you have with your advisor.

CLOSING WORDS

Many years ago I was flipping through a magazine and I stumbled across an ad that covered the two centre pages of the publication. I can't remember the name of the magazine, and I cannot recall what company placed the ad. But I have never forgotten the message.

The picture spanning the two pages of this ad was that of a grand piano, draped with a white dust cover, sitting in a beautiful, sun-lit atrium filled with lush green plants and flowers. The left-hand page said something like this:

I decided not to learn how to play the piano, because
I heard that it took 10 years to learn to play it well.

The right-hand page concluded the statement:

Unfortunately, I made that decision 10 years ago.

The point of sharing this with you is quite simple. You need to pull things together, get some help, do some planning, and most importantly take action. And, you need to do this now. Planning is of no value if no action is taken. So many times we meet people who say, "I wish I would have done that," or "I wish I would have known that," or "I wish I would have met you...10 years ago." The implication is that if they could only go back, they would have planned better, done things differently, and, in so doing, have realized better results. You can't turn back the clock, but you can rewind it.

Now is the time to take action on the concepts you have seen in this book, so that 10 years from now you do not have to be lamenting about what you could have done—you will have done it! It is never too late for constructive planning to make a meaningful difference as long as you implement the planning steps that are designed to get you to where you want to be.

As stated at the outset of this book, the intention of this work is not to be the definitive technical resource for each of the four planning channels. Each of the four areas could easily be a book unto itself. It is, however, our desire to have this book serve as a conceptual resource. If there is one area of particular interest for you, it is our hope that this book will serve as a catalyst to push you to investigate that subject further.

Our ultimate goal is to give you some insight into how the four planning areas do work, can work, and should work together in an integrated fashion. The key objective of integrated planning is to allow retirees the opportunity to fulfill their life goals during their best retirement years while addressing health-risk contingencies and wealth-transfer objectives in the most cost-efficient and tax-efficient manner. This is how you can use money to buy time.

The principles outlined in this material apply not only to those in the baby boomer demographic but to their parents as well. If your parents are able to realize their Time Hub and Money Hub priorities in the best way, then there will be some very important results for them, and for you, too.

1. They will enjoy their retirement years to the maximum.
2. They will feel secure, knowing that plans are in place for their future.
3. You will have the knowledge that there are mechanisms in place regarding their care as they become older.
4. You can accomplish the above without seeing your inheritance go to pay for care facilities and/or for taxation.

That said, all of the knowledge and planning in the world doesn't count for much until action is taken. This is one of the main reasons that we urge you to work with a qualified planner, ideally one who specializes in the area of retirement *income* planning.

Work with this book and your advisor to implement an integrated planning strategy to get the most out of your retirement experience. It should be the best time of your life. Using what you've learned about the four planning channels and the Prime Approach will enable you to enjoy your time and money, rather than worry about it, and that should be the reward you expect after a lifetime of work. May your retirement be, as it truly deserves to be, the best time of your life.

DATA FORMS

The accuracy and detail with which this information is completed will determine the quality of the report that your advisor is able to prepare on your behalf. Please take the time to review and carefully answer the questions in this profile.

INFORMATION GATHERING–PART ONE

There are two types of information required. The first type deals with some personal data and includes an inventory of statements and documents. The most recent copies of the following are required. You may not have certain items, but please collect as many of them as you can.

Document Checklist

_____Current written financial plan

_____Current Investment Policy Statement

_____Copy of your current, written financial plan

_____CPP statement of contributions (may be ordered from HRSDC)

_____Current investment statements for mutual funds, GICs, etc.

_____Statements of debt servicing (mortgages, loans)

_____Income tax returns

_____CRA notice of assessment

_____Statements and booklet of employer-sponsored programs (retirement, life insurance, and health benefits)

_____Will

_____Power of attorney and health-care directive

_____Life and health insurance contracts

Personal Information

Name	Date of Birth	SIN	Sex
Client _____	_____	_____	_____
Spouse _____	_____	_____	_____

Address

Home _____ Postal Code _____

Home Phone _____ Email _____

Employer

Client _____ Phone _____ Ext. _____

Spouse _____ Phone _____ Ext. _____

Children

Name _____ Age _____

Grandchildren Number? Names? _____

Name _____ Age _____

Grandchildren Number? Names? _____

Name _____ Age _____

Grandchildren Number? Names? _____

Name _____ Age _____

Grandchildren Number? Names? _____

Income from Last Year	Client	Spouse
Earned _____	$ _____	$ _____
Investment _____	$ _____	$ _____
Rental _____	$ _____	$ _____
Trust _____	$ _____	$ _____
Other _____	$ _____	$ _____
Total _____	$ _____	$ _____

INFORMATION GATHERING—PART TWO

Initial Considerations

What is your projected retirement date? _____

Why is this the time you have chosen? _____

Will your spouse retire or be retired at the same time? _____

If not, when? _____

What percentage of your final year's earnings would you like to see as your initial retirement income?

You _____ %   Spouse_____%

Or

What is the total amount of monthly after-tax income you think you will require when retirement begins? $ _____

Do you expect any rental or employment income after your retirement date? If so, what is the amount, how long will it last, and in whose name will it be received? _____

_____

Is there any potential for an inheritance in the future? If so, what are the details? _____

_____

Are you servicing any debts or mortgages? _____

Institution_____ Balance Remaining $ _____

Amount/Frequency of Payment_____

Date of Final Payment _____

Once you are retired, what are your plans for your principal residence?

_____

How many months of the year do you plan to reside outside of Canada?

_____

Do you have any major concerns as you approach retirement?

_____

_____

_____

Do you anticipate making a major purchase at the time you start your retirement that will require a lump sum of capital or a repayment commitment? If yes, please provide details.

_____

_____

What would you like to do in these years?

_____

_____

_____

How much additional income do you feel this would require?
$ _____

Would you like to explore options that involve creating additional income in the earlier years of retirement? _____

Do you feel that you have a good understanding of finances? _____

Are there any other family members who should be involved in the planning process? _____

_____

How would you describe your current state of health? _____

How would you describe your spouse's current state of health? _____

Do you know how much the survivor income pensions will be when you or your spouse pass away?_____

Do either you or your spouse smoke tobacco products?
You _____ Spouse _____

Taxes and Tax Planning

Do you understand the difference in tax treatment for interest, dividends, and capital gains? _____

What percentage of your assets would you estimate are non-registered (tax-exposed)? _____%

If you and your spouse have been splitting assets, what is the approximate percentage that is held in each name? You _____ % Spouse ____%

What would you estimate to be your marginal tax rate on your current income? You _____ % Spouse ____%

Your Government Retirement Benefits

Have you made contributions to CPP? You _____ Spouse _____

If yes, for how many years since 1966? You _____ Spouse _____

If you are already in receipt of a CPP survivor or disability benefit, please provide details.

_____

_____

Employer-Sponsored Retirement Programs/Pension Plans

Do you know what type of annuity is being used to show future amounts of retirement income in your pension statement? _____

Do you or your spouse have locked-in accounts from previous pension plans? _____

If yes, would you be interested in exploring options for unlocking some of this money prior to retirement? _____

Registered Retirement Savings Plans

What amount of annual RRSP contributions do you plan to make until retirement?
You $_____ Spouse $_____

Amount of unused RRSP contribution room:
You $_____ Spouse $_____

Amount of RRSP overcontribution (if any):
You $_____ Spouse $_____

If you are making contributions to a spousal plan, when was the last contribution made? _____

_____

Income from Non-Registered Assets

Are you currently letting taxable distributions or interest stay within the investments or are you having these taxable amounts paid out as income?

_____

Are you familiar with the substantial tax advantages of mutual fund corporations? _____

Investing for Retirement Income

Are you aware of the significant impact that even a small difference in rates of return have over an extended period of time? _____

Do you know the rate of return on all of your investment holdings? _____
If yes, what is it? _____ %

What do you estimate the average rate of inflation will be over your retirement years? _____ %

Have you ever had someone look at your situation and structure an investment portfolio tailored to you? _____

What percentage of your assets is invested in:
Stocks? _____% Bonds? _____% GICs? _____% Cash? _____%

Can you describe the current investment strategy that is in place for your assets? _____
_____

Has this been done with consideration to ALL of your assets, including your pension and your government benefits? _____

Do you have an investment policy statement (IPS) in place? _____

Do you currently have all of your assets consolidated with one advisor or institution? _____

If not, why not? _____

Is the timing right to consider consolidating your assets? Why?
_____
_____

What do you expect from the person who advises you on your portfolio management? _____
_____

Are your expectations being met? _____

When was the last time you completed an investor profile to determine your asset mix?_____
_____

When was the last time you examined your portfolio to see if it contains the most efficient asset mix for you? _____

If there was one investment decision you could change, what would it be? _____

What would you do differently? _____

Do the guarantees offered by segregated funds sound appealing to you?
_____

What is your intended use for your assets?
☐ No income, grow assets instead?
☐ Take out growth, keep asset values constant?
☐ Maximize income, deplete assets?

Managing Health Risks

If you required care today, what family member would be the primary caregiver? _____

How would costs for services, facilities, and equipment be covered? ____
_____

Who do you know that has just gone through a critical illness and survived it? _____

What difficulties have they encountered? _____
_____

Do the following statements accurately reflect your feelings and objectives?
I want to:
• Continue to enjoy a certain quality of lifestyle
• Ensure my spouse can enjoy retirement
• Be able to make choices
• Maintain my independence and dignity
• Have access to the amount of care and the type of care that I will need

I don't want to:
- Be forced to accept the lowest form of care and/or facility
- Go on long waiting lists
- Reduce or exhaust my retirement assets by paying for my long-term care
- Be a burden to my spouse or my family
- See my children and grandchildren lose their inheritance
- Create unnecessary emotional and financial hardship for my spouse or family

Is it important to you to have choices in the event that a critical illness strikes you or your spouse or one of you requires long-term care?

_____

Is it important that you have some way of funding these costs other than using your retirement assets? _____

Wealth Transfer

When was your will last updated? _____

What are the plans for the ultimate distribution of your estate?

_____

Are you aware of how estate taxes would be levied in your situation?

_____

Would you be interested to see how you can pass more of your estate to your heirs or charities instead of the tax department? _____

_____

Do your assets have named beneficiaries or are they owned jointly?

_____

Is there a particular charity or religious cause to which you would like to see a bequest made from your estate? _____

If yes, please provide details. _____

_____

Are you providing, or thinking about providing, some form of gifting to children or grandchildren while you are living? _____

If yes, has this been done or is this an area where suggestions are welcome?

_____

Do you own any real estate aside from your principal residence?

_____

If yes, how are these assets to be handled by the estate?

_____

Have you appointed a power of attorney?_____

If yes, who?_____

Is there a health-care directive in place? You _____ Spouse _____

Do you currently have any individually owned life insurance? _____

What are the details of coverage (if copies of actual contracts are not available)? _____

_____

Personal Advisors

Lawyer _____ Firm _____

Accountant_____ Firm _____

Executor _____ Address _____

Special Needs Planning

Have you or your spouse been married previously? _____

If yes, are there agreements, settlements, or personal objectives that affect your assets, pensions, or conditions of estate distribution? _____

Please provide details. _____

_____

Are there any special needs situations with children, grandchildren, or parents for whom you would like to make special provisions?

_____

Have you had the opportunity to investigate the use of trusts for estate purposes? _____

Would you like to be made aware of the benefits of these vehicles as they might apply in your situation? _____

Are you aware of the deferred tax liability of your registered programs?

_____

Have you discussed your estate plans with your children? _____

Have appropriate wealth-transfer plans been put in place for your parents' assets? _____

Advisor Relationship

Do you currently have one primary advisor with whom you work?

_____

Are you satisfied with the relationship and the service provided?

_____

What, if anything, could be improved?

_____

Is your advisor providing you with a financial plan or simply products?

_____

What level of communication would you like to have from your advisor?

Face-to-Face Meetings _____ Frequency_____

Account Statements _____ Frequency_____

Telephone Contact _____ Frequency_____

Would you like to receive information by and be in contact through email? _____

_____

Are you receiving your desired level of communication now?

_____

Intergenerational Considerations

Your Parents	You	Your Spouse
Name _____	_____	_____
Age _____	_____	_____
State of Health _____	_____	_____
Living Accommodations _____	_____	_____
Number of Living Sisters and Brothers _____	_____	_____

Is there still commonly owned property within the family (business, farm, cottage, or lake property)? _____

How will this property be handled through the will?

_____

Are you aware of how current your parents' wills are? _____

How will your parents' assets be divided between you and your siblings?

_____

Are you or one of your siblings responsible for care of your parents?

_____

What duties and time commitment does this involve?

_____

What plans have been put in place in the event that long-term care is required for them?_____

How will the costs be handled? _____

_____

Would you like to explore strategies to minimize costs for their care?

_____

Do they have a health-care directive in place? _____

Do you know what it says? _____

Are you or any of your siblings an executor to your parents' estate?

_____

Would it be appropriate to discuss all of these issues in a meeting where most, if not all, family members could be present? _____

_____

How familiar are you with your parents' financial details? _____

_____

If fairly familiar, how are their retirement assets structured (registered/non-registered amounts, pension income, value of house)?

_____

_____

Is it important to you not to lose part of your inheritance to tax?

_____

Is this something that would also be important for your parents to discuss? _____

_____

YOUR TIME HUB PRIORITIES

These are not yes/no kinds of questions. They will take some serious thought, but this is what makes them worthwhile.

Think about and list those things you would like to do over the next year, three years, five years, 10 years. Be specific in terms of activity, location, and time frame. For example, "We would like to go hiking just outside of Banff and take pictures of the wildlife for two weeks in June of each year."

Next year _____

_____

_____

Three years _____

_____

_____

Five years _____

_____

_____

Ten years _____

_____

_____

In addition to financial plans, what other plans do you have?

_____

_____

What is the most important thing that your money gives you today?

_____

_____

What are the three most important things in your life besides your money?

_____

_____

What does a "successful retirement" look like to you?

_____

_____

_____

Who do you know that has "retired successfully"?

_____

What has made their retirement work for them? _____

_____

_____

How do your views on money relate to your views on life?

_____

What are you looking forward to the most in the next 10 years?

_____

_____

If you had all the money you could ever use or want, what would be the first five things you would buy, and why?

1. _____
2. _____
3. _____
4. _____
5. _____

What are the 10 things you want to do while your health permits you? Rank them and indicate a time frame for completion.

1. _____
2. _____
3. _____
4. _____
5. _____
6. _____
7. _____
8. _____
9. _____
10. _____

YOUR MONEY HUB PRIORITIES

Rank the following in terms of their importance to you. The higher the rating, the more important the issue.

INCOME SECURITY
Being certain you will not outlive your income
1   2   3   4   5   6   7   8   9   10

HIGHEST POSSIBLE INCOME TODAY
Using all assets to create the largest income immediately
1   2   3   4   5   6   7   8   9   10

COPING WITH INFLATION
Having your income grow to maintain purchasing power
1   2   3   4   5   6   7   8   9   10

ESTATE TRANSFER
Leaving assets to family rather than the tax department
1   2   3   4   5   6   7   8   9   10

USING CAPITAL ASSETS
Willingness to reduce the value of your assets to create your income
1   2   3   4   5   6   7   8   9   10

HEALTH-RISK MANAGEMENT
Minimizing the use of your personal assets for health-care costs
1   2   3   4   5   6   7   8   9   10

TAX REDUCTION
Exploring strategies to pay less tax on your income
1   2   3   4   5   6   7   8   9   10

YOUR RETIREMENT BUDGET

	Budget	Actual		Budget	Actual
HOUSING			**HOUSEHOLD**		
Mortgage/Rent	$ _____	$ _____	Furnishings	$_____	$_____
Property Taxes	$ _____	$ _____	Improvements	$_____	$_____
Water	$ _____	$ _____	Gardening	$_____	$_____
Heat	$ _____	$ _____	Repairs /Maintenance	$_____	$_____
Hydro	$ _____	$ _____	Food	$_____	$_____
Telephone	$ _____	$ _____	Clothing	$_____	$_____
Cable TV	$ _____	$ _____	Other	$_____	$_____
Condo Maintenance	$ _____	$ _____	Cottage Expenses	$_____	$_____
TRANSPORTATION					
Other	$ _____	$ _____	Car Payments	$_____	$_____
Car Repairs	$ _____	$ _____	Gas/Oil	$_____	$_____
MISCELLANEOUS					
Instalment Loans	$ _____	$ _____	Life Insurance	$_____	$_____
Auto Insurance	$ _____	$ _____	Property Insurance	$_____	$_____
Alimony/Child Support	$ _____	$ _____	Club Memberships	$_____	$_____
HEALTH CARE					
Govt. Health Insurance	$ _____	$ _____	Dental Care	$_____	$_____
Prescription Drugs	$ _____	$ _____	Non-Prescription Drugs	$_____	$_____
Glasses/Hearing Aids	$_____	$_____	Other	$_____	$_____
Out-of-Canada Coverage	$ _____	$ _____			

	Budget	Actual		Budget	Actual
RECREATION			*GIFTS*		
Vacations	$_____	$_____	Religious	$_____	$_____
Restaurants	$_____	$_____	Charitable	$_____	$_____
Entertaining	$_____	$_____	Personal	$_____	$_____
Hobbies	$_____	$_____			
Other	$_____	$_____			
OTHER			*OTHER*		
_____	$_____	$_____	_____	$_____	$_____
_____	$_____	$_____	_____	$_____	$_____
_____	$_____	$_____	_____	$_____	$_____
_____	$_____	$_____	_____	$_____	$_____
_____	$_____	$_____	_____	$_____	$_____
TOTAL	$_____	$_____	*TOTAL*	$_____	$_____

HOUSEHOLD NET WORTH STATEMENT

ASSETS

SAVINGS AND INVESTMENTS

Chequing Account(s)	$_____	Bonds	$_____
Savings Account(s)	$_____	Mutual Funds	$_____
Canada Saving Bonds	$_____	Life Insurance Cash Value	$_____
GICs	$_____	Receivables	$_____
Stocks	$_____	Other Investments	$_____
RRSPs	$_____	DPSP	$_____
Pension Plan Values	$_____		

REAL ESTATE

Home	$_____	Other Real Estate	$_____
Farm Property	$_____		

PERSONAL PROPERTY

Vehicles	$_____	Jewellery	$_____
Furniture	$_____	Other Assets	$_____

BUSINESS INTERESTS

Value of Business Interests	$_____

LIABILITIES

NON-DEDUCTIBLE DEBT

Mortgage on Home	$_____	Personal Loan	$_____
Other Mortgage	$_____	Income Tax Owing	$_____
Credit Cards	$_____	Loans from Family	$_____
Car Loans	$_____	Other Debts	$_____
Business Loans	$_____	Investment Loans	$_____
RRSP Loans	$_____		

FOR ADVISORS

This document is designed to help advisors sort though the client data, documentation, and responses delivered through the data forms. It is not a complete list of issues, but will allow you to cover key planning points with your client. While most questions can be answered with a simple yes or no, space has been provided for elaboration.

General Considerations

Are the income objectives in line with pre-retirement income?

_____

Is the income target realistic given the assets and benefits available?

_____

Are there sufficient assets to allow for some growth, as well as the delivery of income? Or does the investment allocation need to be more aggressive to cope with inflation?_____

Is there rental or business income that will be received? _____

Does the client plan on having any income from employment? _____

Do the clients understand the effect inflation has on their income/assets?

_____

Are there any sources of income that are either inflation-adjusted or non-taxable? _____

_____

What is the client's view on asset usage (encroaching upon capital to meet income objectives)? _____

What areas of the retirement priority list received higher ratings? Are these reflected in the plan recommendations? _____

_____

How can idle assets or redundant income be used to enhance other objectives in the plan? _____

_____

Are there business holdings that need to be included in the planning process?

If so, what are the details?_____

_____

_____

Canada Pension Plan (CPP)

Has the client confirmed the amounts of income expected from
this benefit? _____

Has the client inquired about any "dropout years" to enhance benefits?

_____

Has application been made to CPP/QPP to commence benefits?

_____

Is there any advantage to splitting CPP benefits?

_____

Are clients aware of how to apply for splitting of benefits?

_____

Notes

_____

_____

_____

_____

Old Age Security (OAS)

Has application been made to OAS to commence benefits?

_____

Has calculation been done in regard to possible GIS entitlements?

_____

Is there any danger, within 12 months of eligibility, of taxable income reaching the clawback threshold? _____

Notes _____

_____

_____

_____

_____

Pension

Are there bridging or benefit integration opportunities that would be part of an annuity through the employer, which would enhance the payout?

_____

If an annuity through the employer's plan is elected, are there health benefits that continue after retirement? _____

Does the pension plan prevent the option of commutation after a certain age? _____

Does the pension plan allow for partial commutation (i.e., take part in the form of a company annuity and roll part to a LIF/LRIF)? _____

Is there an option or desire to split the pension benefit between annuity and LIF/LRIF? _____

Are there defined periods of pension accumulation that have different rules and commutation formulas (e.g., pre-1986 contributions, 1986 to 1993, 1993 to present)? _____

_____

If yes, are there advantages to leaving certain accumulations and commuting others? _____

_____

Have you looked at pension maximization from all perspectives and not solely through income comparisons?_____

Have all aspects of the LIF/LRIF option been considered in addition to the initial income amounts? _____

_____

Notes _____

_____

_____

_____

_____

_____

LIF/LRIF

Is the client comfortable with the potential for variance in the amount of annual income?

_____

Are other assets available to make up income differences in years of lower LIF/LRIF payout?_____

_____

Is the client aware of eventual tax liabilities when the account balance flows to their estate? _____

Has a spousal waiver form been completed to allow for this type of income to be elected? _____

Is there any different investment allocation for this account, given the locked-in status of the money? _____

_____

Does the client wish to have more than the required amount of tax withheld and remitted?_____

_____

Is any transfer of existing LIF/LRIF going to prohibit further income for the rest of the year? _____

_____

Is there an opportunity to begin conversion of LIF/LRIF income to an RRSP? _____

_____

Notes _____

_____
_____
_____
_____
_____

Registered Assets

Is the client taking sufficient income into taxation to make full use of the lowest tax bracket?_____

_____

Is RRIF income needed, for clients over age 65, to be eligible for the pension tax credit? _____

_____

Is it best to employ a total deferral strategy, or to draw amounts out sooner if it can be done at a lower marginal tax rate?_____

_____

Is it necessary to create a RRIF to provide periodic income, or would RRSP withdrawals suffice?_____

_____

Are there tax attribution issues in using spousal RRSP assets? _____

Notes _____

_____

_____

_____

_____

Non-Registered Assets

Is the amount of non-registered assets sufficient to consider some alternative strategies? _____

_____

Does the investment allocation create tax-advantaged income/growth in the form of dividends and capital gains? _____

Is interest on GICs compounding or is it being paid to the client? _____

Is it appropriate to have distributions paid out rather than reinvested?_____

Should non-registered capital rather than fully taxable assets be used at higher income levels? _____

_____

Are there deferred taxable gains that could be triggered and offset with RRSP carryforward room? _____

_____

Notes _____

_____

_____

_____

Health-Risk Management

Do any employer-sponsored benefits continue after retirement?

_____

How does current health affect availability of health coverages?

_____

Are clients aware of health-related per diems? _____

Are there sufficient after-tax income or non-registered assets to fund insurance programs? _____

_____

Are the children willing to fund part or all of their parents' health coverages? _____

What sources of income disappear at the passing of the individual or their spouse? _____

Is there a current health-care directive in place? _____

Has a financial power of attorney been appointed? If so, who? _____

_____

Notes _____

_____

_____

_____

Survivor Income Issues (If there is no survivor, skip this section.)

Are there benefits or income streams that discontinue or are reduced at the client's death?_____

Does this reduction/discontinuance occur immediately or after a certain time period/age? _____

What percentage of the total income(s) do the reductions or terminations represent? _____

What level of income does that leave for the survivor? _____

Is this amount of income sufficient to meet the survivor's objectives? ___

Are all assets currently delivering income, or are there some that could be used later?_____
_____

Are there asset allocation changes to be made to the investments? _____
_____

Are there any locked-in income streams that can be unlocked?
_____

Is asset ownership set up to allow simple and immediate transfer? Is this appropriate given other estate plans? _____

What effect will this have on taxation when that income is only in the name of the survivor, and not the couple? Are there steps that need to be taken? _____
_____

What are the new beneficiary or estate arrangements that will need to be made to the income-producing assets? _____

Notes _____
_____
_____
_____
_____

Estate Planning/Wealth Transfer

How significant is the need for estate planning? _____

What are the client's feelings on providing an inheritance? _____

How can estate taxes be paid most efficiently? _____

Is there any gifting that should occur while the client and/or his or her spouse is alive? _____

Are there any charitable bequests to consider? _____

Are there sufficient assets and/or objectives to warrant the use of trusts?
_____

Are there any special situations that require separate consideration?
_____

Notes _____

_____

_____

_____

_____

_____

_____

Checklist of Additional Points

❑   Make sure that where individuals are eligible, they are in receipt of income that qualifies for the pension credit.

❑   Make sure clients are having sufficient tax withheld from their various income sources to avoid large tax bills.

❑   Make sure clients are taking advantage of personal credits. For example, at least $7,600 of fully taxable income should be received each year. A tax-free dollar is better than a one-dollar tax deduction.

❑   Make sure you do not use non-registered capital for income in a lower tax bracket, unless your client is attempting to qualify for certain government benefits or entitlements.

Index

AUTHOR CONTACT
AND WORKSHOP INFORMATION

Daryl Diamond CFP CLU CHFC is available for speaking engagements, keynote presentations, and half- and full-day workshops. Daryl is the Retirement Income Planning Lifecycle Coach for Evelyn Jacks Productions Inc. and the Knowledge Bureau. For more information on these services or to book Daryl as a speaker, please visit www.knowledgebureau.com or call: 1-866-953-GROW (4769).

Employer-Sponsored Educational Workshops
The Prime Approach(™) to Retirement Income Planning
PlanSmart Financial Planning Workshop
Professional Development Topics for Advisors
Building a Practice in Retirement Income Planning
Risk Management in Retirement Income Planning
Retirement Income and Rock Music Trivia
The Prime Approach(™) to Retirement Income Planning
The Structure of Retirement Income

The Prime Approach™ to Retirement Income Planning workshops are offered regularly in educational facilities across Canada and can be delivered on a corporate basis. For further information, please visit www.personalfinanceseries.com or call 1-888-949-7743.

Daryl Diamond, can be reached at www.diamondretirement.com, by email at ddiamond@diamondretirement.com, or by calling 1-888-949-7743 toll free or 204-949-4749 in Manitoba.